Education, Exclusion and Citizenship

Permanent exclusions from schools in England have reached a level which causes widespread public concern. As schools compete with neighbouring schools for 'good' pupils, headteachers are implicitly drawn to using their powers to exclude disruptive pupils who might affect school image.

This book provides a hard-hitting account of the realities of exclusion, examining the background to behaviours which typically result in exclusion, and asks questions about a society which subscribes to the communal neglect of those most in need. The author looks at the experience of excluded children, the law regulating exclusion, the obligations of the LEAs, and the prospects for inter-agency work with examples from Europe and the United States.

Finally, the book looks at the deeply embedded cultural and political factors which inhibit the development of prevention and early intervention strategies. It points to the need for fundamental shifts in values, policy, budgeting and law, and in the defined functions of social institutions if school exclusions are to be prevented, pupil disaffection is to be better managed and the prospects of developing some of the most challenging children into citizens are to be fulfilled.

Carl Parsons is Professor of Education at Canterbury Christ Church University College.

Education, Exclusion and Citizenship

Carl Parsons

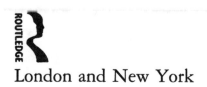

London and New York

First published 1999 by Routledge
11 New Fetter Lane, London EC4P 4EE

Simultaneously published in the USA and Canada
by Routledge
29 West 35th Street, New York, NY 10001

© 1999 Carl Parsons

Typeset in Garamond by
BC Typesetting, Bristol
Printed and bound in Great Britain by
Creative Print and Design (Wales), Ebbw Vale

British Library Cataloguing in Publication Data
A catalogue record for this book is available from the British Library

Library of Congress Cataloging in Publication Data
Parsons, Carl
    Education, exclusion and citizenship/Carl Parsons.
        p.   cm.
    1. Student suspension–Great Britain.   2. Problem children–Great
Britain.   I. Title.
[LB3089.4.G7P37   1999]
371.5'43'0941–dc21   98-35361
                                                          CIP

ISBN 0–415–17496–1 (hbk)
ISBN 0–415–17497–X (pbk)

For Daniel, Christopher, Stuart, Robert, Richard, Melanie, Peter, Naomi, Tommy, Michael, Ryan, Philip, Shaun, Dan, Shane and many others we have known who have experienced permanent exclusions from their schools

Contents

Figures

Tables

Preface

This book is essentially an intellectual project seeking to locate school exclusion within a matrix of social forces and discourses of legitimation which include national and local government decision making, professional teachers' concerns and public opinion. It also extends understanding of what school exclusion is, what it means, what it arises from and what it is related to. As an exercise in policy scholarship, the book attempts to demonstrate that exclusions from school are direct consequences of socio-cultural arrangements. There are powerful factors which legitimise the exclusion process, for some children and for other disadvantaged and disaffected groups. That being the case, those wishing to change policy will need to address the deep-seated interests which sustain exclusions and cannot expect moral exhortation to bring about that change.

Engagement in this area of research and the writing of this book have been motivated by witnessing damaged individuals who were further damaged by the administrative action of exclusion. These experiences, and the emotions they generate, have been kept largely in the background. I was involved in attempts to inform politicians about the extent of, the impact of, and solutions to the exclusions problem in the run-up to the 1997 Education Act but found the election agenda driven by concerns other than social justice and a broader and longer term view of the public good. The pique and feeling of impotence at that experience have also been kept in check. I hope that there is in the book a contribution to thinking about social justice and how we might understand and address the expensive and almost criminalised behaviour of young people whom we permanently exclude from schools. But again, it must be said, this is not a moralising, social change text.

This project is pursued at a time when 'minister knows nowt about the curriculum' and the 'secret garden' are long gone, replaced by an approach informed by the then Prime Minister, John Major's, 'We should understand less and condemn more' stance. In the ascendancy in the 1980s and 1990s there has been 'authoritarian populism' which readily labels and condemns. At the same time, and quite consonant with brutalising and simplifying stances, there has been the 'marketisation' of education dedicated to promote choice, efficient use of resources and 'drive up standards'. In its first eighteen months in office the Labour government, through policies expressed in Green and White Papers from the Department for Education and Employment (DfEE), Home Office and Social Security, displayed some continuity but also distinct, cautious signs of intervention and preventive work. More time is needed, however, to judge the impact of the *Third Way*, Labour's balancing act between welfarism and *laissez-faire* capitalism.

A team, based at Canterbury Christ Church University College, has chronicled the school exclusions phenomenon in England from 1993. Numerous articles have been produced for a wide range of audiences varying in tone from the dispassionately analytical to moralistic exhortation (Parsons, 1996a; Parsons and Howlett, 1996).

Like most researchers, we wish for our work to be used. We want policy makers to take note and act, at least to some extent, on our findings and interpretations. Three particular incidents prompted the commitment to write this book with this content. First, one boy, the first of the cases studied in *Excluding Primary School Children* (Parsons, 1994), was 10 years old in 1993, had been excluded the year before and had the most alarming poverty and family circumstances; he was in a young persons' prison at the age of 14. At the time of writing, he was in prison for a stabbing incident. The exclusions problem has some very negative short and longer term consequences and can involve great financial cost but immeasurable human misery and waste. Our later studies have shown such consequences elsewhere. Thus Chapter 4 looks at the whole range of disaffection and alienation, Chapter 5 at the sort of factors – such as poverty – which correlate with exclusion, and Chapter 6 looks at the costs arising following exclusions – for very poor returns.

The second incident arose from a presentation I made in January 1996 to an All-Party Parliamentary Committee on Children. I talked of exclusions being a punishment in effect and also in intent. One of the noble lords questioned what I meant by punishment – was it retribution or deterrence? I replied that it was not deterrence. At the conclusion the same lord told me that he had said to the minister that more should be spent on prevention; the minister replied, 'There are no votes in prevention'. We agreed that there were votes in retribution and punishment! Therefore, there is a very important chapter on the law, its current character in relation to exclusions, and the forces which shape and sustain legislation.

The third incident is related to this. I tried to place an article in *The Times* just before the final reading of the Education Bill which was passed through Parliament in March 1997. It was my second attempt with that prestigious paper to get a piece published which might affect policy at the crucial point. (It argued that the discipline parts of the bill were counter-productive and a doomed attempt to repair fundamentally flawed legislation.) I was told over the telephone when I enquired, 'Look, we can't use this. It is not the line the paper is taking and you don't propose any alternatives'. So *The Times* has a 'line'. So the purposeful shaping of opinion goes on to this extent and even here. Was I naive to think otherwise? Chapter 8 examines how the media have presented accounts of the school exclusions and pupil indiscipline. The interaction between media and public opinion is a crucial backcloth against which law drafters and vote-conscious politicians work.

The motivation to write the book is riddled with anger and anguish at the situation. We have spoken and written with various voices for a variety of audiences – though it has to be said that most were already converted. We have attempted to drive our messages into the policy arena, especially as the new Labour government was approaching a reality, and since. It was instructive, if frustrating, to experience an impotence in the face of larger, unseen forces which shaped policy. We continue to speak at conferences and write for a range of outlets to disseminate our findings, offer interpretations and tell anyone who will listen what should be done. That strident voice is absent from this book. This project is different and would not be helped by heat and righteous indignation.

In seeking to understand exclusion the context has been set wide. School exclusions can be viewed as a 'local difficulty' within a nation-state. It would be an impoverished sociology that worked with that view. Much as policy makers may try to support the fiction, no nation-state's education system develops in isolation. As we move towards acceptance of a 'global culture' (Featherstone, 1990), so we acknowledge that the purposes set for education, the arrangements made and the problems encountered are influenced and informed by happenings elsewhere in the world. Britain's disaffected youth are not unique and have not sprung uniquely from some dynamic Anglo-Saxon social fray; cultural influences, family structures, ethnic mixes and welfare provisions are among the background factors held with some commonality across western Europe and North America. This book takes note of the international, the global and particularly the nascent Europeanised context within which the legal and administrative framework is set, and within which the legitimised social processes and the personal tragedy of exclusion takes place. Furthermore, while rooted in a conflict sociology paradigm (Karabel and Halsey, 1977), this analysis adopts a historical social science approach informed by politics, economics and law. Whether middle-range theorising can endure into the late modern era (Giddens, 1991b) is open to challenge – but that is what is on offer here.

Acknowledgements

In the production of a book like this, which has grown out of a number of different projects, debts build up. I have received funding from the Department for Education, the Joseph Rowntree Foundation, the Commission for Racial Equality and Canterbury Christ Church Univeresity College and for this I am very grateful. In various ways the following have contributed through conversation, critical comment or just reassurances in the production of these chapters: Jan Adamson; James Arthur; Louise Benns; Shane Blackman; Eric Blyth; Chris Cherry; Tricia David; Christopher Day; Alan Dyson; Jennifer Evans; Ken Fox; Philip Garner; Carol Hayden; Dennis Hayes; Keith Howlett; Ric Mellis; Robert Melville; Amanda Petrie; Mike Presdee; Ken Reid; Brian Salter; Keith Sharpe; Peter Taylor-Gooby; Sally Tomlinson; Guido Walraven. Brenda Didman, Wendy Field and Alison Greenaway did marvellous work word processing my scripts in various forms and tolerated with good humour the multiple revisions called for.

I owe special thanks to my colleagues at Canterbury Christ Church University College who have worked with me on various elements of the exclusions research. Ray Godfrey has been a most disciplined statistician who prevented any excesses of interpretation which appeared tempting; he co-authored Chapter 5. Frances Castle was a tower of strength in the costings work we carried out for the Commission for Racial Equality and has co-authored Chapter 6; Richard Harris magisterially brought his learning in law to bear in co-authoring Chapter 7.

Stephen Steadman read through the whole manuscript and was insightful in his comments and did what he could to urge clarity upon me. I am grateful for the time he spent on it when writing school inspection reports might have been more pressing. Gill Zarnecki read, with astonishing patience, the drafts and redrafts of some chapters and kept up the support and encouragement through to the end.

Nina Stibbe and Jude Bowen did with stick and carrot what good publishers should do and made me get my act together and deliver. Christine Firth copy-edited ruthlessly to sort out my omissions, oversights and imperfect referencing.

The work is unfinished as policy and practice move on.

1 Educational functions, education provision and social selection

Introduction

Education may be viewed as functioning to support societal enterprises or to nurture individual development or to facilitate some mix of the two. Whichever interpretation applies, the act of exclusion of children from formal mainstream schooling is a paradox. There is confusion over whether the child, when excluded from school, has lost a right or received a punishment. In the last years of the twentieth century we witness an unusual degree of individualisation of blame and what Newburn (1996) terms 'authoritarian populism'. It has resulted in unprecedented numbers of children being excluded from school, the rate being far in excess of that in any other western European country. This book attempts to explain why, with so little questioning until recently, the legally sanctioned exclusion of children from schools and its relatively high rate of use has become established in the UK, most particularly England and Wales. The Labour government's plans, and new urgency directed at the problem (Social Exclusion Unit, 1998; DfEE, 1998b), mark a distinctive, broad and multi-agency response. The Social Exclusion Unit report commits the government to targets for the reduction of exclusion and truancy by one-third by 2002, and to the provision of full-time education by that date for those outside school. This allies well with the Education and Employment Committee report, *Disaffected Children* (House of Commons, 1998a, 1998b) and the government's response (House of Commons, 1998c).

In 1998 there were 29,000 maintained schools in the UK catering for nearly 8.8 million pupils. From a peak in 1985 pupil numbers had fallen but rose slowly through the 1990s nearly reaching again the total of 1988. Educational expenditure on schools in 1994/95 was almost £20 billion, nearly 3 per cent of the gross domestic product. In England alone in 1995 there were 7.3 million children of school age and nearly half a million teachers. Even with reductions in 'real' funding, schooling is a big enterprise, a hugely expensive public institution burdened with great expectations which it cannot fail to disappoint.

Demands for 'efficiency' in education, as in other public services, were coupled with a lower rate of growth in resources and reduced discretion for frontline professionals. Pupil–teacher ratios rose over the period 1994–96, from 22.7:1 to 23.2:1 at primary level and from 15.9:1 to 16.5:1 at secondary level (Audit Commission, 1996a: 12). The speed with which local education authorities (LEAs) drew up statements of special educational needs, the availability of local authority support and schools' capacity to vary the curriculum for special groups of pupils were all adversely affected. The centralisation of the curriculum, regular school inspection (originally four yearly – now six yearly), national assessment procedures at 7, 11, 14 and 16 with league table results both disciplined the education workforce and narrowed its role. This established a discourse within education in which the moral responsibility of schools was diminished as attainment in 'subjects' became the overriding technical goal.

Permanent exclusions affected 13,041 pupils in England in 1997/98, 0.172 per cent of the school population, 1 in 581 pupils. Rising to a peak of over 13,500 in 1995/96, the number and proportion still remain small but represent the most extreme end of the disaffection spectrum. Other pupils voluntarily exclude themselves through truanting while still others may remain passively disengaged in school. The creation of a legally defined group actually excluded from full-time education revealed an enigmatic and punitive policy response in England and Wales (Scotland and Northern Ireland operated under different legislation and regulations). The problems of pupil indiscipline and disaffection facing schools are shared by all the societies of late modern western democracy. These are not small local difficulties, but part of the international experience. As Professor Mary Evans writes for the Organisation for Economic Co-operation and Development (OECD):

> Many industrialised countries are experiencing unacceptably low levels of educational attainment and high levels of school drop-out among youth who are not disabled and who appear to have the capacity to follow a normal curriculum.
>
> (OECD, 1996a: 7)

The discussion later (Chapter 10) proposes that the problems of unmotivated and disaffected young people should be seen more broadly as part of the changes in youth transitions, within a restricting welfare policy architecture and as part of the continuing social uncertainties of the late modern age.

Leaving these contexts aside, a perplexing set of questions arise in relation to the provision of education for the nation's young: why should exclusion from school be the response to unmanageable behaviour in schools in some parts of the UK? Why is it that other countries in Europe and North America do not respond in this way? Why is there such limited questioning of this response? What conditions led the three major political parties to agree on the discipline sections of the Education Bill 1996 as it passed through its third reading in Parliament in January 1997? Why does a Labour government devise policy and legislation which only slowly reverses from the position of its Conservative predecessor? And how are we to understand this enterprise of schooling and how construe its role and goals, when a proportion of children are denied it?

This chapter goes on to examine the aims and functions of education. The analysis is applied to the peculiar position of UK education on a number of continua related to functions, speculates on the 'movement' over thirty years towards a more controlling role and considers the extent of a turn-around towards a more nurturing and empowerment position in the first eighteen months of a Labour government. A theoretical framework is proposed which builds on conflict sociology and links cultural, political and economic forms of domination and the legitimisation of discourses on social policy and inequalities. This background and the theoretical framework are necessary to inform a discussion of the meanings of, and reasons for, school exclusions.

The stated aims of education

The aims for a nation's education system(s) are diverse, even contradictory, and change over time. As a theoretical premise let it be said that aims, policy, practices and outcomes do not emerge from some amorphous entity called society but are the results of the purposeful decisions of powerful social groups and players. Furthermore, such decision makers may not work consistently, may attend to the issues with different degrees of energy, are influenced by a range of pressure groups and certainly do not work with a grand and consistent plan. Indeed, one worries at times about the simple myths that political decision makers draw on or attach to their policies in preference to addressing complex realities.

With amusement one may review the aims of education as expressed by the 'greats' of the philosophy of education and the too-recent-to-be-great. These may be set alongside the aims pushed forward by the quality press, the tabloids, professionals, politicians, industrialists, intellectuals and ordinary people. It is not possible to cover in any depth the philosophy and ethics of education. It is enough to show the practical irrelevance of such abstract debates compared with the analysis of the social roots of purposes actually ascribed to education.

The UK has not had a Dewey or Bruner (or even a Skinner) and no commanding philosophical vision to compete in defining the grander purposes of education. Despite what has been clumsily referred to as the 'massification' of higher education and large numbers participating in further education and training, the education system of England and Wales appears deeply divisive. Carr and Hartnett (1996) argue, with an air of exasperation, that this is partly because English society never experienced the kind of political revolutions that had occurred in France and America in the eighteenth century and therefore has never felt the need to reflect seriously and publicly on the type of education system which would be appropriate to a democratic society. As a result cultural, economic and social change in England has often been used not as an opportunity to radically rethink education policy, but rather as an excuse for retreat into spirits, fantasies, vocabularies and dreams of the past.

(Carr and Hartnett, 1996: 107)

We suffer from not having had the trauma of a revolution since the sixteenth century, a successful invasion or Romanian-style communism which would have required reconstruction. So our idealist philosophers from MacIntyre through Peters back to Whitehead operate with only a light touch on political and professional realities.

Whitehead (1962 – originally published in 1932) warns against inert knowledge and speculates about 'the rhythmic claims of freedom and discipline' (1962: 45) which, in different guises, lie at the very heart of continuing debates about education. Is education to empower individuals or prepare people for roles in society? Does it fulfil a generalist parenting role for pupils or concentrate on inputting particular skills, roles and dispositions? Is it high culture transmission to an elite, meritocratic or otherwise, or a technocratic, egalitarian and reconstructionist endeavour? The questions, as put, polarise the situation and are best understood as asking where the balance should lie between the poles and how the compromise should be made.

MacIntyre (1987) is particularly troubled by the necessary compromises. One compromise which he sees as both essential and impossible for teachers is between the requirement

to shape the young person so that he or she may fit into some social role and function that requires recruits [and] teaching young persons how to think for themselves, how to acquire independence of mind, how to be 'enlightened'.

(MacIntyre, 1987: 16)

Arguably this tension exists in parenting, counselling, education and in any situation where advice and guidance are given. It can be seen as a healthy tension and teachers need not be seen pessimistically as 'the forlorn hope of the culture of western modernity' (MacIntyre, 1987: 16).[1]

It is odd, looking back, that so much philosophical energy was dispensed on the Hirst–Peters debates about what is an 'educational process' and what are 'forms of knowledge'. It is peculiarly English, just as Bloom's most influential and equally dumbing 'behavioral objectives' (Bloom et al., 1956) were part of the mechanistic American project of the 1960s and 1970s. The logic which the analytical philosophers and their students traded in was internal to itself and scarcely acknowledged the social processes wherein decisions are made about what to teach, how to teach and how to package it. Debates about education or indoctrination, about finding out for oneself or instruction, have also lapsed as coercive control of the curriculum and teachers' work has tightened. It is as though, left to themselves free of political intrusions, as in earlier times in the twentieth century, education philosophers 'play'!

Her Majesty's Inspectorate (HMI) used an adaptation of Hirst and Peters's (1970) seven 'forms of knowledge' to designate eight 'areas of experience' (Department of Education and Science (DES), 1977, 1980, 1981). It represented, briefly, a bridge from academic philosophy to policy but was wiped from the board by the government's more direct *The School Curriculum* (DES/Welsh Office, 1981) which restated the traditional subject areas. A chance to intellectualise what education was about, involving the powerful, mediating role of the inspectorate, disappeared. Maybe vestiges of this survived in the Desirable Learning Outcomes (School Curriculum and Assessment Authority (SCAA, 1996) for 5 year olds.

Issues, contests and crises in English education

Seemingly, discussion on the aims of education were left to the academic freedom and irrelevance of the seminar room. However, schooling is an institution, designed, evolved, compromised and seriously contested over more than a century, to achieve a mixed bag of ends. These 'ends' are relative to the social context, usually the national economic context, within which they arise and relative to the dominant players' interests. Political, economic and cultural elites contest about the ends which schooling should seek to attain, the form it should take and who it should serve. A contest also takes place among professionals, the newly enfranchised 'customers' and the wider public, though arguably as a sideshow or even audience to the elite contests. From the mid-1980s onwards the contests have been very highly politicised. These notions of elites, contests and legitimations are developed further in the last section of this chapter.

It is puzzling to view the changing crisis agenda addressed with increased bile and heat since the post-war consensus on education disintegrated in the late 1970s. The complacencies and crises have affected aims stated for education and what is allowed and disallowed in compulsory schooling. The post-war focal issues for education have been:

1945–65   tripartite system of grammar, technical and modern schools operating
concern over working-class access and success
comprehensive schools

1966–75	falling standards
	trendy teachers
	challenge to teachers' professional autonomy
	selection
1976–80	education's role in economic decline
1981–87	school self-evaluation
	falling rolls
1988–90	centralised curriculum
	local management
	'marketisation' of education
	standards of attainment
	school effectiveness
1991–97	inspection
	corporate culture and the sciences of management, league tables, school effectiveness, school improvement, value-added
1997–	social exclusion
	a new educational consensus.[2]

Until the Labour government assumed power in 1997 the trend in these focal issues had been inexorably away from the 'big issues' of class, equal opportunity, the social purposes of schooling and, in relation to curriculum content, any policy debate about what the young should learn. The focus had been narrowed and individualised down to the units in the market place – teacher and school effectiveness, excellence through competition 'driving up standards', and national decision making seemingly distanced from the functions and resourcing of education. Despite this policy movement there was still the ebb and flow (or ebb and ebb) in the functions of education as they are actually played out.[3]

Increasingly in the UK, most especially in the 1990s, there has been an emphasis on the cognitive and intellectual processes of education with proportionately reduced attention given to personal and social development and to notions of citizenship, community and co-operation. We see the narrowing of the formal functions of education, a legitimisation of attention to basic skills and curriculum subjects and a corresponding devaluing of relationships, growth and acceptance of diversity.

Functions of education

It is worth revisiting old questions about what education is for which go beyond philosophical and rhetorical claims and move into politically and socially contested realms. As suggested above, education has no aims or functions; people shape education and invest it with aims and functions. Historically, schooling in the UK has served a number of functions. Six are discussed here and the form each takes has to be seen within the overarching tension between individual development and discipline to which Whitehead,

MacIntyre and others refer. The six functions are: custodial; civilising; creating a national identity; skilling; credentialling; and selecting, organising and transmitting public knowledge. In France and Germany over the same period, these same functions, varying from time to time as to which were the most important, have also been addressed. Indeed, in the United States, education has been second only to religion in providing a 'melting pot' for the immigrant populations, fulfilling a national identity function.

It is instructive to consider the way these different functions are addressed in the UK in relation to decisions which actually remove children from the experience of formal education and, therefore, from the impact of these functions.

The custodial function

From 1870 when the Forster Act filled the gaps in provision of education through the establishment of local school boards, there has been a sense that *all* children belong in school from the time when they move away from babyhood and easy containment in the family until they reach maturity and employment. Partly, for the poor, this could be seen as keeping the children off the streets, keeping them out of crime and more easily freeing parents for paid employment (Midwinter, 1970). What they did at school, the curriculum, was arguably of secondary importance.

Further education colleges and schools can be viewed within this function as occupying surplus youth labour. This has become more difficult overall as the demand for workers falls and as the lower level occupational positions reduce in number. Children and young people are being 'warehoused'. It was unquestioned in the twentieth century that children should be at school. 'Education otherwise' has not been easily achieved (Petrie, 1993) and the home education movement is probably more common in the UK than in mainland Europe; indeed in Germany since the 1930s education at home has been illegal.[4]

The custodial function may be different for different groups in different age ranges: the opportunity to socialise and 'give mum a break' for the youngest; the provision of a safe place and time to grow for the 8–12 year olds; the chance to keep out of crime, sex and drugs for the adolescents. It makes sense. At its most benign and unprison like, school is a healthy place for associating and growing. It is a place of safety and is resourced for young people in a way that the home and street cannot be.

Whether the emphasis is on control and containment or on the care and nurturing of the independence of the young is a key ideological divide. Childhood activity, and roles proper for it, are social constructions, varying across national cultures and history. We see child workers in the Indian subcontinent and gun-toting 12 year olds in Africa.[5] In the UK, probably more than other countries in the 'developed' west, children have no legitimate voice.

Most schools do not seem like places designed to satisfy children's expressed wishes. Edward Blishen, reading children's competition essays on 'the school I'd like', admits 'the image of the prison returned to me again and again' (Blishen, 1969: 14). A sad truth?

The civilising function

The young, growing up in a civilisation with its culture and language, are considered to require professionals and specialised institutions to induct them into the culture. Writers as diverse as Oakeshott (1989), Peters (1973) and Stenhouse (1971) elaborate on this. Anthropologists have reported on the apparently less formalised, usually shorter, educational processes of less developed societies (Mead and Wolfenstein, 1955).

Education is about the all-round development of the young and schooling has its part to play alongside the family, community, media and other formal and informal sources of learning. Disputes exist about how directive the civilising function should be and Archard (1993) usefully reviews the 'liberation or caretaking' thesis. There is an expectation that the family and school will see that a young person growing up acquires basic skills and knowledge and knows how to behave. Dawson reports of a south London mother's requirements for her sons' education: 'I want you to teach 'em to read proper, write proper, add up proper and behave themselves!' (Dawson, 1981: 3–4).

Education for citizenship has a long but peripheral presence in educational debates from nineteenth-century legislators, through Tawney, Laski and others in the early twentieth century and through Marshall's (1950) codification of citizenship to the more specific work of authors like Heater (1990) and the Citizenship Foundation.

Personal and social education is directed at being more individually enabling than socially conforming. TACADE (Teachers' Advisory Council on Alcohol and Drug Education) and other organisations have produced exciting material in this area (TACADE/Lions, 1986, 1990, 1994). Pastoral care may be in many respects a safety net for the troubled child and the soft side of discipline but Best *et al.* (1983) see it as having a wider ranging and developmental role. It could be, as Hargreaves (1994) argues, that the traditional 'non-denominational core RE [religious education]' has lost its legitimacy. Barber sees matters thus:

> The only moral community to which all young people are entitled – indeed compelled – to belong to is the school . . . If we want young people to learn the rules of living and working in communities – how to solve differences of opinions, how to respect a variety of beliefs . . . then these must feature in the curriculum of schools.
>
> (Barber, 1996: 187–188)

Hargreaves judged that schools would have to respond by improving civic and moral education or 'more authoritarian solutions to law and order problems will be adopted by politicians' (Hargreaves, 1994: 40). Civics, moral education and personal and social education (PSE) all have places formally in the Education Reform Act 1988, the inspection requirements of the Education Act 1992 and the National Curriculum Council (NCC, 1990b) guidance. However, in the marketised, league table education system, these cross-curricular elements were marginalised.

Creating a national identity function

The school is the most tangible, interpersonal arrangement for developing a general sense of common and shared experience, of commitment and of belonging in the nation-state.[6] This is not necessarily a nationalistic and xenophobic process but one which seeks to create like-minded and like-knowing individuals committed to each other. The nation-state has no chronic need for this outside of wartime; indeed international trade and co-operation are necessary and commonplace. Many citizens work for foreign companies. Jingoism and support of national teams are expressions of the sense of belonging. The nation is the object of responsibility and a source of support, especially social welfare, which arises within national boundaries. The concept and role of the nation were challenged by globalisation and by ideas about world or European citizenship, on the one hand, and regionalism on the other.

Schools do much to celebrate Britishness in their curricula. Sharpe *et al.* (1997: 9–10) point to interesting differences in French and English children's expression of national identity, with French children much more likely to express pride in national 'belongingness'. If we look at intent rather than effect in British education, the swing to a traditionalist, backward-looking and xenophobic position is evident, as J. Beck (1996) points out.

Nicholas Tate, then Chief Executive of the School Curriculum and Assessment Authority, in urging a wider curriculum invited criticism and praise from different sections of the media. He wrote, 'If we included other fundamental purposes such as the transmission of our culture and social cohesiveness, we would end up with a very different national curriculum' (Tate, 1995: 8). 'Britishness' has been on the rise and anti-racist projects and policies have fallen from favour. The message is that there are choices made, within histories and traditions, about the nationalistic (and class) character of education. Sharpe *et al.* (1997) usefully contrast the French construction of an education system, with the state assuming responsibility for welding the people into 'a common national culture built around republican values' (1997: 17) with the English response being piecemeal in funding local initiatives to supplement what was already provided privately. Little surprise that the education systems in the two countries function differently and evoke different responses from children in their nationalistic feelings.

The skilling function

Much has been made of the function of education as generating in the young the skills needed for life, or more particularly work. From earlier claimed needs for a literate workforce through the white heat of the technological revolution (Harold Wilson's 1964 speech) to the Technical and Vocational Education Initiative (TVEI) (Hopkins, 1990) the signals and actions have been strong in demanding that education serve the needs of industry.

That a prime goal for education should be, or could be, directly supportive of economic enterprises has been debated hotly. Bowles and Gintis (1976) presented the classic modern Marxist argument for the hegemonic effect of education. Brown and Lauder (1997) certainly point to a disjunction between what they see as a neo-Fordist education system and the needs of the post-Fordist, globalised economy.

Barnett (1986) and Weiner (1981) have attacked the failure of British education to deliver what industry requires. Berg (1973) argues, in his book subtitled *The Great Training Robbery*, that we kid ourselves that schools and colleges can do that job, and Jamieson (1996), committed to the idea of school–industry links, questions how tight the link can or should be. Stronach (1988) proposes the amusing parallel of blaming schools for economic decline as being like attributing lost battles to poor discipline in the Brownies!

As well as economically useful skills there are other life skills – moral and spiritual development too – which can claim a place in education. This is where the post-Fordists and the socialisers and civilisers come together in proposing educational reforms.[7] They still remained relatively unheard at the end of a year of Labour government.

The credentialling function

Arguably, providing a status passage has long been the most powerful function served by education in the UK, in other developed countries and in many developing ones (Dore, 1976). Education provides a credentialling system which interfaces with employment and other forward routes into adulthood. Educational qualifications are cultural goods or capital (Bourdieu and Passeron, 1977). They are achieved to a considerable extent through family sponsorship and are a key factor in occupational position and income potential. Bourdieu and Passeron (1977) argue that privileged groups amass cultural capital in the form of credentials. These ensure access to occupational and societal positions.

The credentialling function of the school has grown in scope and importance. The school, college or university credential is the clearest communication medium between educational institutions and those of commerce and industry. Some see these as an anachronism and ill-fitted to post-Fordist structures of production and management (Brown and Lauder, 1997). None the less, it has been and remains the case that, as Eggleston has put it, 'Success in competitive examinations is, for most people, an essential prelude to the legitimate exercise of power, responsibility and status throughout modern societies' (1984: 32).

Dore argues credibly that schools are 'testers rather than creators of talent' (1976: 30) and that 'the teaching profession in Britain seeks to maintain the fiction that what counts is education, not pieces of paper' (1976: 502).

Arguably the vocal, articulate, Galbraithian comfortable middle classes strive to maintain the kind of discriminating credentialling system which gives advantage to their children. The system of public examinations disguises as a meritocracy a class-based selection ritual. It legitimises inequality. With economic restructuring, increased competition for jobs and growing uncertainty, credentials assume more importance. Collins's (1978) 'credential society' lives on.

The selecting, organising and transmitting of public knowledge function

The selection of knowledge that goes to make up the curriculum in schools has dubious rational and philosophical bases. Indeed its utility to economic or social life is questionable. The National Curriculum of England and Wales is certainly more of a traditional concoction of standard school subject material than the outcome of contemporary, philosophical thinking or analysis of the needs of the very late twentieth century. Nor is the content of the curriculum something over which professional educators have latterly had much control. It is worth recalling that, in the UK from the mid-1960s to the early 1980s, professional autonomy appeared at its greatest even if mischievously underused and misused.[8] The decline in that autonomy and its consequences for professionalism are an important part of the exclusion story.

Professional autonomy, thought to exist in the UK since the Education Act 1944 and reinforced by non-intervention and no threat of intervention for thirty years, has to be an aberration. Certainly, proud though we were of the facade, we were out of step with other western democracies; in Denmark it was said that education was too important to be left to professionals – Parliament must decide the content of the curriculum. Arblaster made the telling point that 'relative autonomy . . . tends to flourish only when the dominant forces in society feel secure' (Arblaster, 1974: 24) which is an important message for educationists at any time. The teaching profession had its control of curriculum content comprehensively removed.

The work of Goodson (1985, 1995) has done much to place curriculum making in a social context. Choices have always been made about what to teach and the beginnings of compulsory education did not initially borrow models from private education. The curriculum took the form of an extension of the provision made in elementary church schools with the concentration on basic skills and facts. It is in looking back on the decisions leading to the content of universal state education that one is struck by the social class based provision of education – evident still today. A philosophical basis for the set of subject matters making up the school curriculum, and the righteousness of their position to impose it, is a helpful fiction for the whole hierarchy of professional educators to believe in and promulgate.[9]

Before Goodson's work, the text, *Knowledge and Control* (Young, 1971), had reverberated through those parts of the education system vulnerable to excitement and perturbation. Knowledge, it was convincingly declared, was socially controlled. Bernstein (1975) elaborated the parallels between society's and education's classification and framing and, on a broader front, Archer (1979) had discussed the 'insertion' of progressive ideas during the 1920s and 1930s, even if they did not become established as stable and mainstream. The content of subjects was open to contest and power. Layton's (1973) seminal book, *Science for the People,* describes the tussle at the beginning of the twentieth century between the proponents of the science of common things and those who stood for laboratory science. Utility, in the sense of being of practical use in everyday living, was not the main criterion. Goodson's own work and books edited by Goodson show similar conflicts over mathematics, religious education, English, modern languages, even the play house and the sand tray. More recent writings present in a different form the scheming that went on in the National Curriculum writing groups.[10]

Simplistic egalitarian thinking behind the National Curriculum avoided identifying different groups of children who should have different curricula; the view was that all should have an entitlement to the same. Justification of a National Curriculum was accepted as a response to the need for some uniformity across the nation with its mobile population. These are more firmly grounded practical considerations than those which argue that equality is best served by a fixed offering for all. The further argument rested on the belief that there was objective worth in what was taught, a belief uninformed by the social histories of the curriculum movement. The other part of the argument was that pupils would be disadvantaged in progression to further stages in education by the omission of some parts of the National Curriculum. Yet if pupils truant or behave in ways which get them excluded, that results in drawbacks and costs for society and the individual regardless of what might have been learned. Negotiation of the curriculum appeared dead. Flexibility to adjust to what the pupils would/could take was out of the question. As part of the solution to addressing school disaffection curriculum negotiation, selection and tailoring were ruled out.

Whose aims? Whose functions? Who benefits?

The six continua

The six functions are all present in some degree in any schooling system and can be played out in different ways. The poles are intended as equally tenable ideological positions and no expression of the writer's preference is intended.[11]

custodial	benign and nurturing	or	controlling and limiting
civilising	democratising and humanising	or	subjugating and inducting
national identity	open and questioning	or	closed and nationalistic
skilling	generic and flexible	or	specific and fixed
credentialling	egalitarian and communitarian	or	elitist and competitive
public knowledge	conjectural and open	or	received and authoritative

The social democratic and humanistic approach is evident on the left. The controlling and classical is found on the right. It will be argued that the position on the continuum for each of these functions affects the likelihood of policies favouring exclusion.

Movement 1966–98

On each of the continua, movement to the right will favour the achievement of some favoured goals, e.g. high standards in basic skills and traditional subjects, a (self-)controlled population, etc. It will run counter to 'inclusion', will be less tolerant of difference and will increase pressure to conform. Equally, movement to the left resonates with many of those 'weak' words to do with social work, freedom, kindness. It is accepting and inclusive.

Figure 1.1 shows the movement for the thirty years to 1996 with the solid arrow and detectable movement from the start of the Labour government by the dotted arrow. The trends are not always clear and in depicting the continua in this way some licence is necessary.

Schooling has always had a custodial role. In the 1990s policy moved in an authoritarian direction with diminished attempts to shape education content and processes in a way which acknowledged young people's preferences, anxieties and changed futures. The variety of curricula in the 1970s arising from the Schools Council's projects for the young school leaver and the practical and 'real world' elements of the Technical and Vocational Education Initiative (Hopkins, 1990) were replaced by the 'curriculum of the dead' (Ball, 1994: 28). This is represented by the substantial movement to the right along the continuum in Figure 1.1. A slight change of direction was evident by Labour's commitment to nursery education and homework clubs. Or was this more controlling?

The civilising function of the school was diminished when PSE, personal, social and health education (PSHE) and other cross-curricular generalist courses lost out to the push for 'standards' and 'basics'. The National Curriculum confirmed the expressed view of teachers that, 'I am not a social

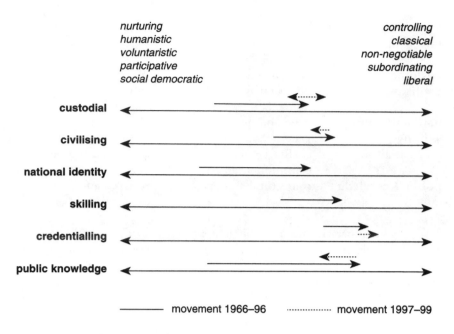

Figure 1.1 Dimensions of education and 'movement', 1965–99

worker', and reduced the pastoral power of schools generally. At a time of damaged morale and high pressure on teachers, extra-curricular activities occurred less frequently. Yet movement to the right on the continuum did not prevent the persistence in most schools of a distinct element of 'civilising' PSE; a profession less wedded to its public service tradition and more responsive to political pressure would have dropped it! Distinct signs of a reversal in the rightward movement on this dimension was evident in the establishment of the Advisory Group on Personal, Social and Health Education (Department of Health, 1998) and in reports on *Education for Citizenship* by the Qualifications and Curriculum Authority (QCA, 1998).

The national identity movement towards a narrow ethnocentric position is definite and explicit. Hall (1988) sees one of Thatcherism's major appeals lying in the defence of 'Englishness' and making Britain 'great again' (1988: 132). In the making of the National Curriculum, Kenneth Baker organised subject committees to devise a nationalistic curriculum. He wanted to make sure that

> our children would leave school with real knowledge of what has happened to our country over the last thousand years . . . helpful preparation for life if they could distinguish between Charles I and Cromwell, and know something about the Victorian age and the Second World War.
> (Baker, 1993: 193)

Ball saw this as a 'cultural restorationist agenda' (1994: 28). Despite a title proclaiming 'Choice and Diversity', the White Paper had a protectionist ring with its stricture that, 'Proper regard should continue to be paid to the nation's Christian heritage and traditions' (DfE/Welsh Office, 1992: para. 8.2). The movement in geography, mathematics and English was likewise substantially to the right along the continuum.

In terms of skills there was still great stress on achievement in the core subjects of English, mathematics and science. Barber's (1998) notion of a world class education service was also still wedded to high performance in narrow, school subjects. There is, however, some evidence of a slackening of this position and a willingness to adjust the curriculum provision for the disaffected. Work experience at 14 and further education college placement for some 15 year olds were proposals in the White Paper (DfEE, 1997b) which were manifestations of this new attitude. The reduction of pressure on the foundation subjects at primary school and the National Literacy Strategy, literacy hour and the Mathematics Strategy may be seen as a movement back along the skilling continuum towards the generic and flexible.

The examination system remains a block on possibilities for change and inclusiveness. For schools the A Level remains the outdated gold standard. Vocational qualifications have established their place and education ministers have sought to argue for parity of esteem. While the system acts to sustain competition it will support a commodity view of education, confirming the belief that it is the certificate that counts and not what was learned.

In terms of movement on the public knowledge continuum, the centralisation of control of the examination system limited choice and flexibility for teachers.[12] Opportunities to pursue locally relevant issues or follow a line that gripped the interests of pupils was largely ruled out. A fundamental sign that the notion of pupils as thinkers was to be encouraged would be the reappearance of flexibility and also the involvement of the young in knowledge which is presented as conjectural and open. This is not yet apparent. Arguably, a major disincentive for children at school is the absence of an agenda over which they have some control. The schooling system does not convey a sense of developing agency, empowerment and capacity in learners, or valuing learners as genuinely thinking young people struggling to understand; it is, arguably, their willingness to struggle that must be nurtured not that which, for the moment, they come to understand.

School exclusions: a theoretical framework for a policy scholarship

This chapter provides a deliberately broad, though necessarily abbreviated, background within which to place the analysis of exclusion from school. It is intended as 'middle range theorising' (Layder, 1993; Merton, 1968).[13] This background will be extended and developed to a deeper level in the final chapter and at points where poverty, youth culture and changing economic and social conditions are discussed. It is asserted here, that elites achieving control of the education agenda at various times have defined the issues, shifted the emphasis between the poles on the six functions, and, through control of the political apparatus, have shaped schooling processes. This section locates the controlling groups, the divisiveness and individualisation of education and the 'struggle for rare goods' which occurs in this contrived politicised context. How the situation is defined and legitimised is examined and how this leads to authoritative constructions of 'reality'. Finally, there is the need to take account of how the managerial state has diminished professional control and autonomy of teachers and exposed them to the further individualising forces of the market.

Contest and control

The outcome of the competition for control was, until 1997, an increasingly exclusive schooling system. The Conservatives were tied to gentry values and economic interests. The ideology was strongly and successfully (in electoral terms) that freedom allows the economy to prosper and, with it, the whole society. A Labour government may allow itself to represent the interests of capital similarly, also with the belief that national prosperity is best advanced this way. It will also have, to a greater or lesser extent, a redistributionist agenda. In the uncertainties of a global economy, government machinery offers control by legislative, fiscal and ideological means. The government must keep its electoral support and thus attends to, and is influenced by, the comfortable and included section of society, who have some wealth and security and wish to see it preserved for their children. Middle-class hegemony in alliance with a 'beyond left and right' government is a winning mix. In these circumstances it is likely that the government will be restrained in its redistributive zeal, maintain some divisiveness for the security of the comfortable classes, demand contributions from those on social welfare and maintain a clear law-and-order profile. Government is decisive in creating the structural architecture but one needs to look to the body of opinion and the socio-economic groups whose influence is strong. Bernstein's (1975) insight applies still:

> How a society selects, classifies, distributes, transmits and evaluates the educational knowledge it considers to be public reflects both the distribution of power and principles of social control.
>
> (Bernstein, 1975: 85)

Tony Blair's echoing statement in 1997 of a Labour government's top three priorities as 'Education, Education, Education' did not disguise the service role of schools. Education is a subservient institution which is sometimes supported, often disregarded and, since 1988, was explicitly dominated after a decade of vigorous attack by political, cultural and economic elites representing controlling interests in society. Bernstein (1990) in later writings points not just to the subservience of education as an institution but to its dynamic, linking role.

> Education is a relay for power external to it . . . The education system's pedagogic communication is simply a relay for something other than itself. Pedagogic communication in the school, in the nursery, in the home, is the relay for class relations; the relay for gender relations; the relay for religious relations, for regional relations. Pedagogic communication is a relay for patterns of dominance external to itself.
>
> (Bernstein, 1990: 168–169)

It is important to establish that, in serving as a 'relay', education is a controlled set of institutional processes. It is not an equalising and democratising system but one which functions to legitimise inequality and the unequal life chances of young people. As well as fostering learning and development, schools may also serve to identify, stigmatise, alienate and debar from education and its rewards a small number of young people. Permanent exclusion from school, the most explicit form of debarring, is arguably paralleled in welfare, employment and housing. Individuals can lose rights to welfare support and to a home which sometimes stems from job loss. Indeed the competitiveness, individualism and uncertainties of the 'Risk Society' of the late modern era may have given rise to these greater polarisations.

Division and individualisation

Brown and Lauder's (1997) analysis challenged the inevitability of these polarisations; they saw it as a choice made between neo-Fordist and post-Fordist forms of organisation with the former leading to 'increasing social and economic polarisation in education, training and the Labour market' (Brown and Lauder, 1997: 31), while the latter heralds the coming of an age of flexible, multi-skilled workers moving in and out of work, guaranteed a social wage which protects families from poverty, regarded as an important foundation of a learning society. While locked in a neo-Fordist age, divisiveness is *known* to be an inherent feature of the chosen system and not a *surprising* and unfortunate by-product (see Wright, 1995, and further discussion in Chapter 10).

Struggles for rare goods

Foucault's (1972) analysis of knowledge and power is helpful in that it points to the purposeful power exerted to define and legitimise positions, relations and persons.[14] Bourdieu, in an equally complicated way, writes of 'reality' and the 'established order' as socially constructed. Indeed, he sees any moment of stability in the social world as:

a temporary equilibrium, a moment in the dynamics through which the adjustment between distributions and incorporated or institutionalised classifications is constantly broken and restored. The struggle which is the very principle of the distributions is inextricably a struggle to appropriate rare goods and a struggle to impose the legitimate way of perceiving the power relations.

(Bourdieu, 1990: 141)

So here is an expression of the view that there is a struggle, it is over rare goods and about defining or classifying people, events, decisions and policies. And it is about legitimising the classifications and the distribution of rare goods or societal benefits.

Definitions and legitimations

A writer who magnificently reveals our subjugation to authoritative classifications, meanings and attributions of worth is Gillian Fulcher. She describes 'the cultural politics of disability' (1993: 19) and the 'policy struggle' (1993: 9) through which groups with disabilities are construed and treated. These processes go on with pupils presenting behaviour problems. There are choices about whether the individuals themselves, as autonomous beings, are defined as responsible, or whether the causes are attributed to psychological disturbance outside their control or to family, social background or trauma-related sources. Then there is the valuation put upon them as individuals and the extent of their perceived deservingness. The answer to this determines whether there will be intervention or support or costly punitive responses. Finally there is the expression of the collective social response through policy.

The Conservative government legitimised definitions of the ill-disciplined in school and set the increasingly authoritarian exclusion legislation and regulations in place. As Brown saw it,

> In a political climate where the Right have claimed a moral legitimacy for a market system of education under the rhetorical slogans of 'choice', 'standards' and 'freedom', those parents who can exert their market power to gain a competitive advantage for their children are increasingly likely to do so, given an evaluation that educational success has become too important to leave to the chance outcome of a formally open competition.

(Brown, 1997: 745)

In the *Third Way* pursued by Labour when it came to power in 1997, there was a determination to share costs with private enterprise, to raise the prestige (legitimation) of partnership. With this came a reduction in commitment to pursue radical socialist responses to welfare problems based on old ideological principles. Policies were not adopted if these did not accord with existing meanings and valuations of the electorate. So a common interest with a so-called working class did not emerge. Instead there emerged a willingness to govern within the discourses of law and order, standards and conditional deservingness. As Apple (1986) has asserted, our learners are not just seen as individuals with needs and potentials,

> We see specific classed, raced and gendered subjects, people whose bio-graphies are intimately linked to the economic, political and ideological trajectories of their families and communities and to the political econo-mies of their neighbourhoods.
>
> (Apple, 1986: 7)

Authoritative reality

From the analyses of Brown (1997) and Apple (1986) a 'reality' can be con-structed where schooling is matched to support economic interest (however badly that match is made) but, more importantly, it is shaped to suit the status acquisition or maintenance requirements of a progressively insecure middle class. Schools are not community building institutions in this 'reality' but competitive, credit earning arenas to assure later life chances. Privileged access to the political machinery is vital both to command the decisions made but equally to voice powerfully the legitimations of why circumstances created *have to be so*.

Excluded pupils are markers of the limits of acceptability in an individual-ised and commodified education system, and set the limits of mainstream school professionals' efforts. Policy has legitimised their rejection and the extent of the resources directed to them. It is the outcome of the struggle to classify people and actions, the struggle over scarce social goods (maintain-ing an education system in which some children can thrive) and the legiti-mating processes to justify the situation. Seen like this, exclusion is a *natural* consequence. Why it should appear natural in England, but not in most other countries of Europe, is the focus of the book.

The final chapter sets the policy and practice of exclusion firmly within the national politics of welfare. Exclusion, it is argued, whether from school or from society, is a purposeful choice made by controlling groups, drawing on contrived or existing legitimacy. Pupil exclusions from school, like the poor and criminals, are *created* and *managed*. A competitive, stratified society needs these failures, as Gans (1995) and Wright (1995) argue in their different ways!

The managerial state, markets and deprofessionalisation

As professionals are required increasingly to work to targets so their job is narrowed but, more importantly, the opportunities are fewer for them to exercise their educated judgement. Schooling placed in a competitive market economy, however 'quasi' that market may be, will experience forces which affect its receptivity to some children. These are central planks in the policy architecture (Cerny, 1990) within which inclusion and exclusion must be played out. Some children will find it less easy to achieve some objectives, such as maximising Key Stage assessment results or the achievement of five-plus A*–C grades in their General Certificate of Secondary Education (GCSE) examinations. Badly behaved children make it more difficult, not simply by depressing results by their own low achievement, but also by disrupting classes and drawing resources away from other children. From 1988 onwards there was a distinct shift towards schools being required to impart personal status passage credits and away from fulfilling a community shaping function. The Education Reform Act 1988, a fixed entitlement curriculum, testing and published league tables, are all likely to push exclusions up. Teachers' professionalism was narrowed by the political/administrative context that prevailed up to May 1997. Thereafter, policy changes which might broaden their professionalism once again began to appear slowly with changes introduced by the Labour administration.

Until 1997, under the Conservative administration, school level education was undoubtedly promoted resolutely by government and the New Right as a private good rather than a public right. That being so, it was a logical consequence that the exclusion of children from education would constitute an individualised punishment. Were education a communal responsibility it would be expressed in policies, institutional arrangements and practices to ensure continued education for every child without exception. The child excluded from school is judged as not deserving of education. From another viewpoint the child could be assessed as even more in need of education. In essence, this is the distinction in the wider debate between the liberal and social democratic forms of social exclusion insightfully reviewed by Hilary Silver (1994). This is discussed in Chapter 10.

Notes

1 This is to dismiss MacIntyre too briefly, but on the point of dealing with tensions and compromises he appears to point out the contradictions, and the impossibility of dealing with them, yet professionals function daily without great problems in this regard.

2 The appearance of consensus on educational matters from May 1997 may be the result of a large parliamentary majority or because the Conservatives are regrouping ideologically. However, there is a significant degree of continuity in the Labour government's emphasis on standards, on the punitive inspection arrangements and pragmatic adjustments on the discipline front.

3 The experience was almost always in the direction of making education more market-oriented within a centrally defined curriculum, and less and less recourse to any further tinkering to respond to social or economic needs at the national level.

4 Education Otherwise, or the home education movement, has a long history in England, once the standard practice for the rich. It has been promoted latterly by a range of groups dissatisfied with the provision available for their children. There is a Home Education Advisory Service, an Education Otherwise Helpline and a Schoolhouse Home Education Authority. It has a small though significant presence in the United States also.

5 In 1998 there were stories of gun-toting school children in the United States and in England. Differences across the world may not be that great.

6 The family and local community may once have served to develop the sense of nationality and nationhood. Its decline or transformation has reduced its reliable ability to fulfil this increasingly complex function.

7 The post-Fordist idea, even the term, has not caught on. It fits with the post-structural and post-modern theorising and is applied to what is argued as the educational (personal development) needs of newly emerging successful economic enterprises. A big question is about what proportion of the population is touched in practical terms by these cutting edge economic developments.

8 The Schools Council for England and Wales, 1964–82, was potentially a powerful institution through which curriculum creation, as well as the more prosaic curriculum development, could be pursued. Union politicking, the failure to make a credible proposal for a national curriculum and the failures to legitimately establish curriculum reform led to its abolition by the Conservative education minister, Sir Keith Joseph, in 1982. Plaskow's (1985) *Death of the Schools Council* is less moving than the tragic title suggests and more about fond memories.

9 All professional groups have preferred stories about their importance, the unchallengeable bases of their work and their right to status and respect. It is part of the social and ideological struggle of a work group to maintain its advantages.

10 There were intriguing press stories in 1987–88 about writing attainment targets on the train journey to meetings and of subject working parties falling out and being cajoled back into line. The intrigue and struggles were played out in many arenas!

11 The writer's preferences are clear. Integrity demands that the poles are, for analytical purposes, constructs to help understanding and not moral positions.

12 There were more than twenty General Certificate of Education (GCE) and Certificate of Secondary Education (CSE) examination boards in the 1970s. There were numerous syllabi to choose from. More importantly Mode III CSE (and a few Mode III GCEs) allowed teachers even more scope in devising the syllabus, establishing the modes of assessment and conducting the examinations. It would amaze teachers in the 1990s to know the freedom exercised at that time and the enthusiasm of teachers to engage in these creative efforts.

13 The approach and scale of the theorising in this book does at times approach the 'grand' level but restraint is used and the focus is mainly on a limited historical period, and a limited geographical and political area. As 'middle range theorising' it seeks to look beyond the ethnography of incidents or the decision making of, say, ordinary teachers. The premise is that structure exerts more power than individual agency. Therefore, the hunt is on for the *structures* and *processes* through which the imposition of definitions, meanings, valuations and legitimations are managed.

14 The excesses of post-modern non-theorising which pay tribute to Foucault's work are unhelpful. Of great value are Foucault's fundamental questioning of our language, categories and taken-for-granted routines and the expectation that these are expressions of the powerful to gain authority over the powerless. It is an important stance to be able to adopt in a work of policy scholarship.

2 School exclusions in the UK
Numbers, trends and variations

The dimensions of the exclusions problem

The data presented in this chapter come from three sources: first, from surveys of LEAs carried out over four years with funding from DfE, Christ Church College and the Association of Teachers and Lecturers; second, from the Office for Standards in Education (OFSTED) school inspection reports; and third, from DES/DfE/DfEE reports. The earliest figures on exclusions available are acknowledged to be inaccurate by the DES; hence the discontinuous line above the markers on the graph in Figure 2.1. Indeed, that monitoring covered years from April to April rather than school years.

Undoubtedly the problem has been 'made'. Exclusions surprised and troubled politicians of all parties but they were the direct outcome of Tory politics. A preliminary discussion of the marketisation, commodification and deprofessionalisation of schooling, deliberate acts of the Thatcher and Major governments which promoted exclusion, is given in the penultimate section of this chapter. Though first sanctioned by the Education (No. 2)

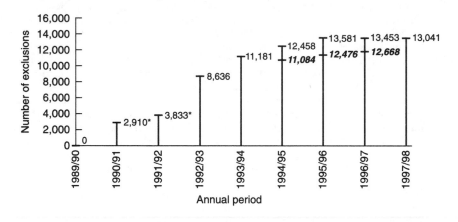

Figure 2.1 Permanent exclusions from schools in England, 1990–98
Note: *Known to be under-recording by National Exclusions Registration System.

Act 1986 (sections 23–27), exclusion was a rare occurrence at the beginning of the 1990s. School exclusions have risen to become educationally and socially significant and costly. Figure 2.1 shows the steady year on year rise to 1996/97, where a slight fall occurred with the downward trend continuing into 1997/98.

The excluded population

The percentage annual increases, as set out in Table 2.1, can be reliably used only from 1993 onwards. Before this time LEAs were not required to keep accurate data, no reliable surveys were conducted across the country and the government's National Exclusions Recording System was known to have collected incomplete data and not compensated for non-response (hence the hatched line above the first two figures). The lower, bold italicised figures for 1994/95, 1995/96 and 1996/97 on Figure 2.1 are derived by the DfEE from the addition to the Form 7 which is completed by all schools in January each year (DfEE, 1997d, 1998c). The fact that the figures from school level data differ from those based on LEA level data raises questions about

Table 2.1 Numbers of permanent exclusions from schools in England and annual rates of increase/decrease, 1990–98

Year	Primary		Secondary		Special		Total
	Number	Increase/ decrease %	Number	Increase/ decrease %	Number	Increase/ decrease %	
1990/91[a]	378		2,532		**		2,910
1991/92[a]	537	42	3,296	30	**		3,833
1992/93[b]	1,215	126	7,421	125	**		8,636
1993/94[c]	1,291	6	9,433	27	457		11,181
1994/95[d]	1,438	11	10,519	12	501	10	12,458
1995/96[e]	1,872	30	11,159	6	550	10	13,581
1996/97[f]	1,856	−1	10,890	−2	707	29	13,453
1997/98[g]	1,796	−3	10,639	−2	605	−14	13,041

Notes:
** = no data available
a The National Exclusions Reporting System figures are an under-recording, based on incomplete responses from schools. The yearly figures were also April to April rather than for a school year.
b From Hayden (1994).
c The figures for permanent exclusions for 1993/94 for all 109 LEAs in England were estimated from responses from 101 LEAs (DfE, 1995a).
d The figures for 1994/95 for all 109 LEAs were estimated from responses from 41 LEAs.
e The figures for 1995/96 were estimated from returns from 91 of the, then, 117 LEAs.
f The figures for 1996/97 were estimated from returns from 102 LEAs.
g The figures for 1997/98 were estimated from returns from 119 LEAs.

what the 'real' figures for permanent exclusions are. There are motivations for schools to under-record. Exclusions are held to be a performance indicator and schools want to show themselves in the best light they can. There is also the problem that exclusion names and numbers are historical data; schools are recording events that happened some six and eighteen months before, while simultaneously completing a form about numbers on roll at the present time which affect income in the coming year. There are similar motivations for LEAs to over-record but this is likely to be variable. Over-recording for the LEA would usefully exaggerate the problem they face. The fact that LEAs receive the Form 7 from all LEA schools, and the DfEE expects the forms to be checked by the LEA, offers little in the way of safeguards, especially when it is numbers on roll that are regarded as most important for that exercise.

Primary school exclusions are a small proportion of the total, a remarkably constant 13.8 per cent in 1995/96 and 1996/97 (13.9 per cent in 1997/98), but the rate of exclusion for this group had been accelerating while the rate of increase at secondary level was slowing. The time period is too short to make much of trends but the problems in terms of individual children and the nature of primary schools as institutions marks them out as different from secondary schools. Primary schools, with class teachers working most of the week with their own classes, have an intrinsic pastoral quality. The problems facing the primary school child who is disruptive are manifold – poor prior learning, disruptive and disorganised home circumstances and psychological disturbance. The child is not in control of its behaviour. This contrasts with some seemingly truculent 14 and 15 year olds who are often making rational choices about their behaviour in the light of competing forces and attractions. Carol Hayden's (1997) research vividly conveys the problems which many excluded primary school pupils and their families already face in terms of poverty, family breakdown and other misfortunes serious enough to involve Social Services. These problems may not be peculiar to the primary phase but they certainly characterise the exclusion-related problems there.

At primary level permanent exclusion is almost exclusively a problem associated with boys; that is largely the case in special schools also, as set out in Figure 2.2. An examination of Figures 2.3 and 2.4 suggests that not until Year 9 (Y9) do girls significantly approach the boys' rates of exclusion.

Exclusions from special schools are small in number but a worryingly high percentage of the special school population. It is not rare to hear of statemented children with emotional and behavioural difficulties (EBD) being excluded from residential EBD schools. They may then be placed part-time in Pupil Referral Units (PRUs) which are less well resourced and staffed to deal with them. In the 1996/97 school year, permanent exclusions fell very slightly in primary and secondary schools but they rose by 29 per cent in special schools. In 1997/98 special school exclusions fell by 14 per cent.

The distribution of exclusions across secondary school years shows few surprises. Fixed term exclusions are about eight times more numerous than

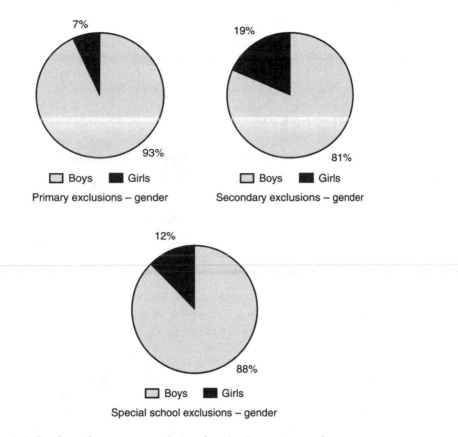

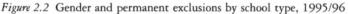

Figure 2.2 Gender and permanent exclusions by school type, 1995/96

permanent exclusions and excluded boys at secondary level outnumber girls by approximately four to one. This pattern mirrors truancy rates (see Chapter 3) and fits with a frequently held view of young people who increasingly 'buck the system', particularly a compulsory system, as they get older. A more sophisticated account of contemporary youth and the social and economic environment which they inhabit is given in Chapter 3.

Figures 2.3 and 2.4 show that for both fixed term and permanent exclusions the rates increase with age to peak at Y10 and drop back in Y11.[1] This is possibly due to the effective shortness of the school year for Y11s who (until September 1998) had been able to leave at Easter (the end of the spring term) if they had reached the age of 16. The same pattern applies for boys and for girls, though the fall off in permanent exclusions for girls in Y11 is more marked. Boys have much higher rates of exclusion in every year. The difference between boys' and girls' rates is least in Y9. DfEE (1997d) figures confirm this overall trend and distribution. Either their explicit oppositional behaviour arises later and/or schools' tolerance of it diminishes for 13–14-year-old girls.

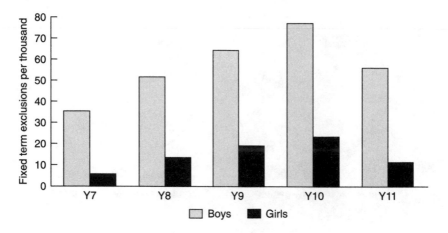

Figure 2.3 Fixed term exclusion rates by National Curriculum year, 1995/96

The difference between different types of LEAs is marked. Figure 2.5 shows that, while metropolitan and county authorities differ little in their rates of exclusion, London authorities exclude at much higher rates, with Inner London boroughs having double the rates for metropolitan authorities and counties. The permanent exclusion rate for Inner London authorities at secondary level is equivalent to 1 in every 130 pupils. This amounts to almost one pupil for every four classes for 11 to 16 year olds. There is considerable variation within LEA types. Variation among LEAs in rates of exclusion is such that they are ten times higher in some LEAs than in others. This variation is greater than can be explained by the socio-economic characteristics of the area alone. Chapter 5 examines how much of the variation is explicable in terms of factors such as unemployment, overcrowding and ethnicity.

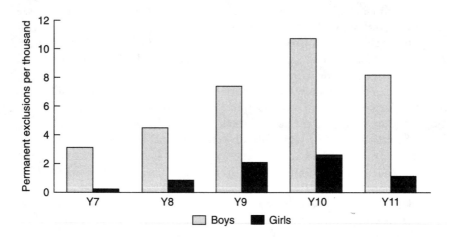

Figure 2.4 Permanent exclusion rates by National Curriculum year, 1995/96

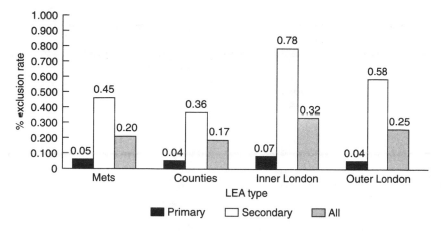

Figure 2.5 Permanent exclusion rates by school type and LEA type, 1995/96

Interestingly, rates of permanent exclusion change from one year to another in LEAs. In 1995/96 exclusions overall rose by nearly 10 per cent, yet for six out of the thirty LEAs for which there were also figures for the year before, there was a fall of more than 10 per cent. In 1996/97, out of the seventy-seven LEAs for which there were also figures for the previous year, five LEAs experienced a rise of more than 25 per cent and four a decrease of more than 25 per cent. In 1997/98 in ten LEAs, increases of more than 25 per cent were recorded, and in seven, decreases of more than 25 per cent, suggesting considerable volatility in permanent exclusion figures. Overall the fall was less than 1 per cent in 1996/97 and a bare 3 per cent in 1997/98. It would be most instructive to examine policies and practices in low excluding LEAs, which manage to reduce exclusions still further. The inner cities, most particularly London, suffer from the greatest deprivation and have the greatest concentrations of ethnic minority pupils. Table 2.2 shows the great over-representation of Black Caribbean pupils, over five times as likely to be excluded compared with white pupils. Other ethnic minority groups are also excluded at higher rates than their presence in the population would lead one to expect. Indian, Bangladeshi and Chinese pupils are exceptions to this pattern.

The interrelation of socio-economic status and ethnicity has never been well examined. The contributors to *Outcast England* (Bourne *et al.*, 1994) write emotively about the exclusion of black children but do not explore the link with class. Blyth and Milner (1996b) and Sewell (1997) point to cultural and other interactional factors of importance. The OFSTED (1996b) report on exclusions from secondary school presented evidence that excluded black pupils did not have such severe home and social problems and were not under-achievers as frequently as white pupils who were excluded. This evidence alone supports the case that there is a racist response to black children's 'difficult' behaviour which lies behind the exclusions. It needs to be

Table 2.2 Permanent exclusions by ethnicity in 1994/95 and 1995/96

	Number excluded		Percentage of excluded pupils		Percentage of school population	
	1994/95	1995/96	1994/95	1995/96	1994/95	1995/96
White	8,785	10,096	83.8	82.6	89.8	88.9
Black Caribbean	769	867	7.3	7.1	1.1	1.5
Black African	148	216	1.4	1.8	0.6	1.0
Black Other	182	241	1.7	2.0	0.8	0.7
Indian	98	109	0.9	0.9	2.7	2.5
Pakistani	208	255	2.0	2.1	2.1	2.5
Chinese	46	14	2.4	0.1	0.8	0.4
Bangladeshi	11	58	0.1	0.5	0.4	0.9
Other ethnic group	241	366	2.3	3.0	1.5	1.7
Total with ethnicity data provided	10,508	12,232				

recognised, however, that if there were *no* ethnic minority permanent exclusions in 1995/96 the remaining total (white) permanent exclusions would still have been over 10,000 and this is on the DfEE's lower number of exclusions on the 12,232 where ethnicity is known.

Provision for excluded pupils

Figures 2.6 and 2.7 show the pattern of provision made for permanently excluded primary and secondary school pupils. The survey (DfE, 1994a) indicated that the 238 Pupil Referral Units in the 101 LEAs responding to the questionnaire accommodated 8,685 pupils, 90 per cent of them secondary. One-quarter of excluded primary pupils for whom there were records and 39 per cent of pupils excluded from secondary school attended PRUs during the autumn term 1994. Home tuition catered for 27 per cent of secondary pupils and 38 per cent of primary pupils. The earlier DfE recording of exclusions (DfE, 1993) reported that 45 per cent of those permanently excluded received home tuition. Return to mainstream schooling appeared more common with primary pupils than with secondary. This is understandable in view of the challenges presented by Year 10 and 11 pupils who have set themselves resolutely against the school regime as the point of leaving approaches.

The proportion of excluded secondary school pupils returning to mainstream school was recorded as low as 14.8 per cent during that period (autumn term 1994), while 27 per cent of primary school pupils managed the return to full-time mainstream education. This is set out in Figures 2.6 and 2.7. The questionnaire asked how many pupils, who were registered as excluded in the autumn term of 1994, returned to mainstream during that

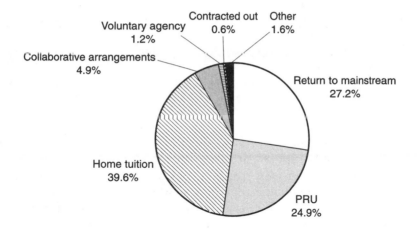

Figure 2.6 Proportions of permanently excluded primary school pupils in different types of provision, autumn term 1994

period. A larger proportion of pupils would have returned after a longer period out of school. Our judgement is that the figures underestimated by 25 per cent the proportion who eventually returned to mainstream education (reproduced as a note in OFSTED, 1996a: 60) and this figure may still be low.[2] If less than 50 per cent return and complete their schooling, there are serious implications for the young people themselves, for the community and for society, the adult membership of which they are to join. There are questions to be posed about the extent to which these young people are equipped with skills, during the exclusion period, to manage themselves on return to school, whether schools are disposed as institutions to face the challenges and responsibilities of receiving an excludee, and whether

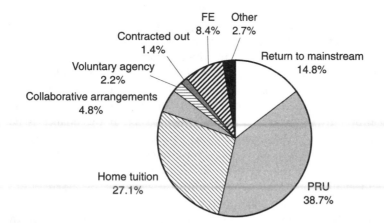

Figure 2.7 Proportions of permanently excluded secondary school pupils in different types of provision, autumn term 1994

individual teachers have the skills and attitudes to do what is necessary to support reintegration.

The more recent study, carried out for the Commission for Racial Equality (CRE), identified only seven out of twenty-six pupils (27 per cent) returning to mainstream school (CRE, 1996, Table 3: 22). Of the remaining nineteen, five were leavers who did not return to school. It was calculated that 46 per cent of excluded pupils continued as excluded into the following school year (CRE, 1996: 26). It is unlikely that the situation in autumn 1998 was better. This same research illustrated the variety of experiences following exclusion with a small number (three out of thirty) finding a place within fifteen days in a new school but most remaining out of school for a long period.

The existence of Pupil Referral Units may encourage exclusions. Some LEAs or areas within LEAs have closed PRUs down with a view to reintegration after an interim period of home tuition. The effects of this measure are, as yet, unrecorded. PRUs in some areas have filled their places quickly, even with part-time provision, with the result that they have waiting lists.

Collaborative provision, usually with Social Services, was a feature in thirty-eight LEAs, but in only fourteen cases did this involve more than ten pupils in any one project. Voluntary agency and contracted out provision, often difficult to separate (e.g. Cities in Schools/INCLUDE), accounted for 297 pupils altogether, 3 per cent of all those for whom provision was being made. Further education (FE) provision for Year 11 pupils, sometimes associated with a PRU placement, was made for 658 pupils, 8 per cent of the secondary pupils.

Figures 2.8 and 2.9 show that, while a proportion of LEA PRUs provided full-time and half-time education, for the large number of pupils receiving home tuition it was mostly for under ten hours per week; indeed over half those receiving home tuition received less than five hours per week This was the case with over 60 per cent of the 338 primary pupils in receipt of home tuition and over 50 per cent of the 2,122 secondary pupils in the same position. These figures have two direct implications which relate to the main themes of this book: first, the withdrawal of opportunities for learning takes the form of a punishment for the family, and for the child whose examination chances are diminished; second, many of these excluded pupils need more, not less, time with professionals, usually to address problems of low educational attainment and basic skills but also to resolve social and emotional problems. A subsidiary implication is that, if the finance is not allocated to meet these needs, the decision which could be interpreted as a legitimised withholding of funds from the undeserving.

Judgement of the value and success of PRUs must await further experience, evidence and evaluation. They were a new initiative for excluded pupils, established from September 1994, often catering for other categories of pupils as well those permanently excluded from school. Evidence at the time of the survey (spring 1995) indicated that provision for excluded pupils was patchy and stretched. While inspectors may have been looking

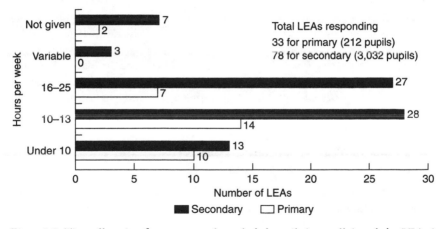

Figure 2.8 Time allocation for permanently excluded pupils 'normally' made by LEAs in PRUs, autumn term 1994

for the wrong things, the report of the first twelve inspections (OFSTED, 1995b) began very negatively.

> Standards of attainment in the pupil referral units (PRUs) inspected thus far are variable, but generally too low, even when the educational history of pupils is taken into account.
>
> (OFSTED, 1995b: 5)

The Education White Paper (DfEE, 1997b) suggested a continuing dissatisfaction, 'The quality and cost-effectiveness of many Pupil Referral Units need to be substantially improved' (p. 57). However, later reviews suggest that only five out of a hundred PRUs inspected had been found to be failing,

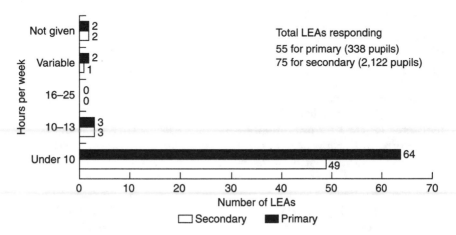

Figure 2.9 Total time allocation for permanently excluded pupils on home tuition, autumn term 1994

and generally, 'PRUs are becoming more successful, in improving attendance and stimulating positive attitudes to learning and behaviour' (Social Exclusion Unit, 1998: 12).

OFSTED inspections of PRUs (as 'schools') have been in place only since 1996. In a number of cases a negative judgement was reached because of the part-time nature of the educational provision and the admission that suitable progress cannot be made with this limited input.

Exclusions in Wales, Scotland, Northern Ireland and countries of the European Union

Exclusions in Wales are covered by the same legislation as applies in England. Figures supplied by the Welsh Office put the numbers of permanent exclusions at a fairly low level.

1994/95	476 permanent exclusions
1995/96	543 permanent exclusions
1996/97	473 permanent exclusions

The Scottish system has always been different. The power to exclude a pupil from school and the circumstances under which this power may be exercised were originally set out in the School's General (Scotland) Regulations 1975, and have been amended subsequently. A key difference, compared with England, is that the responsibility for exclusion rests with the education authority, not with the headteacher or principal. It is possible for an authority to devolve the ability to exclude to school level. Some Scottish education authorities do not allow permanent exclusions. Even when estimates are added in for authorities where small but undisclosed numbers of pupils (recorded as 'fewer than five') were excluded, the picture for Scotland is of falling numbers of permanent exclusions.

1994/95	343 permanent exclusions
1995/96	185 permanent exclusions
1996/97	117 permanent exclusions

It is with some interest that one views the list of Scottish education authorities for 1996/97 which reveals that the numbers of permanent exclusions registered for the City of Edinburgh and for Glasgow City are nought.

In Northern Ireland the situation is again different. Article 49 of the Education and Libraries (Northern Ireland) Order 1986, amended by article 39 of the Education and Libraries (Northern Ireland) Order 1993, regulate the procedures to be followed in relation to the 'suspension' and 'expulsion' of pupils from schools. As in England and Wales, a pupil may be suspended by the headteacher or principal. As in Scotland, where the local authority has powers to put a brake on exclusions, so in Northern Ireland regulations built into the 1995 statutory rules make expulsion more difficult and have a somewhat different orientation to the regulations prevailing in England. The regulations state:

> A pupil may be expelled from a school only after consultation about his expulsion has taken place between the Principal, the parent of the pupil, the Chief Executive of the Board or another Officer of the Board to be authorised by him and the Chairman of the Board of Governors . . . The consultations referred to shall include consultations about the future provision of suitable education for the pupil concerned.
>
> (Department of Education Northern Ireland – Schools)
> (Suspension and Expulsion of Pupils) Regulations (Northern Ireland)
> (1995: 3g–h)

It is the requirement that expulsion meetings 'shall include consultations about the future provision of suitable education for the pupil concerned' that marks the Northern Ireland approach as less punitive and more balanced. The number of pupils excluded in 1995/96 was 62 out of a population of 343,000 pupils; 76 were permanently excluded in 1996/97.

Comparing the four countries of the UK is not straightforward. Suspensions may be applied in Scotland and Northern Ireland like indefinite exclusions were used in England and Wales until September 1994, but this is unlikely to explain the differences. Table 2.3 shows that for 1994/95, permanent exclusions in Wales occurred at only two-thirds of the rate current in England. Scotland's rate was one-quarter of England's. For Northern Ireland it was close to one-tenth of the exclusion rate in England.

The countries of western Europe from which information was obtained about the management of behaviourally difficult children showed some contrasts with the law and practice in England and Wales. These other countries have young people with similar characteristics and in similar proportions found in schools in England and Wales. The management of such pupils has not been characterised by easy solutions but a *fundamental principle* in all these countries is that all children who are nationals of that country or resident in that country should be receiving a full-time education. There are not the provisions for regulating the exclusion of a child that exist in English law

Table 2.3 Permanent exclusions from schools in the countries of the UK, 1994/95

	Wales	Scotland	Northern Ireland	England
Total school population	492,600	820,800	349,500	7,824,600
Number of permanent exclusions	476	343	62	12,458
% rate of permanent exclusions	0.097%	0.042%	0.018%	0.159%

(discussed in Chapter 7). It remains commonly the case that, if a child is to be expelled from school, it is the headteacher's responsibility to find another placement for the child before the exclusion occurs. This is the situation in Denmark, the Netherlands, Belgium, France, Germany, Austria, Luxembourg, Spain and the Republic of Ireland. In the last case, the Irish Department of Education and Science Circular 20/90 makes plain the limitations on fixed term exclusion, and Rule 130 forbids permanent exclusion 'without the prior consent of the Patron and unless alternative arrangements are made for the enrolment of the pupil at another suitable school'.

Conclusion: the social function of school exclusion

In the management of exclusions we witness an example of the atomisation of the services for these young people when it is well known that there are multiple causes for the many social problems which lead to their difficulties (see Chapter 9). There is a punitive response which accords with an attribution of blame which is highlighted by significant media responses to stories of school exclusion (see Chapter 8). In the provision of public services, exclusion from school serves as an exemplar of the way the attribution of blame has changed in British society since the late 1970s: public issues are rendered personal choices, and intervention and support are withheld or reduced in favour of punitive responses.

Careful consideration needs to be given to what is seen as an 'effective school' and *effective for whom* (Slee and Weiner, 1998). Currently the effective school is seen in government and research terms as one with good academic results – learning is proven to have taken place. The 'good' school may be different, placing an emphasis on its caring role (without detriment to its academic functions). The 'very good' school, very much a moral project, may be the inclusive school which keeps its clients and retains the responsibility to cater for their needs – however demanding these may be.

There are forces which increase the likelihood of exclusion from school and these operate at the macro level of socio-economic and cultural factors, at the institutional level and at the personal/individual level. Our argument is that, while 'inclusion' has much rhetorical and moral backing, inclusion is not for these challenging children. Indeed, exclusion is designed into the system at macro level, shaping the institutional response, and limiting options at the individual level. These forces are considered in detail in Chapter 3.

Notes

1 These rates of exclusion are calculated from the data drawn from 388 OFSTED Inspection reports, which form the basis of the analysis in Chapter 5.
2 It is an estimate based on too little firm data. That data have not been required by the DfEE on numbers returning to mainstream full-time education adds to the evidence that these young people are placed outside the system and their rights to continued education of little official concern.

3 The changing social context of education and school exclusions

Introduction

Institutionalised schooling in the UK receives all eligible children as they become 5. For many there is also provision for pre-school education. The possibility of proceeding to further education and higher education is greater now than ever before, though the policy intention behind this expanded opportunity may legitimately be seen as concerned with countering unemployment or promoting a nation's economic investment rather than the empowerment of individuals. The functions of schooling in the different countries of Europe (discussed and illustrated in the English context in Chapter 1) are underpinned by different ideological positions and historical developments. The provision of other welfare services is affected by the same forces. Chapter 1 laid the theoretical foundations for discussion of these issues, for the interpretation of the data and to support the middle range argument and theorising contained in Chapter 10.

The perceived wealth of the nation affects the amount of investment in education. It also affects the goals of education with a more mechanistic outcomes orientation when politicians cut or peg public expenditure. It is important to note that it is not absolute wealth, or even the trend that matters here, but its interpretation and especially politicians' representation of it. The proportion of gross domestic product invested in education is a matter of value and choice, not of economic imperative. As Eric Hobsbawn says, looking at the late modern world moving towards the millennium,

> It was absurd to argue that the citizens of the European Community, whose per capita share of the joint national income had increased by 80% from 1970 to 1990, could not 'afford' the level of income and welfare in 1990 that had been taken for granted in 1970.
>
> (Hobsbawm, 1995: 577)

Education may yet be a medium for countering inequality and social exclusion but that has not been possible under a Conservative government committed to markets, choice, competition and inspection to raise standards, nor will it be if the Labour government relies on prosperity spin-offs from other policies and the competitiveness and exhortations of the White Paper *Excellence in Education* (DfEE 1997b).

Social structure and human agency in school exclusions

The level of theorising adopted throughout this book is one best described as 'middle range theorising' (Layder, 1993: 19–37; Merton, 1968; Parsons, 1987: 198–200). In keeping to this level it incorporates macro-social forces which limit access and opportunity for some and shape life experiences and cultural forms. It also accepts that, at the situational or micro level, individuals and social groups have some autonomy and scope to control, reinterpret and transform their actions and contexts. This position accepts that construing social actors 'as both bound and free does not make for simple explanation, but it is honest to the experience of what it is to be social' (R. King, 1980: 20).

The specific nature of this research focus, school exclusions and related social factors, has led to an interpretation of the situation which is structural rather than individual. It has looked at the social forces directly impinging on the lives of young people and their families and the network of institutions and processes around them. The research has examined correlates of exclusion (Chapter 5) and one powerful defining context of exclusions – the law (Chapter 7) and, in this chapter, identifies forces promoting exclusion which are built into the social structure and cultural system.

Theoretical stances which stress the agency of individuals as reality definers (Schutz, 1970) and reflexive creators of their own biographies (Giddens, 1984) have limited explanatory strength in relation to society's least favoured groups. Shilling's (1997) notion of 'the undersocialised conception of the embodied agent' is particularly telling with youth, especially alienated youth. Inequalities in terms of wealth, housing, disability and ethnicity severely circumscribe the room for their social agency. Post-modernists celebrating the crumbling of social controls, excited about the expansion of choice, extolling the virtues of individual freedom, both as personal emancipation and as explanatory theory, are peddling what amounts to 'a cruel joke' (Robinson and Gregson, 1992: 46) for marginalised young people and a mischievous hoax with regard to social science theorising. For those with little left to lose, freedom is just another word for absence of support, zero tolerance and social exclusion.[1]

The explanation for policy and practice in school exclusion will be sought in theories of labelling and social control as applied in a stratified society. They draw on related Weberian conflict theory as manifest in the defined roles of professionals and their performance in welfare and education.[2] Within constraining structures Chapter 10 develops this analysis. Disadvantage and inequalities overlap and join together to socially exclude significant proportions of young people in a general sense and contribute to the more specific exclusion from school.

Social exclusion is a relatively new notion which has had currency on the mainland of Europe for some time (Room *et al.*, 1991). Katherine Duffy writes:

> Social exclusion is a broader concept than poverty, encompassing not only low material means but the inability to participate effectively in economic, social, political, and cultural life, and, in some characterisations, alienation and distance from the mainstream society.
>
> (Duffy, 1995: 33)

The number of disadvantaged families, as indicated by available statistics, the numbers of children from single parent and 'reordered' households, serious crime, numbers on Social Services child protection registers and the unemployed continue on an upward trend.[3] Numbers of young children with problems and adolescents with psycho-social illnesses are also rising.

It is important that the social and environmental factors which correlate significantly with social and school exclusion are recognised as the same as those which are related to a range of other undesirable outcomes in terms of breakdown in family relationships, lack of employment, low pay, poor health and criminality. School exclusions are part of wider social exclusions related to inequality and poverty. Individual choice, determination, responsibility and other attributes of the person inevitably play a role in how individuals function within societal institutions, but this occurs within a structure of access to resources, opportunities, pressures and life chances. Social and economic disadvantage consists of low educational attainment, poverty (which is often associated with lack of employment and poor housing), poor health prospects and increased likelihood of criminality. These factors are often associated with unstable family relationships and psycho-social problems. These four areas are considered below.

Educational attainment

The debate about class and educational performance has a long history in the UK. It was once a dominating theme in educational sociology with much intellectual effort spent on explaining the under-performance of the working class and their under-representation in the higher levels of the education world. From Hoggart's (1958) lyrical *Uses of Literacy* through the arithmetic of Titmuss (1962) and Douglas (1964) to the neo-Marxist and phenomenological writings of Bernstein (1975), Sharp and Green (1975) and Young (1971), the social class basis of educational processes, curriculum content and assessment is sustained. Success through education has been a minority experience for the lower social classes.

The correlations between disadvantage measures and school performance, examination results and league tables are politically unwelcome, but stubbornly present. The OFSTED (1993a) report on *Access and Achievement in Urban Education* is cautious to suggest that much can be done within present funding arrangements to improve. This is based on demonstration of the moderate variability in disadvantaged urban areas and evidence of some very good practice. The argument, deployed vigorously by ministers and the Chief Inspector of Schools, Chris Woodhead (1996), is that if good practice, and correspondingly good results, can be found in *some* difficult areas then it can appear in *all*. The 'blame' is mostly placed with local providers. 'The residents of disadvantaged urban areas covered by this survey are poorly served by the education system' (OFSTED, 1993a: 6) and 'The quality and standards of much of the work revealed by this survey are inadequate and disturbing' (OFSTED, 1993a: 7). The reasons for this are again part of a matrix of negative factors which make the job of teaching harder, recruitment more difficult and sustaining an effective staff with high morale a very real challenge in such areas. The report acknowledges that 'most schools in these disadvantaged areas do not have within themselves the capacity for sustainable renewal' (OFSTED, 1993a: 45). The authors do not refer to resources as part of the solution.

Smith (1996), necessarily acknowledging the variation in achievement within categories of disadvantage, states that 'overall the difference in proportions gaining five-plus A–C GCSEs between the highest and lowest disadvantaged areas is approximately twofold' (1996: 38). He reports that the favourability of school inspection reports varies in relation to the social context represented as seven categories of increasing disadvantage (1996: 39–40); the favourability of reports falls as disadvantage increases. Smith writes that:

> It seems very unlikely that any one set of explanations could fully explain what is a complex series of events and processes. Thus school-based explanations are not in themselves sufficient, as average performance differences emerge almost as soon as assessment can be conducted and before school entry.
>
> (Smith, 1996: 41)

Commentary on the first primary league tables suggested that 'there is generally a correlation between performance and poverty' (TES, 1997: 20). Jencks's (1972) work long ago said as much of American society and Mortimore (1996) sums matters up from more contemporary research in the UK. He concludes from an analysis of a range of studies that the student intake factors account for around 60 per cent of total variance between individual students' examination results and that 10 per cent can be attributed to the school. While Mortimore may argue that a large part of 'student intake factors' is ability or attainment on intake it seems reasonable to regress this to the web of disadvantage in family, income, housing, ethnicity and community backgrounds.

Mac an Ghaill writes of the 'erasure of social class' (1996: 163) from education discourse and empirical research. The 'incorporation' of academia, mainly effected through funding, including that from the Economic and Social Research Council, has led to attention to what can be improved within existing resources and structures. The *effective school* movement has been all about how school-based and school-controlled factors can enhance prospects of narrowly conceived and measured success. OFSTED's various publications, Barber (1998) and Woodhead (1995) have used this conveniently to press the case for individualising success and failure down to institutions and pupils. Within this policy context it is amusing to witness the most uneasy rapprochement between the 'school improvement' movement and 'school effectiveness' research. Publications have been produced which contain contributions from the two camps (Reynolds, 1996; Gray *et al.*, 1996). However, the public, albeit intellectual, row between Elliott (1996) and Sammons and Reynolds (1997) has revealed neatly both theoretical and implicit political allegiances of each. Elliott claims that the central assumptions of the school effectiveness research paradigm are

> a mechanistic methodology, an instrumentalist view of educational processes and the belief that educational outcomes can and should be described independently of such processes . . . their research findings are best viewed as ideological legitimisations of a socially coercive view of schooling.
>
> (Elliott, 1996: 200)

Sammons and Reynold's (1997) unconvincing defence of school effectiveness research is that 'Elliott knows little of the knowledge base, misinterprets what he knows and fails to support his criticisms with evidence' (p. 123). This is to mistake the fundamental criticisms that Elliott levelled at the school effectiveness movement. Elliott sees the approaches being urged on schools to make them 'effective' as narrow and disempowering, and the drive to compete to raise standards as counter to processes which support and generate debate among professionals.

The National Commission on Education (1993) acknowledged that, where multiple disadvantages combine, the dice are loaded against educational success:

> The link between disadvantage and educational performance has so far proved too difficult for policy makers at a national level to break.
>
> (National Commission on Education, 1993: 5)

Yet the National Commission's (1996) *Success against the Odds*, subtitled *Effective Schools in Disadvantaged Areas*, is about documenting those exceptions where the link has been broken. The report acknowledges that it is nothing less than heroic that the schools whose stories are told here make such a difference to so many children and their families.

(National Commission on Education, 1996: 356)

Pilling (1990) gives an account of the means by which some disadvantaged young people 'make good'; researchers, politicians and citizens need to decide whether the instances of 'escape from disadvantage' and 'success against the odds' override the strong statistical associations between family prosperity and educational achievement. We need to choose similarly between narrowly 'effective' schools and morally 'good' schools.

Poverty

The incidence of families in poverty and of reordered and redisrupted families is increasing (Cockett and Tripp, 1994). The increasing number, indeed increasing proportion of the population, experiencing social and economic disadvantage is associated with a range of negative outcomes in health, crime and education.

The Joseph Rowntree Foundation reports that the proportion of the population with less than half the average income has more than trebled since the mid-1970s (1995: 15). The Commission on Social Justice (1994) makes many of the same points, that there is a matrix of linked factors which make up disadvantage and are associated with a range of negative social outcomes. The poor have got poorer and become more numerous in the period 1977 to 1997. Families with children figure disproportionately in this group.

Drawing on Department of Social Security (DSS) average income figures and the Social Security Committee's Low Income Families data, Oppenheim and Harker (1996) report that,

> Between 1979 and 1992/3 the real incomes (after housing costs) of those in the poorest tenth fell by 18 per cent; the average rose by 37 per cent, whilst the richest enjoyed a staggering rise of 61 per cent.
>
> (Oppenheim and Harker, 1996: 1)

British governments have refused to set out an official definition of poverty. It is difficult to define, either in absolute terms, or in ways which demarcate clearly between those in and those outside poverty. Townsend sets down a moral, if not scientific, marker:

> Individuals may be said to be in poverty when they lack the resources to obtain the types of diet, participate in the activities and have the living conditions and amenities which are customary, or at least widely encouraged or approved, in the societies to which they belong.
>
> (Townsend, 1979: 32)

In 1990 11 million people in the UK, one in five of the population, lacked three or more from a list of seven 'necessities' (reported in Oppenheim and Harker, 1996: 11). Using criterion levels – below the supplementary benefit/income support thresholds or households with 50 per cent of average income after housing costs – leads to a conclusion that by 1992/93 between 13 million and 14 million people in the UK – around one-quarter of British society – were living in poverty. This affected children disproportionately with over 3 million in households with less than 50 per cent of average income in 1996/97 (Howarth *et al.*, 1998).

Health

A number of research studies show that there is a strong link between social class, more specific measures of disadvantage, life expectancy and a range of diseases. Townsend and colleagues' (1992) work shows that there is, and has long been, a consistent class gradient in relation to most diseases and standardised mortality ratios (SMRs). In sixty-five out of the seventy-eight disease categories for men, SMRs for social classes IV and V were higher than for either class I or II (Townsend *et al.*, 1992: 231). This applies also in the case of coronary heart disease and ulcers, normally thought of as executive diseases. It is clear that in adults of working age, death rates have declined, but more rapidly in the higher occupational classes contributing to a widening of the gap. Owner occupiers have lower rates of illness and death than private tenants, who in turn have lower rates than local authority housing tenants. The unemployed tend to have poorer health than those in work and areas of the country with high levels of unemployment have worse health records (Townsend *et al.*, 1992: 253). Using later data, Margaret Whitehead concludes that,

> The Black working group proposed that we should adopt a national goal for the 1980s of abolishing child poverty. Not only have we failed to make progress towards this goal, but in some respects the situation has grown worse as more families with young children have fallen into the low income category.
>
> (Whitehead in Townsend *et al.*, 1992: 375)

Summed up by Benzeval *et al.* (1995: xvii) the health picture is that 'People who live in disadvantaged circumstances have more illness, greater distress, more disability and shorter lives than those who are more affluent'.

Criminality

Graham and Bowling (1995), like others using data from samples of young people rather than records of conviction, found 'no association between social class and offending or only a weak association' (p. 34). Conviction rates on the other hand show a strong social class effect (Walmsley *et al.*, 1992; Utting *et al.*, 1993). There is an official unwillingness to cite macro-social factors as contributing powerfully to crime. Farrington (1996) prefers a psychologistic position which identifies risk factors such as prenatal and perinatal factors, poor parenting, peer influences and school influences as providing causal forces. He writes that 'low family income and poor housing predicted official and self-reported, juvenile and adult offending' (p. 12), while noting that 'low socio-economic status [SES] was a rather weak predictor' (p. 7) and 'some reviewers have concluded that there is no relationship between SES and either self-report or official offending' (p. 12). But atomising and individualising background factors hardly disguises their remarkable collective similarity to what constitutes class, economic disadvantage and social marginalisation.

The Audit Commission (1996b) report on young people and crime acknowledges briefly the link between poor neighbourhoods and crime:

> Neighbourhoods where large numbers of young offenders live are more deprived, as measured by the DoE Index of Local Conditions . . . The same correlation (0.3) exists between deprivation and reports of juvenile disturbances.
>
> (Audit Commission, 1996b: 60)

The link between truancy and exclusion and offending is stated (quoting Graham and Bowling, 1995: 67) with more than 75 per cent of those permanently excluded offending. Gilbertson (1998), a senior police officer, presents a similar picture for the (London) Metropolitan Police area. It may not be as simple as Reiman argues that *The Rich Get Rich and the Poor Get Prison* (Reiman, 1990), but logic, experience and data can be brought together to support the direction of this argument. Smith (1995), however, concludes that, 'it seems clear that poverty and inadequate housing are *not* among the causes of rising crime' (p. 479). This is because they do not co-vary – if prosperity increases, crime does not necessarily reduce. He argues that the explanation for the increase in crime in most developed countries in the post-war period, most of it committed by young people, must be sought in the weakening of informal social control and social bonds (Smith, 1995: 479).

Smith's assessment is that there is no clear evidence that oppositional youth culture and changes in the usual sequences of life events in the adolescent period are necessarily related to increased criminality. However, he expresses a concern that long-term unemployment will create the conditions for an increasingly distinct section of the population which loses any attachment to the labour market or to the social fabric and that crime will rise rapidly among that group. This speculative notion runs somewhat counter to his earlier stated view that poverty is not a causal factor. It also comes close to identifying an 'underclass', which is discussed in Chapter 8.

A *joined up structural problem*

More young children are growing up in poverty than in the late 1970s. School leavers have poorer prospects when compared with the two previous generations. Those without A Level equivalent education are poorly equipped to participate legitimately in the nation's social and economic world.[4] The number of young people with problems concerning housing, drugs and crime is rising.

Youth transition takes place in increasingly difficult and uncertain circumstances. This transition is taking place within a society-wide set of developments to what has been termed a 'post-welfare society' which is accompanied those other 'post' transitions – industrial, modern, etc. The sections above have illustrated similar trends and a common rationale across the four major personal public services of education, social services, health and criminal justice. Policy is developed in such a way that public expenditure in these areas is viewed as a drain and a burden, and a significant portion of the clients are seen as culpable unfortunates. The services will be ineffective and, indeed, for the nation, will be counterproductive while these negative definitions prevail.

It is interesting to witness the shift in emphasis which was evident from May 1997 in the Health Service towards health promotion and the creation of Health Action Zones, and in social work, to schemes of early intervention and proactive projects. Criminal justice proposals for intervention are emerging (see Audit Commission, 1996b; Social Exclusion Unit, 1998) and in education and training 'Education Action Zones', homework clubs and 'New Start' policies were also devised to intervene earlier in combating disadvantage.

In the face of evidence of continuities of deprivation and disadvantage there have been, as Michael Rutter wrote, 'many opportunities to break the chain' (Rutter, 1984: i) which have not been taken. These opportunities exist with regard to educational achievement, poverty, health (about which Rutter was writing) and crime. It is a matter of political choices that the chain holds so strongly. The Labour government's Social Exclusion Unit is established and run from the Cabinet Office and the nature of the discourse has been moved on; messages are given about the need to focus

> on those who are disadvantaged, . . . have low aspirations, are at risk of dropping out, failing to achieve, or not making a successful transition to further education, training or employment.
>
> (DfEE, 1998c: 9)

Substantial action and resources are awaited. Of particular interest is whether the language of equity, social justice, 'at risk' and 'inclusion', emerge as part of a legitimising narrative that will successfully supplant the 'condemn a little more and understand a little less' world of the then Prime Minister John Major's 1993 speech.

A comparison that should provoke action through political embarrassment on the international stage is revealed by comparative graphs on literacy levels, participation rates in education post-16 and youth unemployment across a range of European countries; Britain shows up in a negative light. Little surprise then if this impacts on disaffection in school, truancy and exclusions from school.

Forces promoting exclusion and inclusion

The causes of the increased numbers of pupils excluded from school may be divided into any number of categories which span macro, institutional and individual levels. Figure 3.1 summarises these. They fall into three groups: socio-economic and cultural factors, institutional factors, and individual factors. The argument of this book is that socio-economic and cultural factors constituting the structural conditions of life exert the greatest forces and only *some* of these are amenable to short-term remedial action.[5] Quite clearly there is interaction between the factors within each level (e.g. poverty and unemployment), and some are causal factors and some are consequent upon the action of others (e.g. anti-school, criminal subculture and poverty).[6] The allocation to a particular level is not always clear cut; the anti-school subculture or socially adjusted stakeholder subculture *could* be a consequence of institutional factors.

Figure 3.1 lists twenty-seven factors promoting or inhibiting exclusion. Some are less 'malleable' than others and there is great temptation to look to institutional and individual levels for solutions rather than to factors at the socio-economic and cultural level. In the case of exclusions the expectation is that schools and teachers should do their job better and parents and children should exercise control and self-control. The factors are discussed briefly below.

The law (1) has defined school exclusion and, until recently, left undefined the substitute educational provision for those out of school. The Education (No. 2) Act 1986 and amendments to it in the Education Act 1993 (see Chapter 7) are primarily about how to manage the process of exclusion. Circulars and regulations which have followed from the DfE/DfEE, as well as documents produced by the LEAs, are to ensure that exclusion is carried out in a judicially and administratively proper way. The law and supporting documents have little to say about ensuring the continued full-time education of the pupil. The law is, therefore, an instrument *for* exclusion and offers minimal protection to excluded pupils' rights to any education. The amendments in the Education Act 1997 (Section 6 (1)) which came into force from September 1998 (see Chapter 6), especially allowing forty-five days of fixed term exclusions to be used in a single term, mostly constitute 'push' factors which are likely to send exclusion numbers up.

Forces promoting exclusion	Forces promoting inclusion
Socio-economic and cultural factors	*Socio-economic and cultural factors*

	S C H O O L	
1 Law: punitive orientation		1 Supportive, interventionist, restorative law
2 Poverty		2 Affluence
3 Poor living conditions		3 'Comfortable' living conditiions
4 Unemployment		4 Steady income
5 Diminished finance for education nationally		5 Priority protected funding for education
6 Education as a personal 'good' and for international competitiveness		6 Education for community building and democratic participation
7 Rigid national curriculum		7 Flexible curriculum
8 Cognitive emphasis of the curriculum		8 Space for personal and social education
9 Separate, professionalised managerialist welfare services		9 Humanistic, integrated and community sensitive welfare services
10 Punitive attitude to troubled and troublesome young people ←		10 Diagnostic and ameliorative attitude towards troubled and troublesome young people
11 Excessive attribution of personal and troublesome young people	←	11 Acceptance of some societal responsibility in the creation of deviance
12 Anti-school, non-stakeholder, criminally inclined local youth subculture		12 Socially 'adjusted' stakeholder youth subculture
Institutional factors		***Institutional factors***
13 School policy implicitly supportive of competitive and conflictual relationships		13 School policy promoting positive school ethos, consensus and negotiation
14 Ineffective recognition and confrontation of racism		14 Effective steps taken to address racism
15 Lack of school effectiveness, leadership and staff skills		15 An effective school with skilful staff
16 Limited initial and inservice training in class management and interpersonal skills		16 Quality training at initial and inservice levels in classroom management and interpersonal skills
17 Inadequate individual attention to, and recognition of, learning needs		17 Considerable individual attention to, and recognition of, learning needs
18 Over-emphasis on school competition in the local area		18 Schools co-operate in local area
19 Excessive concerns over local management and limited resources	←	19 Local management and resource issues regarded as no more than moderately worrying
20 Insulation, friction and conflict in relationships with parents		20 Inclusive and co-operative relationships with parents
21 Lack of locally available support to maintain pupils in school		21 Locally available support to help maintain pupils in school
22 Debate dominated by legal/administrative concerns ←		22 Debate characterised by seeking the best solution for the young person
Individual factors		***Individual factors***
23 Significant family and social problems		23 Few family and social problems
24 Presence of pupils with psycho-social disorders		24 Absence of pupils with psycho-social disorders
25 Decision making influenced by deviant peers		25 Pupils insulated from influence of deviant peers
26 Undetected or uncorrected sight or hearing problems		26 Sight or hearing problems routinely screened and appropriate follow-up measures taken
27 Low self-esteem		27 High self-esteem

Figure 3.1 A framework for understanding exclusions from school

The inter-linked problems of *poverty* (2), *poor living conditions* (3) and *unemployment* (4) have been discussed. Their increase since 1979, the financial insecurity they bring, and the greater number of children in disadvantaged circumstances are fertile conditions for school exclusions.

Diminished finance for education nationally (5) has led to teachers being faced with larger classes, having to ration the resources of time, care and attention that they can give to the most demanding pupils. Schools acting as small businesses experience the tension between the business ethic and the professional ethic: the former urges them to organise their enterprise so that it is most effective and efficient and this may mean removing obstacles to those goals and ingredients likely to lower its standing – behaviourally difficult pupils; the professional ethic urges the school to maintain its service to *all* pupils no matter what difficulties they have or present to the staff.

Education as a personal 'good' and for international competitiveness (6) has reduced attention given to broader goods of schooling. Schooling becomes something that young people are lucky to receive because of the way it enhances life chances rather than something we have to provide to maintain a sense of community and commitment to democratic participation.

The *rigid National Curriculum* (7) has limited teachers' ability to respond to the interests of pupils. It has defined for teachers the content of what should be taught and set an assessment framework that concentrates on the ten core and foundation subjects. Added to this, the *cognitive emphasis of the curriculum* (8) has diminished the importance of personal and social education (which includes health education, citizenship education, etc.) and other cross-curricular themes (NCC, 1990a–e). The message to teachers is one which directs their energies to the academic curriculum. The all-round nurturing of each child is to receive less attention. Pushed further this could be seen as encouragement to remove elements which hinder the academic or cognitive development of the pupils in a class; so-called difficult pupils may constitute such elements.

Increasingly the public services, including education, have been more closely targeted and more precisely costed and they cannot cater for the wider 'good'. Professionals in these services have had their scope for judgement narrowed and requirements of them made more explicit. Problem children fall outside the norm of what teachers habitually deal with and make the attainment of targets in the quality assured world harder.

Separate, professionalised managerialist welfare services (9) have been unable reliably to interrelate their work and address the 'joined up problems'. At the same time there has been a *punitive attitude to troubled and troublesome young people* (10). Excluded pupils were defined as culprits rather than victims. The *Pupils with Problems* circulars (DfE, 1994b) explicitly located the problem with the children. This inhibited a balanced understanding of their problems and discouraged the allocation of resources to 'restorative' solutions. Gillian Shephard referred to 'disruptive pupils', 'unacceptable for a minority of pupils to undermine', 'before problems run out of control' and 'ill-behaved pupils' (DfEE, 1995b). The conventional sense of this view was clear and Lane's (1990) *The Impossible Child* unintentionally gives it further credence. Unfortunately couching the issues in this way obscured the foundations of the problem and narrowed options in dealing with it. The tendency is to 'reject the rejecter' and take a punitive line towards the excluded pupil who is not seen as deserving of help – particularly if he is 15 or 16 (and it usually is 'he'). Furthermore, negative media attention given to difficult or excluded pupils and their families has fuelled unsympathetic reactions to the allocation of resources to support a child and family through their difficulties.

These attitudes are linked with the *excessive attribution of personal and family responsibility* (11) and the individualisation of the problem. While the behaviour of young people has been a very real cause for concern among all agencies, some responses have been such as to generate *anti-school, non-stakeholder, criminally inclined local youth subculture* (12).

At the institutional level the variation in exclusion rates across schools has been considerable and suggests that some *school policies* (13) and practices are more supportive than others. *Racism* (14), however implicit, appears to operate in school as in society at large and some schools have taken more effective steps to address this. School staff may need to look even more closely at the conflict situations that arise with ethnic minority children to see if, in their responses to them, they are sufficiently racially aware and culturally sensitive to the lives of these young people and their families.

In relation to policy and practice at the whole school level, some schools appear to be better at the business of *leadership, relationships and general teaching skills* (15) and maintain reasonable morale. More particularly, *class management and interpersonal skills* (16) are more evident in some schools than others. The curriculum demands have placed emphasis, both at initial teacher education and at inservice training (INSET) levels, on core subject skills and this has reduced the time and importance devoted to generic people management skills and particularly skills of conflict management.

A significant proportion of pupils who are permanently excluded from school struggle with their school work prior to exclusion and it is clear that there has been *inadequate attention to individual learning needs* (17). This may take the form of reading problems, dyslexia, hearing or sight problems, or inability to concentrate or relate to others, or it may be a specific, diagnosed (or diagnosable) condition such as Asperger's Syndrome or Attention Deficit and Hyperactivity Disorder (ADHD). Early identification of, and treatment for, such problems would appear to be crucial.

The special educational needs assessment process has proved to be very slow. The statementing process is completed within the recommended six month period in only a minority of cases. Addressing *learning* needs may help to address *behavioural* problems.

Schools find themselves competing in the local area (18) to attract pupils and do not easily co-operate in organising the movement of a pupil from one school

to another for a new start and demonstrating thereby their collective responsibility for children in the area. Equally, in the manner of small businesses the
local management (19) of limited resources can mean reducing outlay on
services with a poor return, the more so when *relationships with parents* (20)
are not well developed and *LEA support for schools dealing with behaviourally
challenging pupils* (21) is limited. LEAs cannot easily offer the support that
schools request, and certainly have problems in offering it at short notice.
Schools may have to pay for this help which may predispose the school to
remove the problem rather than buy the solution.

The embattled position in which schools have found themselves, the targets
for which they are publicly held accountable and the legal framework available to regulate exclusions appears to *place emphasis on carrying out the exclusion
correctly rather than seeking the best solution for the young person* (22).

There is an increase in *family and social problems* (23), poverty and in family
breakdown. The number of children in poor families increased through the
1980s and 1990s and there were 1.3 million one-parent families caring for
2.2 million children (Office of Population Censuses and Surveys (OPCS),
1995). There is an association between social dislocation, poverty and difficulties at school including the experience of exclusion.

Smith and Rutter's (1995: 781) review of the available evidence suggests
that *psycho-social problems among young people* (24) are on the increase. The
authors are concerned with individual factors, including the process of individual development, and with social structures and conditions which may
contribute to the development of more of these problems. There are more
behaviourally difficult children and young people in schools today.

Schooling no longer leads to employment and many who would leave at 16
to begin work find that this is not an option. The result can be alienation from
the school's purposes and a lack of tolerance for the presumed social function
of schooling. The emergence of *deviant peer subcultures* (25) can result in just
these circumstances.

Undetected medical problems (26) particularly those associated with hearing
and sight can be behind behavioural difficulties. *Low self-esteem* (27) in
young people can also undermine motivation and promote inappropriate
behaviour. Poverty and difficulty in the home situation can sap self-esteem;
so also can a competitive and narrow achievement orientation within the
school.

Social exclusion and exclusion from school

Bringing together the forces promoting exclusion and inclusion and decon-
structing these further leads to the lengthy list presented in Figure 3.1.
This representation both acknowledges the complex, not to say holistic,
nature of school exclusion and social exclusion, and directs attention to
points of intervention which can blunt an exclusion process and promote an
inclusive one. This chapter has dealt mostly with forces promoting exclusions.

In the 1980s and 1990s, there have been more predisposing social factors underlying the rise in permanent exclusions than in earlier periods. Figure 3.1 indicates the range of forces at play in creating or inhibiting exclusions from school in the UK.

The law and finance are predominantly matters for central government.[7] So too, in the main, are key messages about what education is for and whether it is to be seen as a personal, competitive good or a community building necessity. Poverty, poor living conditions and unemployment are not always amenable to speedy government action but eighteen years of a Conservative government led to a substantial widening of the gap between rich and poor and a greatly increased number of children growing up in poverty. Other socio-economic and cultural factors have also to be addressed at that national level and interventions made which will shift the emphasis from blame and punishment to support and restorative approaches.

With open enrolment, money following pupil numbers and parents supposedly informed by league tables, schools are encouraged to sell themselves and are tempted to remove anything which might diminish their reputation – such as problem children. The local school is no longer the community resource providing unconditionally for all in its area. Furthermore, there is a sense in which, if behaviour is bad, education, viewed as a commodity, is withdrawn – as a punishment. These institutional factors related to the school which affect the likelihood of inclusion or exclusion are not divorced from national and regional processes, policies and priorities. The full set of institutional factors are amenable to intervention but time is needed and there are costs associated with changing cultures and spreading skills and attitudes more widely. Indeed, the major levers for action lie with national government in terms of the training it requires of its teachers, the marketing environment in which schools are to operate and the responsibility local education authorities are to take for children.

The last set of factors concerns individual pathologies. Three key points are to be noted from the small number of items in Figure 3.1 which refer to individual factors: first, they are few in number; second, the extent to which these pose 'problems' are matters of definition, policy and provision; third, it is arguable that institutional factors and national policy affect the extent to which these factors appear, are recognised and are addressed.

At each level there are 'malleables' accessible to the influence of structural change or human agency. The high expectation was evident, following a year of a Labour government, that human agency could change much, that better schools and teachers, more self-controlled young people and more effective parents could reduce the incidence of bad behaviour in schools which leads to exclusion. The political, administrative and structural changes which can hugely affect the forces acting to push up exclusions remain somewhat hidden. This is political individualism winning out over social democracy, and central government showing a minimal willingness, up to the end of

1998, to address the inclusion agenda set out in items 1–12 in the right-hand column of Figure 3.1.[8]

Notes

1 'Freedom's just another word for nothing left to lose' is a line from Kris Kristof-ferson's 'Bobbie McGee', most famously sung by Janis Joplin. Tracey Chapman's 'Fast Car' has the line 'started with nothing, got nothing to lose'. Both are expressions of the socially excluded.
2 Weber's characterisation of social action is about the management of conflicts, unequal distribution of power, how certain 'ideas' come to dominate and how that domination is legitimated.
3 The most recent figures available at the time of writing do not relate to the new Labour government.
4 Bynner (1998: 435) writes, 'The increasing value placed on educational qualifica-tions can be seen more as a means of rationing jobs on a class basis in a situation of job shortage'.
5 Selznick (1949) had a view on the non-malleability of important elements of the system. It is important to identify the factors which are difficult to change and these are usually the structural and cultural ones. Clearly, policy makers are keen to accentuate the personal, local and institutional factors which are supposedly exposed to short-term and cheap interventions to bring about improvement. This can bring a denial of any *necessary* link with deep-seated structural con-ditions and glorify human agency placing great (maybe impossible) pressure on it to effect change.
6 The link between crime and poverty is not a simple one. Working-class antag-onisms towards education have been described over many years and the tempta-tions for alienated (socially excluded?) groups to engage in criminal activity are plain.
7 Local government controls some finance and has a limited policy-making role.
8 The Labour government's guidance on exclusion (DfEE, 1999) appears under the ambitious and wholesome title *Draft Guidance on Social Inclusion: Pupil Support*. In attempting to build on the Social Exclusion Unit report it attempts to com-bine a wide range of advice but it still leaves EBD (emotional and behavioural difficulties) to a later Special Needs guidance document; to that extent its 'integrated' nature is compromised. The guidance increases the barriers to exclu-sion and has much emboldened text in sections 5 and 6 on exclusion but it does not constitute a commitment to 'social inclusion'.

4 Disaffection, truancy and exclusion

Introduction

Pupil disaffection has been around as long as there has been compulsory schooling. The Newsom Report, *Half Our Future* (Central Advisory Council on Education, 1963), is about the growing group of young school leavers who had little commitment to the curriculum they experienced and showed little motivation to benefit from it. Though disaffection could flourish even in selective schools (Lacey, 1970), it was mainly to be found with working-class pupils. The formation of anti-school subcultures has been well documented from Hargreaves (1967) through Willis (1977) and Corrigan (1979) to Blackman (1995).

Many of the negative factors which impair pupil motivation, quality of learning and examination results are not susceptible to modification solely by the efforts of the school. These negative factors may be of an economic or social kind affecting whole families as discussed in Chapter 3. The Elton Report (DES, 1989) acknowledged the complexity of disaffection and, although restricted by its remit, produced very good guidelines for the development of whole school policies and strategies for individual teachers which might reduce the degree and scope of the problem. The oversimplifications and limitations resulting from the restricted remit are examined later in the chapter.

This government inquiry, chaired by Lord Elton, reporting under the straightforward title *Discipline in Schools,* was prompted by concern over the problems facing the teaching profession, in particular reports of physical attacks by pupils on teachers in school. However, disaffection is an umbrella term which embraces a range of pupils whose disaffection manifests itself in different ways. It is a generic concept which needs to be unpacked in order to reveal the range of meanings collected together under the common title. Aggressive and violent physical behaviour is the most significant, disruptive and distressing expression of disaffection, particularly for teachers and pupil peers who suffer as a consequence of it. It exposes the teacher to high levels of stress and it causes severe disruption to the education of the other pupils in the class. Where a pupil persistently engages in disruptive behaviour, a school is more likely to exercise the right to exclude that pupil in order, as the headteacher sees it, to secure the well-being of the teacher and the education of the other pupils.

'Disaffection' can also be applied to pupils who truant on a regular basis. These are pupils who vote with their feet because they feel that school has little or nothing to offer them. Such pupils are commonly in Years 10 and 11 (O'Keefe, 1994). Such high levels of alienation from school are extremely difficult to combat, especially when the pupils appear in school so infrequently. In-school truancy, where lessons are skipped by pupils after registration, are lesser but still worrying manifestations of disaffection.

School refusers and school phobics are also classed as disaffected, but some disaffected students do not truant nor do they exhibit unusual behaviours. They attend school but school has little relevance for them; they are not actively engaged in the learning process. They do not volunteer to join in. They do not contribute to debate or discussion and they only go through the motions of working, putting in the minimum of effort required without drawing attention to themselves. They could be described as the passively disaffected, a minority who glide unobserved through the system absorbing little teacher time and little learning.

It is possible to quantify the extent of disaffection in relation to exclusion and truancy, while the numbers of school refusers/phobics and the under-achievers who attend school but are educationally withdrawn remain unknown. Exclusions, particularly permanent exclusions, present most difficulty. These pupils' overt disaffection has led to a decision that the institution does not want them to be there. In general there is confusion about the motives of these pupils and responses to their behaviour. Seeing them as 'mad', 'bad' or 'sad' hardly helps. 'Flight' or 'fight' is also not a helpful distinction. With the stereotyped picture in the background it is no wonder that official and public reaction swings from struggles to comprehend to exasperated condemnation. The Social Exclusion Unit (1998) set a very measured agenda to reduce truancy by one-third by 2002 and 'ensure that education ceases to be optional' (1988: 2), but the tone is largely one of compulsion rather than inducement.

Understanding school disaffection

'Disaffection' is a wonderfully sanitised term. It is hardly jargon, yet is not commonly applied by teachers, still less by pupils themselves who might be 'disaffected'. 'Disaffection' and 'disaffected' carry with them a neutral though sad shading, a sense of slight worry and disappointment. 'Troublesome' pupils, 'disruptive' behaviour (Social Exclusion Unit, 1998: 11) and 'pupils with problems' (DfE, 1994b) energise thinking and debate far more and lead to responses with tones ranging from serious concern to outrage. Indeed it is the location of blame and responsibility which is the decisive factor and what alliances of groups centre their judgements upon in the contest of discourses.

Professionals dispute the terms, and 'troubled and troublesome' is sometimes used to indicate a pupil's internal state which should be acknowledged as well as the effect it has on others. Arguably, a dominant public view and dominant teacher professions' view, set within limited educational resources and league tables, define disaffected pupils negatively and locate blame with the pupils themselves, the parents or the community. Where the discourse takes this form and is legitimised, schools and teachers are not required to adjust. Thus, it is more a matter of understanding others' *understanding* of school disaffection than developing a clear account of the 'objective reality' of disaffected behaviour.

The degree of explicit oppositional behaviour from disaffected pupils varies and their accounts of why they are negatively disposed to schools have both a consistency and a conditionality about them. They do not like school, do not like some teachers, some subjects or some activities but they express the wish not to be there, and might act on that wish; however, they also want school to change to make it more attractive and motivating to attend. It is well known that some schools produce more disaffection among pupils than others and that some arrangements and practices can reduce disaffection, or at least the recording of symptoms of it like boredom, non-involvement, lesson disruption and truancy. Both pupil definitions and school context deserve more attention.

As pupils in any one school are drawn from varied family and community backgrounds it may be viewed as odd that order prevails in schools to the extent that it does. Children are regimented into groups of around thirty and placed in rooms with furniture, decor and activities which are separated from much else that they know and do. For those children who attend school, the teacher is vested with a certain authority. The school can be viewed as a setting which is not in need of legitimation. Therefore, efforts to generate pupils' approval or willing participation are rarely considered necessary or appropriate.

In the 1920s there existed a mood of liberal and optimistic expansion and a calm acceptance that we knew what young people needed and deserved from their education. The introduction to the Hadow Report, *The Education of the Adolescent* (Board of Education, 1927), is a delight.

> We have been profoundly interested by the question propounded in the terms of reference, which we desire to thank the board for remitting to us, and to which we have devoted a prolonged and anxious consideration. After hearing and weighing a large amount of evidence, and after some study both of the development of the past which is recorded in our first chapter and the tendencies of the present which are examined in our second, we cannot but feel – as we unanimously do – that the

times are auspicious and the signs favourable, for a new advance in the general scope of our national system of education . . . There is a tide which begins to rise in the veins of youth at the age of eleven or twelve.
(Board of Education, 1927: xix)

This is the language of the gentry benevolently extending education to provide secondary level schooling for all, proposing a 'practical bias' for the new Modern Schools (p. 176) and, 'a new Leaving Examination to meet the needs of pupils in selective and non-selective Modern Schools' (p. 179). The school leaving age was raised to 14 in 1930. In 1948 it became 15. Even in the 1990s teachers talk of ROSLA buildings (Raising of the School Leaving Age Nissen huts and other temporary buildings) put up for the 1948 expansion, not that of 1970.

The plan for raising the school leaving age to 16 was undertaken with a greater measure of trepidation.

The raising of the [school leaving] age could mean little more than the extension of a struggle between pupils who feel that school has little to offer them and teachers who feel they meet little other than boredom and resistance.
(Central Advisory Council on Education, 1963: 111)

The teaching profession was clearly worried about this 'extension of a struggle'. Part of the research commissioned in preparation for the raising of the school leaving age was to look at 'what stage in their school careers some pupils became allergic to education' (Schools Council, 1965: 28).

When the ROSLA decision was confirmed, however, there began a programme of curriculum development to meet the needs of the oddly named 'Young School Leaver', oddly because such individuals were less *young* as leavers than had been previously possible. The Schools Council delineated a wide range of exciting developments. The imaginative approaches, the speculative curricular offerings and the gentle pace of the late 1960s and the 1970s were a contrast to later times in the UK experience of curriculum reform. The investment on this scale in curriculum packages was an acknowledgement that the education service accepted the major responsibility for negotiating a settlement with reluctant learners. These curricular initiatives and TVEI received great praise. Circumstances, mainly funding and legislation, took them out of existence. From the 1980s onwards the UK has not succeeded in reducing disaffection through developments in school organisation or curricular changes.

While schools were held in great esteem by parents (Schools Council, 1968. 43), teachers rated educational objectives differently from both parents and pupils. 'Examination achievement' was rated low by teachers and heads but high by parents, 19–20 year olds and pupils. The same held for job-related goals. For attributes like 'independence' and 'personality and character' the ratings are reversed with teachers attributing much greater importance to these (Schools Council, 1968: Figure 6, p. 43). It would be interesting to have the questions posed again. One suspects that nearly twenty years of an instrumental ethic driving educational reforms would have changed teacher opinion to some degree.

Raven (1975: 22), surveying 4,000 pupils in the Republic of Ireland, found 'More than half of them considered more than half of their school subjects either boring or useless.' Raven's research indicated that teachers attached great significance to the development of social characteristics of students and, indeed, (at that time) Raven (1976: 14) affirmed that research 'suggests that these qualities seem to be a more important determinant of performance in the job pupils will enter than examination achievement'.

So there is a sense of irritation and disbelief in Raven's 'analysis' that while teachers agreed that many of the social objectives were important – development of qualities of character, patterns of thinking, feeling and behaviour, independence, initiative, a sense of duty towards the community – they did little to promote them. He contends that teachers were locked into a narrow, certificating view of their function yet clung to a rhetoric that described objectives they could no longer pursue.

A range of forces, and funding from different bodies, resulted in developments in the 1980s which were aimed directly at providing for the less academically inclined. The Lower Attaining Pupils Programme (LAPP), TVEI, partnerships with employers, such as 'COMPACT', and the development of Records of Achievement (ROA) were directed or adapted to appeal to the older pupils who gained less from their schooling. Ability matching, 'relevance' and recording the positive were prominent aspects of this movement. The National Curriculum from 1988 marked an end to this adaptation of curricular opportunities for the less able or the less motivated.

The initiatives in the 1990s to address truancy and disaffection largely ignored the curriculum. In the main, official strategies for countering truancy and disaffection attention have moved away from curriculum, school organisation and teacher–pupil relationships to a focus on the 'erring pupil'. The blame and responsibility has been shifted. The strategies now funded are more akin to policing – truancy watch and computerised registration systems.

Pupil disaffection and school rejection have been more elaborately theorised in a way which goes beyond Furlong's claim that 'one of the most consistent findings in studies of the relationship between indiscipline and school factors is that deviant pupils do not like school' (Furlong, 1985: 52).

The conflict of values – working-class home vs middle-class school – has been explored by Hargreaves (1967), Willis (1977), Corrigan (1979), Blackman (1995) and Sewell (1997). Their school rejectors are respectively called 'the anti-school subculture', the lads, the smash street kids, mods and rebels. Whatever the bases of these contractions, and they may apply more

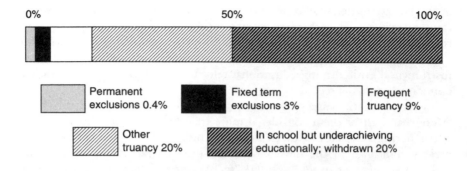

Figure 4.1 Secondary school disaffection

Note: The Keele University National Database of Pupil Attitudes to School (Mackereth, 1997) states that the disappointed (24%), the disaffected (15%), the disappeared (5%) make up a worryingly large proportion of the school population.

successfully in one place at one time – 1960s Manchester for Hargreaves (1967), 1990s London for Sewell (1997) – school rejection is not uncompromising and absolute. Though complex, the school rejectors' views need not necessarily be viewed as contradictory, confused or illogical. The most extreme of the disaffected in one sense, the permanently excluded, do not want to be out of school (CRE, 1996; Garner, 1997). There is great distress that results from being removed not just from mainstream school but from mainstream life.

Three forces in the 1990s operate to generate disaffection: school will not lead on to job – the continuity incentive is gone; children are adult in behaviour earlier yet forced to wait until later for adult status – especially economic status; the school curriculum is inflexible and teachers' jobs more narrowly defined.

Figure 4.1 above illustrates the possible extent of the disaffection problem.

Truancy

The DfE research into truancy in English secondary schools (O'Keefe, 1994) reported on the extent and likely causes of truancy in English schools, in Years 10 and 11. Findings revealed that 8.2 per cent of all pupils in Years 10 and 11 were frequent truants (i.e. that they truanted *at least* once a week). For Year 10 only, the same statistics became 6.4 per cent, while for Year 11 it rose to 9.9 per cent, nearly one in ten pupils who were frequent truants. Other pupils truanted less frequently. Of all Year 10 and 11 pupils, nearly one-quarter truanted less often than once a week (i.e. up to three times each month). For Year 10 this becomes almost one in five pupils (18.8 per cent). For Year 11 it rises to more than one-quarter of pupils in that year.

Just under one-third of all pupils in Years 10 and 11 (30.5 per cent) had truanted at least once in the previous half term. The level, however, was markedly higher in Year 11 than Year 10. One-quarter (25.2 per cent) of pupils in Year 10 had truanted, compared with more than one-third (35.8 per cent) of pupils in Year 11 (O'Keefe, 1994: 14).

These figures are believed to be understatements. Pupils who truant frequently may well have been absent during the survey in schools. Indeed, the report notes that some 17 per cent of the sample were non-respondents, which means that they were not present in school when the survey was carried out. It is impossible to say how many of these pupils were truanting, but O'Keefe states that 'the survey systematically understates the truancy problem'.

The scale of truancy compared with that of exclusion identifies truancy as a much more widespread problem facing schools. The problematic nature of truancy is also almost certainly greater than that of permanent exclusion. Research has shown that the reason given by schools for excluding pupils is entirely related to aggressive and disruptive behaviour. In the case of truancy, however, various reasons are elicited in the research. Over two-thirds (67 per cent) of all truants truanted in order to avoid a particular lesson. Questioned further about their dislike of particular lessons, 36 per cent stated that these lessons are of no relevance to their lives, 29 per cent said that they disliked the teacher and 22 per cent disliked the subject. The complete list of reasons given by pupils for avoiding lessons is given in Table 4.1.

One particularly interesting finding emerged from Coldman's (1995) further analysis of O'Keefe's research; he describes the situation as follows:

> Just under one half of all truants (49%) stated that they truanted, among other reasons, to avoid school, which initially would appear to suggest the view that truancy represents a complete rejection of the school as an institution. When they were invited to expand on this, however, it became clear that most of these pupils boycott school in order to avoid particular aspects of their educational experience rather than the totality of it . . . only 11% of all truants went on to say that school was generally boring or oppressive. In other words, only about one in ten truants

Table 4.1 Reasons for lesson truancy

Irrelevant lessons	35%
Dislike of teacher	29%
Dislike of subject	22%
Coursework problems	19%
Difficulty of subject	14%
Poor teaching	3%
Bullying	1%

gave the response which would best fit the traditional view of the truant as being alienated from the whole process of schooling.

(Coldman, 1995: 32–33)

The DfE report itself sums up the dislike of school versus dislike of lessons explanations for truancy succinctly:

> Our results point both to the pre-eminence of rejection of particular lessons as a reason for truancy, and to the acceptance of the curriculum as worthwhile by most pupils. This acceptance also embraces most confessed truants, even if less closely than is the case with their non-truanting peers Thus there is little evidence of widespread, outright hostility to the world of school.
>
> (O'Keefe, 1994: 49)

Finally, the report offers a word of encouragement to those who seek to influence the balance of disaffected pupils in favour of the school. The traditional question whether the sources of school behaviour rest within the institution itself, or the background of pupils is raised and responded to in this way:

> None of the leading researchers today is likely to say that truancy is typically to be explained *entirely* by school factors, or alternatively by the personal aspects of individual pupils. The data uncovered in this research point both ways, but more consistently in the direction of institutional explanations. This proposition seems hopeful, at least in the sense that it is easier to work on improving schools than it is to work on improving homes and backgrounds.
>
> (O'Keefe, 1994: 49)

O'Keefe and Stoll were more emphatic in later reporting of this research claiming 'the enormous influence curriculum seems to have on the willingness of teenagers to be in school or class' (1995a: 9). In pressing their position further, they claim

> If educational dysfunctions such as truancy, bad behaviour and idleness, illiteracy, innumeracy and non-certification are to be addressed, then the curriculum for 14- to 16-year-olds needs to be changed radically. The National Curriculum . . . will . . . have to go. It is too coercive, too centralised, too prescriptive and too inflexible.
>
> (O'Keefe and Stoll, 1995a: 24)

This called for a change of curriculum, and for a curriculum pitched at the right level for the pupils. Elsewhere their research cited irrelevance of lessons and dislike of teachers; clearly work is needed at this level. Different content, different resourcing and teaching processes and different relationships.

Teaching by domination is counter-productive in its impact on some young people.

School refusers and school phobics tend to identify themselves but there are no figures available for these categories. Disaffected pupils who attend school regularly and do not draw attention to themselves are a cause for concern. But again, the extent of this problem is unknown. Individual schools will need help in order to identify this category of pupil and to quantify the problem. However, it is possible to conduct a review in each school in order to discover the nature and extent of more overt disaffection expressed through exclusion, blanket truancy, post-registration truancy, phobic behaviour, disruption and more passive withdrawal behaviours that some pupils may adopt.

The Elton Report (DES, 1989) requested that funding be made available 'to encourage innovative projects for meeting the needs of the most difficult pupils and their schools' (p. 158, Recommendation 87). The report recommends that 'the management of pupil behaviour should become a national priority for funding' (p. 78, Recommendation 9). As a result of this recommendation, funding has been made available by the government under wider terms of reference. The DfE invited LEAs in England to apply for a range of grants under the Grants for Education Support and Training (GEST) programme. Among these, bids were invited for grant number 20: Truancy and Disaffected Pupils. Sixty LEAs secured funding in the 1993/94 tranche. Eighty-four LEAs secured funds for a start in 1994/95.

Each year the Pupils and Parents Branch of the DfEE has produced a directory of approved projects listing details for each. The directories are intended to enable GEST project teams to liaise and share experiences with other project teams where they share common ground or common interests. Four such annual directories have been produced. In addition an independent evaluation of the 1993/94 and 1994/95 programmes was carried out by James Learmonth (DfEE, 1995b) and three volumes of reports from LEAs on these projects were produced (DfEE, 1997a). The department let it be known that it supported a newsletter to promote networking and sharing of information about these projects. The newsletter was produced by the London Institute of Education and Lewisham LEA.

DfE Circular 18/94 invited further bids for, among others, GEST 13 projects related to Truancy and Disaffected Pupils. About eighty LEAs were to be supported in 1995/96 from this grant. The means of addressing truancy and exclusion has been through the GEST funding. An examination of the directory of approved projects over three years (DfE, 1995b; DfEE, 1995c, 1996a) reveals considerable expenditure on schemes. In 1994/95 forty-three of the eighty-five projects were related to 'truancy watch' projects. Information technology (IT) based registration systems were also popular. A third factor to which a significant number of LEA schemes paid attention was bullying. In the prevention or reduction of truancy educational welfare officers (EWOs) clearly have a leading role and while much of their work was of the 'liaison' and 'following-up' type, particularly with parents, two specifically referred to legal sanction and Educational Supervision orders. While truancy watch and IT registration schemes were mentioned less in the 1995/96 and 1996/97 directories, there was more mention of PRUs supporting home tuition and of reintegration. Police, educational psychologists and youth workers continued across all the years to receive mention in only a few schemes. Counselling, the development of pupils' coping skills, and pastoral care or PSHE work are also seldom explicit in these documents. Throughout, the picture presented was one of identification and coercion – find the truants, prevent truancy (through computerised registration systems) and persuade them to stay. The problem was located with the child, the family and mainly outside the school.

The attention to training for teachers was a common element across about half the projects (though it was clearly intended that in-school support and behaviour support teams should have spin-offs for mainstream school staff). Whole school approaches figured in only a few projects. Special needs was likewise a minority element and ethnicity, despite over-representation of African Caribbean pupils in exclusion figures, was explicitly mentioned in only one project. Teaching methods and the curriculum were mentioned by fewer than five projects in any one year.

The big increase across the three years is in the mention of PRUs, in resourcing a full National Curriculum, supporting home tutors and even developing distance learning material for pupils out of school. Thus there is a move from 'prevention' aimed at the child in the direction of the institutions providing for pupils. Most emphatically, across all three years, the curriculum is not targeted. The problem of truancy and disaffection has been definitively displaced.

The compendium of reports on these projects (DfEE, 1997a) runs to three volumes and 665 pages. The view offered here is fairly detailed; the reader is at least able to see if the projects (those running in 1995/96) were focused on a small number of 'difficult' schools or across the authority. Materials have been produced, activity is recorded, lists of schools are set out. Three concerns arise: first, much of this could be seen as sound local administration of education that should be going on anyway; second, because these are 'projects' in the context of cash-strapped local authorities, the likelihood that they will continue without the GEST funding is questionable; these 'projects' are bolt-on and droppable; third, the government position on these initiatives was at a distance, granting funding but appearing to have, and want, little control of implementation, evaluation or dissemination.

Though one may question the focus, style and understanding of these truancy and disaffection projects, evaluation of them has been positive (DfEE, 1995b), even if based on mainly qualitative indicators. 'GEST funds had made a very positive contribution to their [LEAs'] and schools' efforts to improve attendance' (DfEE, 1995b: 11).

There have also been schemes of a more targeted sort funded by the DfEE. Pilot Pupil Behaviour and Discipline Projects have been funded in forty-four

LEAs over three years (1996–99) with £18 million. The sixty-three projects funded, and a further seven in grant maintained (GM) schools, were in three categories – multi-disciplinary support teams, secondment of teachers to Pupil Referral Units and in-school centres for pupils at risk of exclusion.

These projects operated alongside others for older disaffected pupils funded under Restart (New Start from May 1997). An education minister of the time claimed of the sixty-three pilot projects, 'The programme will provide an excellent basis for identifying and promoting models of good practice. All schools and LEAs will be able to learn from what proves most effective' (DfEE, 1996b). This level of rationality seems unlikely. The curriculum is built into policy and is to be 'delivered'. Little has been researched on good and bad teachers or good and bad relationships that motivate pupils and make them want to attend.

We should not lose sight either of the claim made in a study of truancy in the 1980s:

> Both truancy and the laws in which it is constituted are rooted in the class and political interests of an increasingly divided society. Not until the politics of compulsory education are driven by a belief that the equal education of all our children is equally in all our interests will more young people believe that they can benefit from the goods that schools have to offer.
>
> (Carlen *et al.*, 1992: 180)

Exclusion

Types of behaviour which lead to permanent exclusion vary hugely: persistently breaking school rules, verbal abuse to staff, violence to other pupils, violence to staff, inappropriate sexual behaviour. However, many incidents are irritating but minor. OFSTED's report on exclusions examined 112 individual cases of which 2 were for carrying weapons and 4 for attacks on teachers (OFSTED, 1996b), which are clearly unacceptable but make up a small percentage of the total.

Causes cannot be assumed to originate within the child. Personal circumstances, the context of the school and LEA and national policy all contain contributory factors. Yet the *Pupils with Problems* circulars explicitly locate the problem with the pupils (Parsons and Howlett, 1996). Redefinition of the problem of exclusions requires recognition of difficulties beyond the control of the pupil. Three pieces of research offer support for such a reorientation. Hayden (1997), in a survey of 265 primary excluded pupils, found that almost all had experienced a variety of stress factors. Among these were:

- family breakdown
- time in care/social work involvement

- multiple moves/disruption
- disability/bereavement
- violence/abuse
- major accident/incident
- special education needs
- previous serious exclusion
- no member of household in paid work

OFSTED (1996b) produced an almost identical list associated with disruption and leading to exclusion, adding four other factors: poor basic skills; limited aspirations and opportunities; poor relationships; and peer pressure to behave in ways likely to lead to conflict with authority. In addition, in more than one-quarter of the cases analysed by OFSTED, pupils had been, or were, in the care of local authorities. There are children with major difficulties to cope with in their lives. These difficulties alone cannot be viewed as the causes of disruption. Responses to them are crucial.

Kinder and her colleagues (1996) at the National Foundation for Educational Research (NFER) reported in rank order the views of pupils on the main causes of truancy and disruption. These were:

- influence of friends and peers
- relationships with teachers
- content and delivery of the curriculum
- family factors
- bullying
- classroom context (individual learning support and classroom management)
- problems arising from their own personality or learning abilities.

(Kinder *et al.*, 1996: 5)

There are other, institutional, reasons for the rise in exclusions. Hayden (1997) found that if a school was suffering financial cuts or staffing problems, or was overcrowded, a child was more likely to be excluded. Many schools serving disadvantaged areas exclude few pupils but some, with falling rolls, experience severe difficulties because they are obliged to accept disruptive pupils excluded from other schools. LEAs may be able to ensure that no one school becomes overloaded with excludees, but not all achieve this effectively (OFSTED, 1996b). This is exacerbated by headteachers feeling under pressure to be seen to take a hard line on discipline which results in higher exclusion rates (OFSTED, 1996b).

Three-quarters of low excluding schools were judged by OFSTED (1996b) to have effective behaviour policies. According to OFSTED, good behaviour policies embody respect and responsibility; set out implications in clear language; accessible to all; give clear expectations to both staff and students, stating sanctions and rewards; and are implemented consistently by all staff and are known and supported by parents.

Applying suitable sanctions and rewards is important. Pupils put this among their four top-ranking solutions (Kinder *et al.*, 1996: 28) and also said it would be easier to behave if things were more fair. Pupils value rewards but some feel that there are too few, that they are unjustly applied and that sanctions are used more than rewards (OFSTED, 1996b). There need to be enough sanctions, or privileges to be withdrawn, so that exclusion is not considered too quickly. Fixed term exclusions are used so often in some schools that they cease to be effective (OFSTED, 1996b).

Pastoral support is ideally co-ordinated and has continuity, with clear routes for referral. There must be the opportunity also for informed discussion (among staff, with parents, involving outside professionals when necessary). Again, because of stretched resources, most support is reactive, unable to anticipate and prevent difficulties arising, and so may become disciplinary (OFSTED, 1996b).

Very few excluded pupils are of above average ability (OFSTED, 1996b). Almost half the cases of permanent exclusion examined in the OFSTED report had literacy difficulties, some of which went undetected. Others were detected too late or could not be allocated a share of the school's scarce support. Children's self-esteem is linked to their success. Repeated failure is demoralising and most children would prefer to hide this, perhaps behind a veneer of disruption. Some children feel that their learning difficulties are being publicly exposed or that their needs are being ignored (Kinder *et al.*, 1996).

Schools' budgets and resources are stretched to the limit. However, some could make more curricular concessions, in setting realistic targets for low attainers. The replacement of one or two GCSE subjects by vocational options works well in some schools (OFSTED, 1996b), a practice which, if more widely applied, could respond to the finding of Kinder *et al.* (1996), that pupils described the curriculum as irrelevant and boring.

Subject and class teachers have not all received adequate training in behaviour management. Some are unsure of the distinction between poor behaviour and behaviour arising from emotional disturbance which requires treatment (OFSTED, 1996b). As a result, referral to specialist services is often too late and sometimes ineffective because the services themselves are stretched. The effectiveness and pupil perceptions of behaviour management have been linked to disruptive behaviour (Kinder *et al.*, 1996). Another favourable development is an increasing tendency to provide training for classroom assistants for which GEST funding has been made available.

Disaffected pupils as a social problem

If young people do not particularly like school and express the wish not to b there, this can be an entirely rational view. Pupils are known to atten 'because my friends are there', as though it is in some respects the natur meeting place for young people. It is the institutional arrangement set

for the containment, care and development of young people. It is a matter of what mix of attractions, incentives and coercive measures work best to get them to school, to attend the lessons when there and to 'engage'.

As Hallam (1997) has indicated, truancy increases as pupils transfer from primary to secondary schools, as pupils progress through secondary school, peaking in Years 10 and 11. Absence is higher in the inner cities (1997: 3). There are good reasons to expect truancy to correlate with the usual indices of disadvantage.

Disaffection, truancy, disruption and exclusion are disproportionately found in disadvantaged groups. To that extent they are a 'social' problem rather than simply an educational one. There are questions about the welfare and compensatory welfare role with regard to these children.

Truancy or exclusion are related to crime though studies are inconclusive. Lewis (1995) reports that

> not all children who truant from school are involved in crime and in the majority of cases it appears that they do nothing in particular. In some cases they are apparently either a nuisance in town centres, or vulnerable to the crimes of others.
>
> (Lewis, 1995: 24)

It is suggested that fewer than 4 per cent of offenders were truanting when the offence was committed yet Reid (1987) reports that where truancy patrols have been established in inner city areas youth crime has been reduced. The Audit Commission is unequivocal about the relationship between youth crime and being out of school.

> Young people who truant or are excluded from school are more likely to offend. Exclusion and truancy are therefore both key indicators of trouble to come if corrective action is not taken. Forty-two per cent of offenders of school age who are sentenced in the youth court have been excluded from school. A further 23 per cent truant significantly!
>
> (Audit Commission, 1996b: 66)

Thus a further social problem is in the consequences of disaffection, truancy and exclusion.

It is finally to be seen as a social problem in terms of youth culture, the structural location of youth and the diminished opportunities for status usually via employment and assured progression for many as they move to the end of compulsory schooling and beyond. Education's role may well need recasting, as suggested in Chapter 3. There are certainly dangers if a state apparatus functions to alienate, marginalise and contribute to the social exclusion of young people. This is, of course, unless such exclusion functions to serve other purposes to which Wright (1995) and Gans (1995) refer.

5 The correlates of school exclusion

Ray Godfrey and Carl Parsons

Introduction

This chapter examines the variation between exclusions within a set of secondary schools and across LEAs in England, considering how far this variation can be accounted for in terms of social disadvantage and to what extent schools differ, despite similarities in the disadvantages they face. It reports on a statistical analysis undertaken for this purpose.

The reader is taken through the steps of the analysis and we attempt to give explanation at every step which will make the whole accessible to those with little statistical background. In multivariate analysis or multilevel modelling the complexity lies in the interaction between variables. For instance poor housing, unemployment and free school meals correlate moderately highly. Good statistical analysis will try to take account of these inter-correlations and weight their part in the final explanatory model in a way which avoids simplistic conclusions.

OFSTED inspection reports provided all the school level data. For each of the academic years 1992/93, 1993/94 and 1994/95 a sample of secondary school reports was selected from twenty-four LEAs. For some of the LEAs there were few or no reports in a particular year. For some of the larger authorities a systematic sample was taken. In total 388 school reports were analysed. These data were combined with information about the twenty-four LEAs taken from the 1991 Census database (Chadwyck Healey, 1994), Local Authority Performance Indicators (Audit Commission, 1996a) and permanent exclusion rates for the twenty-four LEAs in 1993/94 (DfE, 1995a).

Building a statistical model

The analysis described in this chapter builds up a statistical model of the data. It attempts to find a relatively simple set of equations or numerical relationships which provide a reasonable summary of the information and the relationships it contains. This is done in the hope that relationships between data are matched by relationships in the real-world conditions which the data represent, though it is important to be aware that statistics alone are unable to guarantee this match. The point to note is how much of the variation between LEAs, between schools and between cohorts is described by each model and how much of the variation is unaccounted.

In the tables representing the models, the variance columns show that the statistics are complex but are explained in lay person's terms where possible with footnotes for more technical matters. A glossary is also provided at the end of the chapter (pp. 87–88). It is important for the reader to evaluate possible real-world relationships represented in the data and have a sense of the quality and strength of the mathematical relationships that lie behind them.

The purpose is to develop a model which accounts for as much variation as possible in terms of background social factors at LEA and school level and then to see how more variation can be explained by taking into account variables which indicate aspects of LEA and school policy and practice. By allowing background social factors to have 'first bite', how this unexplained variance (see glossary) is distributed between the different levels (LEAs, schools, cohorts) introduces a bias towards a social rather than a school effectiveness explanation of exclusion rates; but the bias is a conscious one and can be taken into account informally. Ideally an analysis would also consider explanations at the level of individual exclusion events. A full account of exclusions would give due weight to the fact that exclusion events happen to individual pupils in unique personal situations, although these situations arise in a school and wider social environment. The model developed here is unable to reflect this important fact. Individual differences always remain part of the 'variance', the variation not accounted for by the model.

There are great difficulties in conducting and interpreting statistical analyses in this context. The data available are not perfectly suited to the task in hand and different variables used may relate to different time periods. For example, unemployment rates and home ownership rates in 1991 have to be taken as (inaccurate) indicators of conditions actually affecting exclusion rates between 1992 and 1995. The business of finding indicators of disadvantage is far from simple (see Department of the Environment, 1991). The forms of analysis required are fairly complex. There is a large degree of ambiguity in the significance of certain variables, which may appear to be important simply because they are closely related to other, more important data which are not available. When all reasonable explanation has been offered for differences between schools, there is still room for disagreement on how far the remaining differences are a matter of school effectiveness and how far we simply have to accept that human affairs contain an element of chance.

Rather than looking just at the total number of exclusions from a school in a particular academic year, it is important to break the figures down into yeargroup and gender of pupils as well as distinguishing between permanent and temporary exclusions. In the analysis undertaken 'temporary' was used as a label to cover fixed term and also indefinite exclusions. The latter were not allowed from September 1994 onwards. This makes it impossible to compare like with like. Possibly indefinite exclusions in some cases would be replaced by a number of fixed term exclusions of the same pupil. Possibly they would be replaced by permanent exclusions.

The basic model

In Chapter 2, Figures 2.3 and 2.4 showed the average rates of temporary and permanent exclusion events for every 1,000 boys and girls in each age group within the 388 schools. The pattern in both cases is similar. Boys are excluded far more frequently than girls. Exclusions increase markedly from Y7 to Y10 and then drop back in Y11. Fixed term and indefinite exclusions are far more frequent than permanent exclusions. It is therefore essential to analyse the data in ways which take account of this. A school which permanently excludes two more Y7 girls than expected is a far more unusual place than one which has ten more fixed term exclusions of Y9 boys. Unfortunately OFSTED reports no longer provide the data for such a detailed analysis to be possible.

The basic model developed here does no more than take into account the variation in exclusions seen in Figures 2.3 and 2.4. It is of little value in itself but serves as a basis for further development. This basic model treats boys and girls separately. It distinguishes between exclusion rates in each year from Y7 to Y11 and distinguishes between permanent and temporary exclusions. All the necessary coefficients could be estimated reasonably accurately. There were not enough data to estimate accurately any differences between years in the way permanent and temporary exclusions were related.

The basic model, which is summarised in Tables 5.1 and 5.2, differs in a number of important ways from ordinary linear regression with which

Table 5.1 Fixed effects in the basic model

		Exclusion rate per 1,000 pupils	Scale factor	Confidence interval (95%)
Boys				
Permanent	Y7	3.90		2.75–5.53
	Y8		×1.58	1.39–1.80
	Y9		×2.15	1.90–2.44
	Y10		×2.75	2.43–3.11
	Y11		×1.90	1.67–2.17
Temporary	Y7–Y11		×9.57	8.88–10.32
Girls				
Permanent	Y7	0.52		0.40–0.68
	Y8		×2.65	1.39–3.41
	Y9		×4.17	3.27–5.32
	Y10		×5.37	4.22–6.84
	Y11		×2.86	2.22–3.69
Temporary	Y7–Y11		×11.97	10.09–14.21

Table 5.2 Random effects in the basic model

Level	Variance	Confidence interval
LEA	0.158	0.038–0.277
School	0.356	0.250–0.463
Temporary[a]	0.241	0.136–0.345
Yeargroup	0.200	0.158–0.241
Exclusion type[b]	0.371	0.329–0.414

Notes:

a This is the amount by which the variance among schools' rates of temporary exclusions exceeds that among schools' rates of permanent exclusion.

b This is the amount of variance within school cohorts between the deviation of boys' and girls' permanent and temporary exclusions from the levels estimated by the model.

many people are familiar. The major differences are explained in the next few paragraphs. The complexities are no more than are necessary to cope with the nature of the data.

First, the model is log-linear (see Lindsey, 1995) which means that the explanatory variables are assumed to have a multiplicative rather than additive effect. This means that any one variable does not add a fixed amount on to the rate of exclusions. Rather it increases the rate of exclusions in a fixed proportion. For boys and girls separately Table 5.1 gives the rate of exclusions per 1,000 pupils in Y7 together with the factors by which this must be multiplied to obtain the rates for Y8 to Y11 and factor by which the result must be multiplied to give the rates for temporary exclusions. For example the rate per 1,000 for permanent exclusions of Y9 girls is

$$0.52 \times 4.17 = 2.17$$

and the rate for temporary exclusions of Y9 girls is

$$0.52 \times 4.17 \times 11.97 = 25.84$$

This does not agree exactly with the rate shown in Figure 2.3 (Chapter 2). The model does not exactly fit the actual level of exclusions in the 388 schools sampled, but the discrepancy is not statistically significant (see glossary). The 95 per cent confidence intervals (see glossary) are given for each coefficient. The background calculations on which these are based are carried out on the logarithmic scale and are symmetrical about the best estimate; but when they are transformed into ordinary numbers the best estimate is not the midpoint of the confidence interval.

Second, the model is multilevel (Goldstein, 1995). This means that local and regional variations can be given their proper consideration. For example the ratio of permanent to temporary exclusions varies between LEAs, between schools, and between the different years in a single school. A multilevel model can take account of this without losing sight of the fact that there is also a national ratio to which all these are approximations. The variations are assumed to fit normal distributions at all levels. Analysis of this kind requires sophisticated software specifically designed for the purpose.[1]

Multilevel modelling also allows an effective approach to the way that rates of temporary exclusions varied more widely between schools than the rates of permanent exclusions, and produces accurate estimates of this variation in the types of exclusion. Note that this variation is measured on a logarithmic scale; so temporary rates vary more than permanent rates even after allowing fully for the fact that temporary exclusions rates are far higher than permanent.

Third, it is assumed that at the very basic level, when for example we are looking at the chance of a girl in Y10 being permanently excluded from school A, all the explanatory variables establish only an expected level of risk. There is still room for chance events to determine how closely the actual number of exclusions matches the expected rate. To use a crude analogy, if conditions in a store make it likely that about ten light bulbs will 'fail' in the course of a week, even when conditions are unvarying there will still be weeks when none 'fail' and weeks when twenty 'fail'. The pattern in failure of light bulbs in a set time period will not follow a normal distribution. The name given to the type of pattern of variation found in the example of the numbers of failing light bulbs is a Poisson distribution.[2] The variation in exclusions is assumed be similar. This Poisson variation is assumed to be constant throughout all the models mentioned in this chapter and is not described or discussed.

Because of the complicated nature of the models of this type, it is not appropriate to judge their success simply by considering the proportion of variance explained. It is possible to judge the effectiveness of a change in such a model by seeing how far it reduces the deviance (see glossary), a measure of how improbable the given data would be if the model were absolutely correct. The significance of a reduction in deviance passing from one model to another can be calculated from the χ^2 distribution. For a single additional explanatory variable, a reduction of deviance of about 4 would be significant at the 5 per cent level. In this chapter no significance level is given for a reduction in deviance when the relevant level is less than 0.1 per cent.

One thing which does emerge from Table 5.2 is that the differences found between LEAs, as measured by the figure of 0.158 in the variance column, are relatively small compared with the figures for differences between schools and for differences within schools. At this initial stage the point to notice is that there is comparatively little variance between LEAs. Even allowing for the fact that some of the variation in the data is attributable to the assumed Poisson distribution of exclusions within individual school cohorts, about half the remaining variance is within schools rather than between them. Schools differ largely in terms of the balance between age, gender and types of exclusion rather than simply in terms of their overall exclusion rates.

In all that follows, as all the parameters are re-estimated at each stage, the fixed coefficients (see glossary) given in Table 5.1 remain virtually unchanged. For the most part changes in the estimates of these coefficients will not be reported. In principle, all fixed coefficients and variances could change drastically as any one element is added to the model. When a coefficient does not in fact change in a number of models, it is usually safe to assume that it reflects the real-world situation. The changes that do occur are in the amount of variation which is left unexplained after each new variable is introduced.

Key factors that might affect the basic model

Before building up the basic model in a systematic way, it is worth considering the importance of three factors which are known to be related to exclusions: the proportion of black pupils, the roll of the school and the year in which the exclusions are recorded.

It is recognised that black pupils are more likely to be excluded. Chapter 1 reported on the disproportionate exclusion of black pupils, particularly African Caribbeans. Unfortunately the inspection data are unhelpful for investigating this effect. Although during the period studied each inspection report gives for each age and gender the number of pupils from ethnic minorities as well as the total number of pupils who are excluded, the important distinction between black pupils and those from other ethnic groups is not made. Further, no account is given of the overall number of ethnic minority pupils in each group, year or school. This makes it impossible to employ the current form of analysis. If six out of ten fixed term exclusions of Y9 boys are of ethnic minority pupils, the significance is totally different if the proportion of ethnic minority pupils in the year is 95 per cent at one extreme or 5 per cent at the other. HMI has done its own analysis in relation to this issue, concluding that 'a disproportionate number of black pupils were excluded' (OFSTED, 1996b: 12). HMI clearly used evidence beyond that in OFSTED reports. In fact HMI, rather than OFSTED inspectors, inspected thirty-nine schools to gather data.

Census data are available on the proportion of black heads of household in each LEA, which will be abbreviated as BLACK HOUSEHOLDS. Adding these data to the basic model produced an impressive improvement in the accuracy with which the model summarises the data. The drop in deviance is 172.2. There is little change in the fixed coefficients. Each 1 per cent increase in the proportion of black households is estimated to multiply exclusion rates by a factor of 1.08, giving the authority with the highest proportion of black households exclusion rates which are 3.33 times those in the authority with the lowest value (confidence interval: between 1.84 and 6.02 times). However, this shows only that those LEAs with more black households also have exclusion rates up to three times higher than those with less. Despite the confirming evidence of the HMI study, it does not establish

Table 5.3 Changes in variance produced by including BLACK HOUSEHOLDS or ROLL as explanatory variables

Level	Variance in the basic model	Variance taking account of BLACK HOUSEHOLDS	Variance taking account of ROLL
LEA	0.158	0.055	0.175
School	0.356	0.436	0.275
Temporary	0.241	0.255	0.258
Yeargroup	0.200	0.236	0.186
Exclusion type	0.371	0.494	0.398

that it is the black pupils who are excluded more frequently. LEAs with high numbers of black households clearly have many other things in common and the BLACK HOUSEHOLDS variable may simply stand proxy for those.

Although the fixed coefficients were not significantly changed from those shown in Table 5.1,[3] the variance at each level was considerably influenced by the introduction of the BLACK HOUSEHOLDS variable. Table 5.3 shows the variance between LEAs reduced to one-third of its value from 0.158 to 0.055. Variance between and within schools is increased. A further elaboration of the model showed that schools in LEAs with large black populations are less varied between themselves than schools in other areas. The between school variance in the authority with the lowest proportion of BLACK HOUSEHOLDS was estimated at 0.65 higher than in the authority with the highest BLACK HOUSEHOLDS (between 0.48 and 0.82). The reduction in deviance for this model was a further 18.00.

McManus (1987) found that the size of the school roll was negatively related to its exclusion rates. This is supported quite strongly by including school roll in the model. There seems to be a very strong link between higher exclusion rates and smaller schools. A difference of 100 pupils between the rolls of two schools might be associated with almost 10 per cent difference between their exclusion rates. ROLL is the number of pupils in the school during the year of the inspection and is only an approximate measure of the number of pupils at the time of the exclusions. Nevertheless, including ROLL as an explanatory variable produced a reduction in deviance of 349.2. Again the fixed coefficients were almost unchanged from the basic model. A difference of 100 between the rolls of two schools was estimated to give the larger school exclusion rates only 91.9 per cent those of the smaller (between 89.5 per cent and 94.4 per cent). Unsurprisingly, since ROLL is a school level variable, the main effect of ROLL on the variances is to reduce the between school variance by about one-quarter from 0.356 to 0.275.

Exclusions rose during the period covered by these data and this is fully illustrated in Chapter 2. Unfortunately, the data analysed here are not strong enough to explore trends. Although the addition of factors for each year involved produce an appreciable drop in deviance ($\chi^2 = 37.4$ with 2 degrees of freedom), the parameters are not well estimated.

The model suggests a decline in overall exclusions rates between 1992/93 and 1993/94, to 94.1 per cent of the original levels (between 76.6 per cent and 115.5 per cent) followed in 1994/95 by an increase to 105.6 per cent of the 1992/93 level (between 85.0 per cent and 131.2 per cent). This accuracy of estimation is hardly impressive.

There are at least three possible explanations of this discrepancy. First, the decline in 1993/94 occurred mostly in low excluding groups and in terms of the total number of exclusions was totally offset by increases in high excluding groups which were smaller in relative terms but larger in absolute numbers. Second, there could well be differences between the schools which were selected for inspection in 1993/94 and those which waited longer. Third, rules governing OFSTED reports and rules governing exclusions have changed in the period since 1992. In 1992/93 indefinite exclusions were permitted in addition to fixed term and permanent exclusions. This makes comparison between years difficult. From April 1996 OFSTED reports ceased to contain the data used in this analysis.

These factors, the proportion of black pupils, size of school roll and the year in which the exclusions were recorded, will be reconsidered when the basic model has been systematically developed using the other explanatory variables shown in Table 5.4.

Correlations

Table 5.4 sets out the LEA level variables used in this analysis and their sources.

Table 5.5 shows those correlations between the LEA level variables which have a significance level better than 10 per cent. The actual significance levels are given, except in cases where this is less than 0.1 per cent. The proportion of statements of special educational needs processed within six months (STATEMENT6) is not significantly correlated with anything other than levels of funding for each secondary school pupil and this correlation is negative. Overcrowding is not significantly correlated with anything except unemployment. All other correlations are very significant. Home ownership, as a measure of affluence, is negatively related to all other variables. The strongest correlation is the negative one between home ownership and unemployment.

The permanent exclusions of secondary pupils is most strongly associated with the proportion of black households, followed by low home ownership rates, high proportions of poor home facilities. Then, with considerably lower correlations, come funding and unemployment.

Table 5.4 LEA level variables used in the analysis

Variable	Definition	Source
BLACK HOUSEHOLDS	proportion of households where the head of household is black	Chadwyck Healey (1994)
HOME OWNERSHIP	proportion of households where the householder owns the property outright	"
POOR HOME FACILITIES	proportion of household with no central heating and with shared shower, bath or toilet	"
OVERCROWDING	proportion of households with more than 1.5 persons per room	"
UNEMPLOYMENT	proportion of males age 16+ who are unemployed	"
STATEMENT6	proportion of statements of special educational needs completed within six months	Audit Commission (1996a)
FUNDING	the mean annual expenditure in the LEA for the mainstream education of a secondary pupil	"
EXCLUSIONS	the rate of permanent exclusions of pupils of secondary school age	DfE (1995a)

Since the variables are closely correlated it is worth looking at their partial correlations in Table 5.6. These show the correlations between what remains of a pair of variables after full account has been taken of their common association with the other variables involved. For example the correlation between BLACK HOUSEHOLDS and EXCLUSIONS is shown as 0.61 in Table 5.5; but when we take into account the values of BLACK HOUSEHOLDS and EXCLUSIONS that each LEA would expect to have on the basis of all the other listed variables, the residual unexplained parts of BLACK HOUSE-HOLDS and EXCLUSIONS have a correlation of only 0.32, shown in Table 5.6. Even so, this partial correlation is still very significant.

After partialling, the correlation between BLACK HOUSEHOLDS and FUNDING is no longer significant. Negative correlations appear between OVERCROWDING on the one hand and BLACK HOUSEHOLDS and HOME OWNERSHIP on the other. STATEMENT6 now has a negative correlation with POOR HOME FACILITIES. All other things considered, statements of special educational need seem to be processed less swiftly in areas where there is more substandard accommodation.

Table 5.5 Correlations between LEA level variables, excluding those not significant at the 10 per cent level

	BLACK HOUSEHOLDS	HOME OWNERSHIP	POOR HOME FACILITIES	OVER-CROWDING	UNEMPLOY-MENT	STATEMENT6	FUNDING
HOME OWNERSHIP	-0.67						
POOR HOME FACILITIES	0.67	-0.46					
UNEMPLOY-MENT	0.55	-0.71	0.36	0.34			
FUNDING	0.50	-0.44	0.54		0.29 (0.4%)[a]	-0.22 (2.7%)[a]	
EXCLUSIONS	0.61	-0.53	0.47		0.27 (0.7%)[a]		0.35

Note:
a Figures given in parentheses are those significance levels which exceed 0.1%.

Table 5.6 Partial correlations between LEA level variables, excluding those not significant at the 10 per cent level

	BLACK HOUSEHOLDS	HOME OWNERSHIP	POOR HOME FACILITIES	OVER-CROWDING	UNEMPLOY-MENT	STATEMENT6
HOME OWNERSHIP	−0.18 (8.8%)[a]					
POOR HOME FACILITIES	0.45					
OVERCROWDING	−0.25 (1.8%)[a]	−0.18 (8.3%)[a]				
UNEMPLOYMENT	0.29 (0.5%)[a]	−0.60		0.51		
STATEMENT6		−0.19 (6.8%)[a]	−0.21 (4.1%)[a]			
FUNDING		−0.23 (3.0%)[a]	0.36			−0.26 (1.1%)[a]
EXCLUSIONS	0.32 (0.2%)	−0.33			−0.28 (0.8%)[a]	

Note:
a Figures given in parentheses are those significance levels which exceed 0.1%.

EXCLUSIONS has a strong negative correlation with HOME OWNER-SHIP and a surprisingly negative correlation with UNEMPLOYMENT. It is not surprising that areas with high proportions of children from privately owned houses exclude fewer pupils. However, the link between low unemployment and high exclusions appeared a number of times in the analysis and requires some explanation. It could be an artefact of the analysis. For example, the residual unexplained part of EXCLUSIONS might be largest where the explained part of UNEMPLOYMENT best fits the data. UN-EMPLOYMENT is measured in 1991 and EXCLUSIONS in 1995. The time lag may be causing illusory relationships. On the other hand it is possible that there really is a relationship between high unemployment and low exclusions. Having a parent around the home more may account for the relationship but this is highly speculative.

The school level variables employed are listed in Table 5.7. Comparison of their correlations in Table 5.8 with their partial correlations in Table 5.9 raises some interesting possibilities.

ROLL is negatively associated with the rate of permanent exclusions (PER-MANENT EXCLUSION RATE) but also with the proportion of pupils eligible for free school meals (FSM). When FSM is taken into account (along with all the other explanatory variables) the partial correlation of ROLL with PERMANENT EXCLUSION RATE is not significant. This may mean that the dependence of exclusion on school size is illusory or that FSM is a better indication of poverty and 'speaks up' the variance that ROLL had to try to account for previously.

Although most of the correlations with FSM cease to be significant after partialling, those of the academic achievement variables (5 A–C, 5 A–G and 1 A–G) remain relatively large. The strong relation between high academic achievement and low unauthorised absence disappears; but that between high achievement and low exclusions remain significant even though originally the correlations with temporary exclusion rates (TEMPOR-ARY EXCLUSION RATE) did not appear significant.

Models using social factors

The investigation of a number of different variables representing the affluence or deprivation of each LEA showed that home ownership rates and unemployment rates were extremely important in relation to exclusions. The number of measures of affluence or deprivation that were investigated made possible a very large number of models; so there was a high probability that some of these would purely by chance appear to be significant. However, by using HOME OWNERSHIP and UNEMPLOYMENT as explanatory variables, a reduction of 402.1 in the deviance of the basic model was produced. This would have been extremely significant even if all the possible explanatory variables were involved. The two new fixed coefficients imply that for two LEAs with a 1 per cent difference in affluence as indicated by the rate of

Table 5.7 School level variables used in the analysis

Variable	Definition	Time of observation
ROLL	total number of pupils in the school	the year of the inspection
FSM	proportion of pupils eligible for free school meals	"
SEN	proportion of pupils with statement of special educational need	"
PUPIL–TEACHER RATIO	ratio of pupils to total teaching staff full-time equivalents	"
TEACHING GROUP SIZE	average teaching group size in Y7 to Y11[a]	"
GOOD	proportion of lessons deemed by the inspectors to be good or very good[a]	during the inspection
SOUND	proportion of lessons deemed by the inspectors to be at least sound[a]	"
5 A–C	proportion of Y11 pupils obtaining at least five GCSE grades A to C	the year before the inspection
5 A–G	proportion of Y11 pupils obtaining at least five GCSE grades A to G	"
1 A–G	proportion of Y11 pupils obtaining at least one GCSE grade A to G	"
FE	proportion of Y11 pupils continuing with school or further education	"
ABSENCE	rate of unauthorised absences	third week of the term before the inspection

Note:
a There was some inconsistency in the manner of reporting and some of these figures were adjusted in an attempt to allow for this.

home ownership, the more affluent area would have exclusion rates 96.5 per cent of those in the less affluent area (between 93.9 per cent and 99.1 per cent). Of two LEAs with a 1 per cent difference in disadvantage as indicated by unemployment rates, the more disadvantaged would have exclusion rates 107.5 per cent above those in the other area (between 100.2 per cent and 115.4 per cent). Both these effects are significantly different from zero, although if any decision were to hang upon the size of the coefficients a much more precise estimate would be required. The chief effect of this

Table 5.8 Correlations between school level variables, excluding those not significant at the 5 per cent level[a]

	ROLL	FSM	5 A–C	5 A–G	1 A–G	SEN	ABSENCE	FE	PUPIL–TEACHER RATIO	GOOD
FSM	−0.23									
5 A–C	0.15 (0.3%)[b]	−0.62								
5 A–G	0.21	−0.72	0.72							
1 A–G	0.22	−0.66	0.61	0.85						
SEN	0.15 (0.3%)[b]		−0.25	−0.12 (1.9%)[b]						
ABSENCE	0.17	0.38	−0.33	−0.43	−0.41					
FE		−0.46	0.66	0.58	0.54		−0.31			
PUPIL–TEACHER RATIO	0.29	−0.23	0.19	0.25	0.21	−0.11 (3.5%)[b]	−0.12 (2.3%)[b]	0.12 (2.2%)[b]		
TEACHING GROUP SIZE								−0.12 (2.3%)[b]		
GOOD	0.18 (0.4%)[b]	−0.36	0.53	0.41	0.36		−0.22	0.45		
PERMANENT EXCLUSION RATE	−0.22	0.43	−0.47	−0.48	−0.48	0.11 (3.5%)[b]	0.24	−0.35	−0.26	−0.30

Notes:
a SOUND and TEMPORARY EXCLUSION RATE had no significant correlations with any variables.
b Figures given in parentheses are those significance levels which exceed 0.1%.

Table 5.9 Partial correlations between school level variables, excluding those not significant at the 5 per cent level[a]

	ROLL	FSM	5 A–C	5 A–G	1 A–G	SEN	ABSENCE	FE	PUPIL–TEACHER RATIO	PERMANENT EXCLUSION RATE
5 A–C		-0.36								
5 A–G		-0.47	0.30							
1 A–G		-0.38	0.15 (3.0%)[b]	0.67						
SEN	0.25									
ABSENCE	0.16 (2.6%)[b]		-0.30							
FE	0.15 (3.7%)[b]		0.45	0.41	0.30					
PUPIL–TEACHER RATIO	0.19 (0.9%)[b]					-0.16 (3.0%)[b]				
TEACHING GROUP SIZE								-0.26		
GOOD			0.19 (0.8%)[b]					0.14 (4.5%)[b]		
PERMANENT EXCLUSION RATE			-0.22 (0.2%)[b]	-0.14 (4.3%)[b]	-0.15 (3.5%)[b]					
TEMPORARY EXCLUSION RATE		0.12 (0.6%)	-0.17 (1.4%)[b]	-0.24	-0.27				-0.18 (1.3%)[b]	0.30

Notes:
a The following groups of variables were taken together and not used as explanatory variables for each other when calculating partial correlations: (a) PERMANENT EXCLUSION RATE and TEMPORARY EXCLUSION RATE, (b) 5 A–C, 5 A–G and 1 A–G, (c) PUPIL–TEACHER RATIO and TEACHING GROUP SIZE, (d) GOOD and SOUND. For example the correlation between GOOD and FE does not take into account the expected levels based on SOUND as well as other variables.

b Figures given in parentheses are those significance levels which exceed 0.1%.

Table 5.10 Unexplained variances in the HOME OWNERSHIP and UNEMPLOY-MENT model and in the FSM model

Level	Variance in the basic model	Variance taking account of HOME OWNERSHIP and UNEM-PLOYMENT	Variance taking full account of FSM	Variance taking account of FSM and STATEMENT6
LEA	0.158	0.032	0.030	0.025
School	0.356	0.457	0.185	0.175
Temporary	0.241	0.204	0.232	0.228
FSM[a]			−0.004	−0.004
Yeargroup	0.200	0.234	0.195	0.194
Exclusion type	0.371	0.471	0.413	0.406

Note:
a This is the change in variance for each 1% increase in FSM.

model, shown in Table 5.10, is to reduce the variance between LEAs from 0.158 to 0.032. That is to say most of the differences between LEAs can be attributed to these two factors, rates of home ownership and unemployment.

The only school level social indicator systematically available in OFSTED reports is FSM, the proportion of pupils eligible for free school meals. Adding these data is enormously successful as a means of reducing the inaccuracy in the way the model summarises the data. Adding FSM^2 (the square of FSM) to the basic model reduced the deviance by 565.8. A more complex model was developed by including FSM^2 as an explanatory variable. This makes allowance for the fact that a difference of 1 per cent in FSM rates for two schools will not have the same effect if both schools have very low FSM rates as if they both have very high rates. This model further reduced the deviance by 69.8. The device of using FSM is not a particularly subtle approach to this issue and a more sophisticated solution to the problem would presumably produce an even greater reduction in deviance. Taking account of the fact that schools with low FSM have more variation in their exclusion rates than schools with high FSM reduced the deviance by another 31.

In the model which takes FSM most fully into account the size of its effects can be seen by comparing the exclusion rates of schools with 9.5 per cent of pupils eligible for free school meals (higher than one-quarter of schools) and those of schools where 30.9 per cent of pupils were eligible (higher than three-quarters of schools). The schools with lower FSM rates would have half (46.7 per cent) of the exclusion rates found in schools with higher FSM rates. Variation between schools around the 9.5 per cent rate is estimated as 0.14 more than variance between schools at the 30.9 per cent rate. As Table 5.10 shows, this model reduces the variance between LEAs by an amount similar to that of the model using HOME OWNERSHIP and UNEMPLOYMENT. It also reduces the between school variance by about half.

No improvement was made by combining HOME OWNERSHIP and UNEMPLOYMENT together with FSM. Since the LEA level variables are effective in explaining differences at LEA level, and since the full FSM model leaves very little unexplained variance at LEA level this is not surprising. Table 5.10 shows the details. The failure of LEA variables to improve upon the predictive power of FSM does not necessarily indicate that general social conditions are irrelevant to a school's exclusion rates. It could be that the LEA is in many cases too large an area for the average conditions within it to be relevant to each individual school.

Models using LEA type and policy variables

Variables such as STATEMENT6, the proportion of statements of special educational needs which are processed within six months, FUNDING, the expenditure per pupil on secondary education, and LEA TYPE were considered only as possible influences on exclusion rates against the background of social factors. To an extent this is unreasonable. LEA type could be considered as a social factor in itself. Metropolitan boroughs and county LEAs differ not only in their organisation but also in the nature of the areas they administer. In the event, this problem was unimportant, since LEA TYPE, like the less ambiguously social LEA level variables, had no significant influence when combined with the full FSM model.

FUNDING might be thought of as purely a matter of LEA policy, but the correlations in Table 5.5 show that the level of funding says quite a lot about the social composition of the LEA, though in fact it made little improvement to the model. The absence of a significant partial correlation with EXCLUSIONS in Table 5.6 suggests that FUNDING would not be a useful explanatory variable in combination with the social variables. It made no significant improvement on the full FSM model.

On the other hand STATEMENT6 made a very definite improvement. Inclusion of this explanatory variable reduced the deviance of the full FSM model by 60.2, very significant even allowing for the fact that searching among a range of potentially useful variables is more likely to produce an apparently significant result than simply testing one selected variable. The fixed coefficients, including those for FSM and FSM^2, were changed only minutely. Values of STATEMENT6 range between 0 per cent and 79 per cent. The model estimates that the LEA with the highest proportion of statements processed within six months (variable STATEMENT6) can expect exclusion rates only 74 per cent of those in the authority with the lowest proportions. The 95 per cent confidence interval is from 48.4 per cent to 114.3 per cent, showing that this coefficient is not very well estimated and that there are significant departures from the expected levels. However, the reduction in deviance is considerable. All the variances in the full FSM model are reduced slightly and, at LEA level, the unexplained variance is reduced by 15 per cent.

Models using academic achievement

The proportion of pupils with statements of special educational needs (SEN), and measures of academic achievement at 16, are not simply indications of the type of pupils which a school has. Schools can undoubtedly make a difference. However, the main determinant of a school's final achievement with pupils at the age of 16 is undoubtedly their achievement on entry to the school and it is worth considering whether the ability profile of a school's pupil population can help account for some of the variation still unexplained in the model.

OFSTED reports contain a range of data intended to indicate academic achievement. Unfortunately these are not consistently and accurately recorded. A number of schools had to be excluded from the sample for this part of the analysis for that reason. Since the defective reports tend to cluster within the LEAs where the offending inspectors operated, this may have had a biasing effect on the results. Comparing variances in the FSM and STATE-MENT6 model in Table 5.10 and the corresponding model in Table 5.11 shows the extent to which the model was influenced by this reduction in the sample. Changes of similar proportion also occurred in the fixed coefficients though the new values were all well within the 95 per cent confidence intervals of the previous estimates. The most dramatic change was in the effect of STATEMENT6, where the estimated exclusion rates for schools in LEAs with the highest proportion of statements processed quickly had expected exclusion rates 70.8 per cent of those of LEAs at the other extreme rather than 74 per cent if academic achievement is not taken into account.

Table 5.11 Unexplained variances in the models employing 1 A–G and FE

Level	Variance taking into account FSM and STATEMENT6 only[a]	Variance taking into account 1 A–G	Variance taking into account 1 A–G and FE
LEA	0.022	0.023	0.033
School	0.189	0.165	0.159
Temporary	0.230	0.202	0.199
FSM	−0.0045	−0.0055	−0.0056
Yeargroup	0.196	0.186	0.181
Exclusion type	0.411	0.381	0.354

Note:
a Discrepancies in the variances given in this column and the corresponding values in this table are due to the reduction in sample size necessitated by missing data from some schools.

The variables considered include 5 A–C, the proportion of Y11 pupils obtaining at least five GCSEs grade A to C, 5 A–G, the proportion gaining at least five grades A to G, and 1 A–G, the proportion obtaining at least one grade A–G. Whereas the first two variables indicate levels of achievement relevant to near average pupils, the third is an extreme measure. Even the least effective school can do little to prevent an average pupil from obtaining at least one GCSE grade. Values of 1 A–G ranged from 62 per cent to 100 per cent and clearly those with considerable numbers failing to achieve one GCSE grade were dealing with very different pupils from those with no such failures. This partly explains why 1 A–G proved to be the most effective variable for improving the FSM and STATEMENT6 model. The reduction in deviance was 204.3. Combining this with other academic achievement variables gave no further improvement.

Models using other school indicators

In addition to achievement at age 16, OFSTED reports also provide data on SEN, the proportion of pupils with statements of special educational needs, on FE, the proportion of pupils continuing with schooling or further education after Y11, and ABSENCE, the proportion of unauthorised pupil absences during the third week of the term prior to the inspection.

SEN is closely related to FSM. Unsurprisingly, therefore, SEN added no significant explanatory power to the model.

The rate of unauthorised absence may well vary with the time of year, so schools inspected in different terms may well have different values for ABSENCE. In principle it would be preferable to use an alternative and more reliable measure of unauthorised absenteeism. OFSTED reports should provide the rates for the whole year given in the last governors' report. Unfortunately many OFSTED reports fail to contain these data possibly because they were not in governors' reports either. Despite the probable association of truancy and exclusion, this variable added nothing to the explanatory power of the model.

FE, which indicates rates of continuance of education beyond 16, appeared in the present context to be a more effective measure of the success of a school than either 5 A–C or 5 A–G. Combining this with 1 A–G reduced the deviance by a further 75.2. The size of the effect can be judged by comparing the predicted exclusion rates for a school at the lower quartile of 1 A–G having 91.2 per cent of pupils obtaining at least one GCSE grade and for a school at the upper quartile with 98.3 per cent of pupils obtaining a grade. The predicted rate for the first school is 128 per cent of that for the second school (between 117 per cent and 140.1 per cent). A similar comparison between schools at the lower quartile for FE, with 58 per cent of pupils continuing in education, and a school at the upper quartile, with 83 per cent of pupils continuing, gives the school with the lower FE rate an exclusion rate of 117 per cent (between 103.8 per cent and 132.6 per cent) above those in the other schools.

SCHOOL TYPE made no appreciable difference to the model. If grant maintained or voluntary do have different overall exclusion rates, the effect is so small that the software was unable to estimate it on the basis of this sample. Grant maintained and voluntary schools seemed to behave very similarly to other schools in similar circumstances. This may seem surprising. However, the evidence of this analysis suggests that any differences in exclusion rates between grant maintained and other schools is attributable to the fact that the schools also differ in FSM rates, levels of academic achievement and so on.

PUPIL–TEACHER RATIO and TEACHING GROUP SIZE similarly had no estimatable effect. Higher pupil–teacher ratios and lower class size had very slight links with lower exclusions, but the individual coefficients were not large enough to estimate confidently and there was no reduction in deviance.

Finally, OFSTED reports are required to state the percentage of observed lessons deemed to be good and the percentage deemed to be at least sound. At the time of the reports analysed here these data were included in a paragraph of text rather than listed among the statistical indicators. The wording of many reports was so vague that it was not possible even to assign schools to one of five 20 per cent bands for each of these variables. Attempting to analyse these data required an enormous reduction in the sample size. Again it is not clear that the sample that remained was representative of the whole sample since the offending inspectors affected some areas but not others. Very slight and statistically insignificant effects were detected, but these might well be explained by a tendency of inspectors to be slightly influenced in their judgement of the quality of a lesson by factors related to discipline and thus to exclusions.

Table 5.12 Unexplained variances in the full models including ROLL and BLACK HOUSEHOLDS

Level	*Variance not taking into account ROLL or BLACK HOUSEHOLDS*	*Variance taking into account ROLL*	*Variance taking into account ROLL and BLACK HOUSEHOLDS*
LEA	0.033	0.032	0.018
School			
Permanent	0.159	0.151	0.171
Temporary	0.199	0.206	0.208
FSM	−0.0056	−0.0054	−0.0062
Yeargroup	0.181	0.179	0.192
Exclusion type	0.345	0.367	0.411

In revisiting BLACK HOUSEHOLDS and ROLL, the proportion of black heads of household in each LEA and the roll of each school taken individually produced quite significant models. ROLL again produced a significant improvement when added to the FSM, STATEMENT6, 1 A–G and FE model, reducing the deviance by 45.0 and adding BLACK HOUSEHOLDS produced a further reduction of 36.2. Table 5.12 gives details of the effects on variances.

Conclusion

The final model is summarised in Tables 5.13 and 5.14. The apparent un-importance of factors not included in this final model may reflect the quality of the data available as much as real irrelevance. For example, the proportion of lessons deemed to be GOOD (OFSTED inspection reports) is omitted. This does not necessarily mean that good teaching has no impact on disaffection and exclusion.

The fixed effects which were included in the basic model have changed little in the final model. The final figures no longer represent expected values for all schools but only for schools with typical values of FSM, 1 A–G, FE and ROLL in LEAs with typical values of STATEMENT6 and BLACK HOUSEHOLDS. This has made little difference. The final rates for Y7 permanent exclusions are lower, but most of the multiplying factors for other types of exclusion have become higher, thus bringing most of the expected values to approximately their original level. The extra fixed effects which were not included in the basic model look very small. Multiplying by 0.997 is very little different from multiplying by 1, which would make no change at all. However, for most of the variables listed the factors are those needed for each percentage increase. Thus an increase of 1 per cent in FSM is estimated to multiply exclusion rates by 1.03, but an increase of 4 per cent would multiply the rates by $1.03 \times 1.03 \times 1.03 \times 1.03$, which is 1.13, 13 per cent higher. The scale factor for ROLL is extremely close to 1, but this represents only the estimated difference made by a single extra pupil.

A considerable proportion of the variance between LEAs has been accounted for only partly by the use of LEA level variables, BLACK HOUSE-HOLDS and STATEMENT6. There is some slight evidence that LEA policy and practice can make a difference to exclusion rates. However, in the final model the coefficient of STATEMENT6 is not very well estimated. The confidence interval is from 0.991 to 1.001. Nevertheless 88.6 per cent of the between LEA variance has been explained, mostly by reference to social conditions in the LEA as a whole and to conditions within the schools.

In the final model there is more variance within schools than between them. About half of the basic variance between schools has been accounted for without recourse to any data which unambiguously reflects school effectiveness. The proportion of pupils gaining at least one GCSE grade A–G and the proportion continuing with education after Y11 are scarcely less indicative of the

Table 5.13 Comparison of fixed effects in the basic model and the final model

		Basic model		Final model	
		Exclusion rate per 1,000 pupils	Scale factor	Exclusion rate per 1,000 pupils	Scale factor
Boys					
Permanent	Y7	3.90		3.04	
	Y8		×1.58		×1.74
	Y9		×2.15		×2.50
	Y10		×2.75		×3.21
	Y11		×1.90		×2.39
Temporary	Y7–Y11		×9.57		×9.59
Girls					
Permanent	Y7	0.52		0.42	
	Y8		×2.65		×2.77
	Y9		×4.17		×4.92
	Y10		×5.37		×6.27
	Y11		×2.86		×3.41
Temporary	Y7–Y11		×11.97		×11.71
FSM[a]					×1.03
FSM^2 [b]					×0.9993
STATEMENT6[a]					×0.997
1 A–G[a]					×0.965
FE[a]					×0.991
ROLL[c]					×0.9997
BLACK HOUSEHOLDS[a]					×1.04

Notes:
a The given factors must be raised to the power equal to the percentage by which the rate exceeds the mean rate for all schools in the sample. For example, a school's FSM rate is 6% above average, the exclusion rates are multiplied by 1.03^6.
b The factor must be raised to the power equal to the square of the percentage difference between the school FSM rate and the average.
c The factor must be raised to the power equal to the number by which the school roll exceeds the average for the sample.

social background of pupils than is the proportion eligible for free school meals. The interesting relation between exclusions and school roll could reflect different and better procedures followed by larger schools, but it could equally reflect that the tolerability of a particular form of behaviour is greater in a larger, less intimate community.

In the analyses in this chapter three sorts of factors have been taken into account. The percentage of pupils on free school meals (FSM) and the percentage of households where the head of the household is categorised as black (BLACK HOUSEHOLDS) are background features independent of

Table 5.14 Comparison of variances in the basic model and the final model

Level	Variance in basic model	Variance in final model
LEA	0.158	0.018
School	0.356	0.171
Temporary	0.241	0.217
FSM		−0.006
Yeargroup	0.200	0.192
Exclusion type	0.371	0.411

the school and LEA policy. The percentage of statements of Special Educational Need completed within six months (STATEMENT 6) and size of school roll are products of education policy at the local level.

One A–G pass at GCSE level and proportions of pupils progressing to Further Education (FE) are, in a sense, school effectiveness factors but are also greatly affected by background features. The claim is not being made that these are direct causal factors, i.e. that pupils on free school meals are personally more likely to be excluded. Nor can it be said that free school meals as such (as opposed to other factors for which it stands proxy) are causally related to exclusion. However, these explanatory variables, or the situations they represent, account for virtually all the differences between LEAs, reducing the variance from 0.158 in the basic model to 0.018 in the final model (Table 5.14). At school level these variables account for about half the differences between schools' rates of exclusion.

The analyses in this chapter have narrowed the scope for claims that schools in similar situations achieve very different levels of exclusion. Social factors play a considerable role in the determination of exclusion rates in schools and LEAs.

There is still plenty of variation, especially within individual schools, which may be explicable in terms of school effectiveness. It may also be explicable in terms of social variables not investigated here. Some of it may even be inexplicable, the residue of randomness in human affairs.

Glossary

Coefficient   The fixed coefficients are the numbers by which the explanatory variables in a regression equation must be multiplied as part of the process of calculating the expected values.

Confidence interval   A confidence interval is a range of values which are not significantly different from the estimated value of a coefficient or other statistic. The 95 per cent confidence interval for a coefficient is the range of values which do not differ from it at the 5 per cent significance level.

Deviance   A measure of how unlikely the data actually observed would be if the model described in the regression equation were 'true'. This is given in the form of minus twice the logarithm of the probability of the data being as divergent as it is from the predicted values. If the model assumes a normal distribution of differences between observed and predicted values, the deviance is closely related to the variance; but not in other cases.

Regression equation   An equation that allows the 'predicted' or 'expected' value of one variable to be calculated by arithmetical manipulation of other 'explanatory' variables.

Significance   A more complex model will always reduce the deviance found in a less complex model for the same data even if the variables introduced into the model have no real importance and are only randomly related to the important data. Even quite large improvements in deviance can be produced by pure fluke. The significance level of a result is the probability of seeing an effect purely by fluke. An effect which has 5 per cent significance is one which is too large to be achieved by fluke more than one time in twenty. However, if two effects are looked at, there is around a one in ten chance that one of them will seem to have this significance level. The more models that are considered, the less significant any nominally significant result will look.

Variance   A measure of the departure of the observed values of a variable from the values predicted by a regression equation. The average of the squares of the differences between observed and predicted values.

Notes

1 In the present case the software used was MLn, developed at the London Institute of Education.
2 A Poisson distribution is not symmetrical about the mean as in a normal distribution. There is a definite minimum value of zero light bulb failures but there is no theoretical maximum value.
3 In principle all fixed coefficients and variances could change as any one element is added to the model. When a coefficient does not change in a number of models, it usually indicates that it reflects the real-world situation.

6 The economics of exclusion

Carl Parsons and Frances Castle

Introduction

Calculating the costs of public services is increasingly important as the perceived pressure on welfare budgets grow. The methodologies for calculating current costs in order to compare with alternatives are still relatively unsophisticated.[1] Costing information is important since policy decisions are, at least in part, decided by likely cost and likely effect. There are too few structured experimental, comparative studies to allow a rigorous and objective comparison of different policy options with the different costs which they entail. We have to make the best of naturally occurring variations which inevitably involve uncontrolled and non-calculable variations. Sometimes it is also difficult to disentangle financial cost, human costs and ethical arguments. The little research there has been into the costs of exclusions suggests that the call on the public purse is substantial (Parsons, 1994).

This chapter has three goals:

1   to set out a framework for estimating the cost to the public purse of exclusions from schools within existing structure, provisions and practice
2   to present an estimate of the costs nationally of permanent exclusions from school from data covering two years gathered in two different ways in six English LEAs
3   to estimate the costs of alternative provision for these young people.

The work reported here on costing exclusions was carried out at Christ Church University College, Canterbury, funded by the Commission for Racial Equality (CRE, 1996). The data were gathered in six English local education authorities.[2] The research design involved acquiring data on the individual or *unit costs* of ten cases of exclusion in three of the LEAs and the *gross costs* of exclusions in three 'matching' LEAs.

Gathering the data

In the unit costing LEAs (Met U, County U and London U) a full, anonymised list of pupils permanently excluded in 1994/95 was obtained and fifteen cases were identified in each. The parents were approached through LEA officers to seek their co-operation, and ten cases were located in each of the three LEAs.[3] Four were primary aged pupils and twenty-six secondary, in line with the national distribution of permanent exclusions across school types. Interviews with parents or guardians were arranged to identify all the agencies which had been involved, the period out of school experienced by the pupil, the extent and duration of the replacement education and the effect on the child and the family. The agencies named were contacted and, with the parents'/guardians' permission,[4] were asked to cost the time and processes associated with the named child's exclusion. Cost data were gathered about the involvement of education officials, educational welfare officers, educational psychologists, social workers, health workers including doctors, young offender teams, police, court work, Pupil Referral Units and special schools. This required the calculation of hourly costs and, by reference to other costing studies, the allocation of a percentage overhead cost (CRE, 1996: appendices 3 and 4 give fuller information). From the cost of ten cases in each LEA a calculation was made for the costs of all the authority's permanent exclusions.

The gross costing required the identification of all costs to the LEAs (Met G, County G and London G) and to the other services, as above, for the totality of its permanent exclusions during 1994/95. Services were asked to provide detailed estimates of the numbers of excluded pupils for whom they made provision, the proportion of their work that this took up and the cost of that provision. Some agencies did not know the educational status of their clients (a fixed term exclusion, a permanent exclusion or a long-term truant). In some cases it was necessary to 'carry across' the costings for services from the matched unit costing authority and check with service managers that the estimates derived for their services were reasonable. It is likely that the figures derived for the unit costing LEAs are underestimates.

Drawing on permanent exclusions data available for the previous three years up to August 1996, an estimate of the cost trends is provided. This has taken account of the increase in the numbers of permanent exclusions, numbers who continue on the exclusions roll beyond the first year and a factor for inflation.[5]

Every effort has been made to acquire the local information on the actual costs of services. This information has been used in conjunction with other published costing formulae. In all cases the aim has been to include ALL costs – salaries, on-costs, expenses and overheads which cover support staff, maintenance and capital building costs. Recognition is also taken of the ratio of client contact time to other time which this necessitates.[6]

The two approaches give a secure basis for demonstrating the variability in policy and practice with regard to permanent exclusions, as well as the high cost of exclusions. The data also reveal much about the quality of education and care received by excluded pupils and the impact on the children and families.

Six condensed case studies were carried out of individual pupils at risk of exclusion who were retained in school. By this means the costs of 'inclusion' have also been addressed.

The costing data represent the best estimates possible in the six months over which the project conducted its work and are likely to be an underestimate of the costs of permanent exclusion to the education service and to the other agencies, particularly police and criminal justice. The costs that are given should, in all cases, be regarded as indicative; further studies would be needed to arrive at more precise estimates.

Calculating the costs

Expressed at its most simple, the additional cost to the public purse of permanently excluding a pupil from school equals the *cost of managing the exclusion process* plus the *cost of replacement education* plus the *cost of other services* called upon as a result of exclusion minus the *cost of the pupil's place in a mainstream school*. Permanent exclusions can be costed in this way on an annual basis. Often the costs of a permanent exclusion persist beyond the one year.

Table 6.1 indicates the range of sources of expenditure which arise in the case of an exclusion and the time-scale over which this expenditure may occur. There are also finance implications for the parents when a child is excluded; data on parents'/carers' additional expenditure arising from exclusion were not gathered for this study because it is even harder to calculate this accurately and because of the policy focus of the work. The longer term costs are also not dealt with as the data from this study do not extend over a sufficiently long time period.[7]

This study calculated the *immediate additional costs* following from the permanent exclusion of pupils in 1994/95. For education, these are the costs of managing the exclusion process (administration, etc.), support (e.g. educational psychologists) and replacement education. There are also the costs to other services (e.g. Social Services). Exclusion causes 'cost-shunting'. This means that other parts of the education system and other services, particularly Social Services, are forced to bear some costs of supporting the excluded child. Police costs for a proportion of excluded children are very high. It is well known (Cohen *et al.*, 1994; CRE, 1996) that the damage from exclusion persists beyond the immediate period. Therefore, in order to gain some indication of these additional costs, we calculated the continuing additional costs in the medium term for pupils excluded in 1994/95 who had continuing provision made for them in 1995/96.[8]

The financial cost of exclusions: 1994/95

There is great variation among permanently excluded pupils which is particularly evident in the periods of time out of school and their eventual destinations. Of the sample of thirty pupils, three were out of school for fifteen

Table 6.1 Costing permanent exclusions from school

Services	Managing the process of exclusion costs	Immediate costs (in the year of the exclusion)	Medium term costs (in the following full year)	Longer term costs (up to ten years)
Education	Communication to Education Office Appeals	Replacement education Assessment Referrals to services Calls upon services	Continued replacement education, induction or phased reintegration	Compensatory/ second chance education Unemployment
Social Services	None	Social worker time for pupil and parents Services to avert family breakdown Increased family monitoring	Costs which may include residential care, residential education, transport and support for stressed families	Excessive demands on services – child and family
Police	None	Police officer time involved in cautions	Remand and multiple court appearances	Recidivism
Health	None	Involvement of GP with stressed parents, referral to psychiatrist	Attendance at child, adolescent and family therapy units	Longer term health problems

days or fewer and returned to continue their education in another mainstream school. Others waited longer for a new school. Four went to special schools, in three cases residential. For the majority the situation can be characterised by first delay and eventually provision being made. Replacement provision was often at a greatly increased level of expenditure which was established only in the year following the exclusion. Another distinct group were the leavers; six left school without returning to mainstream school and without taking examinations.

The variability was reflected in the costings also. For the small number who went to another school with little delay or who left school, the sole cost was to administrative services and this was minimal. By contrast, a small number had high levels of expenditure associated with their cases including police involvement and whole year residential therapeutic unit provision.

The average annual cost for mainstream schooling in 1994/95 was approximately £2,300 for secondary pupils and £1,700 for primary pupils. The costings for permanently excluded pupils in six LEAs reveal that they cost, on average, over £4,300 in full year equivalent replacement education and other education costs. Exclusion costs for the Education Department cover three elements: the administration of the system including appeals; the educational support agents – educational psychologists and educational welfare officers; and the replacement education which takes the form of home tuition or Pupil Referral Unit placement. Return to mainstream often has additional costs associated where induction and phased reintegration are arranged but this did not arise in the thirty cases in this study. Similarly there were no transfers to further education institutions.

Variation in policy and practice was found in the three LEAs where a unit cost approach was used and, as a consequence, different centres and rationales for budget holding. Met U focused its provision in PRUs (eight out of ten of the excluded pupils in the sample) while County U, partly because of travel problems, catered for many of its excludees (again, eight out of ten) through home tuition. Approximately 21 per cent of the expenditure was on *managing* the exclusion process, while 68 per cent was devoted to delivering the *replacement education*.

Table 6.2 includes the three LEAs (U) above with the costs grossed up to represent costs for *all* the authority's permanent exclusions. This is accomplished by multiplying up from ten cases costed in each of those three LEAs to the full number of exclusions, as given in the second column. The other costs are similarly grossed up to offer comparisons with the three LEAs (G) where gross costing figures only for permanently excluded pupils have been sought.

There is similar variation in policy among the gross costing LEAs with educational welfare playing a significant role in Met G and County G and the Administration in London G being largely located in the PRU. EWOs are sometimes located within PRUs working closely with the staff and pupils on site.

mean cost of managing the case of an excluded pupil arrived at by dividing the 'total education costs' given in column 9 of Table 6.2 by the 'numbers of permanent exclusions' given in column 2 of that table. Taking the mean cost of an exclusion (column 4 of Table 6.3) out of a 190 day school year, a full year equivalent cost can be calculated. This is set out in column 5 of Table 6.3. The variation is considerable, in part because individual pupil costs vary so greatly. The mean indicative cost for a full year equivalent education and provision for a permanently excluded pupil is over £4,300.

The amount of education received during the period of permanent exclusion in the unit costing LEAs was under 10 per cent of a full-time education. This is a consequence of the delayed start and the part-time nature of the replacement education. This is inevitably damaging to the individual pupil and makes return to mainstream school more difficult.

The costs to education of 'continuing' permanent exclusions into 1995/96

Some of the costs of exclusion do not arise immediately; if a pupil is excluded towards the end of the summer term it may be the autumn before replacement education is arranged. For some pupils there is a significant delay, sometimes six months, before costs begin to accrue. Of the twenty-six exclusions during the 1994/95 school year in the unit costing authorities, eight were Year 11 and therefore finished their compulsory schooling in May or July 1995. Of the remaining eighteen, twelve were 'continuing' cases for whom non-mainstream educational arrangements were being made. The costs of this are set out in Table 6.4. About 46 per cent of the 1994/95 permanent

Table 6.4 The costs of cases of 'continuing' permanent exclusions in three LEAs, 1995/96

LEA	Number of continuing cases	Home tuition costs	PRU costs	Administration costs[a]	Other replacement education costs	Total	Mean costs to education per case in each LEA
		(£)	(£)	(£)	(£)	(£)	(£)
Met U	4 (out of 6)	1,840	7,594	1,092	[b]	10,526	2,632
London U	2[c] (out of 10)	4,600	4,875	864		10,339	5,170
County U	6 (out of 10)	3,979	471	336	35,955[d]	40,741	6,790
					Overall mean = £5,134		

Notes:
a Administration costs are for half-termly review and maintaining the database.
b Other replacement education costs for one pupil were met by Social Services.
c A third pupil was placed in a special school and his SEN Statement reviewed.
d In respect of residential out-of-area therapeutic unit the bulk of the cost is met by Social Services.

exclusions studied in the unit costing LEAs were 'continuing' cases into the following year. These cost on average £5,134, a more substantial charge on the education budget in 1995/96 than new exclusions.

The trend in the costs of permanent exclusions: 1993/96

Taking account of the mean cost of new excludees in 1994/95 (column 4 of Table 6.3), continuing cases (column 8 of Table 6.4) the trend in permanent exclusions and an inflation factor of 2.7 per cent per year allows a calculation of *actual* expenditure on exclusions by education in the six LEAs. The mean cost for continuing excludees was over £5,000 in 1995/96 compared with under £2,000 in actual expenditure per new exclusion case. The total bill to education in the six LEAs reached nearly £5 million in 1995/96. Table 6.5 sets these calculations out. Though a small part of the education budget, it was a significant allocation which was growing and, arguably, offered poor value for money.

Table 6.5 Costs to education of permanent exclusions in six LEAs, 1993–96

	1993/94		1994/95		1995/96	
	Number	*Cost (£)*	*Number*	*Cost (£)*	*Number*	*Cost (£)*
Exclusions in the current year (6 LEAs)	1,002	1,846,268	1,096	2,073,997	1,236	2,402,075
Exclusions continuing from the previous year (6 LEAs)	357	1,737,734	461	2,304,551	504	2,587,536
Total costs to education in that year (6 LEAs)		3,584,002		4,378,548		4,989,611

The costs to other agencies of permanent exclusion

The costs to other agencies are undoubtedly considerable, though higher levels of inference have been used to arrive at estimates of overall costs. Common frameworks for maintaining data on individuals are not found. Costing data – usually in the form of personnel hours devoted to the case – are *more* difficult to acquire from the other agencies than from within education, and extrapolation from the unit costing LEAs to the other three LEAs

Table 6.6 Estimates of costs to other agencies incurred by permanently excluded pupils in 1994/95: three unit cost LEAs

LEA	Numbers of excluded pupils involved	Social work costs (£)	Numbers of excluded pupils involved	Health costs (£)	Numbers of excluded pupils involved	Police costs (£)
Met U	2	5,035	3	265	3	13,992
London U	1	385	1	106	2	1,235
County U	3	1,346	0	0	3	1,270
Total	6	6,766	4	371	8	16,497
Mean cost to each service per pupil		1,128		93		2,062

has been carried out using 'low' estimates. Table 6.6 gives the costs for the individuals within the sample of ten cases in each LEA who were a charge on the agencies other than education. The figures in Table 6.7 are arrived at by generalising the rates of involvement indicated in Table 6.6 to the populations of excluded pupils in the same way as for education in Tables 6.2 and 6.3 earlier.

It is important that an estimate is arrived at for the full costs to all services so that co-ordinated policies may be formulated in the face of a shared problem and planned budget allocations. On the basis of the data available

Table 6.7 Estimates of gross costs to other agencies incurred by permanently excluded pupils in 1994/95: six LEAs

LEA	Total of permanent excluded for whom LEA must provide, 1994/95	Social Services		Health		Police and criminal justice	
		Estimate of excluded pupils involved	Estimate of Social Services costs (£)	Estimate of excluded pupils involved	Estimate of health services costs (£)	Estimate of excluded pupils involved	Estimate of police and criminal justice costs (£)
Met G	302	60	67,680	31	2,883	81	167,022
Met U	136	27	30,456	40	3,720	40	82,480
London G	145	29	32,712	15	1,395	38	78,356
London U	56	6	6,768	6	558	11	22,682
County G	291	58	65,424	30	2,790	77	158,774
County U	162	49	55,272	0	0	49	101,038
Totals	1,092		258,312		11,346		610,352

to the research team in this short investigation, it is clear that the expenditure incurred by other services is substantial, though it cannot in most cases be attributed solely to the act of permanent exclusion. Table 6.7 presents the total estimated expenditure for all six LEAs.

Approximately 20 per cent of permanently excluded pupils are Social Services cases costing on average £1,100. Social work costs during the year of exclusion amount to only 10 per cent of the costs borne by education. These costs are spread unevenly and even for those young people for whom they make provision, the variation is great with the costs for residential out-of-area units or schools being the most expensive items.

Approximately 10 per cent of permanently excluded pupils call upon health services resources, but they incur little expenditure, amounting to an average of less than £100. Health costs arise from attendance at child and adolescent therapy units and similar centres with some general practitioner (GP) or psychiatric consultations. Information provided by four of the community healthcare trusts suggests that referrals, by parents or schools, of pupils with behaviour difficulties have risen significantly since the mid-1990s.

Costs to the police are calculated to arise in connection with a little over one-quarter of permanently excluded pupils at an average cost of over £2,000. This should be regarded as a low estimate because data supplied from some police areas suggest that up to two-thirds of excludees are known to the police with one-third going to court. Police and criminal justice costs vary from the caution (around £35) to a prosecution which runs to something approaching £3,000; where remand or multiple court appearances are involved, the expense is obviously greater.[9]

Figure 6.2 shows this distribution of estimated costs to the services other than education for the six LEAs. Police and criminal justice costs form

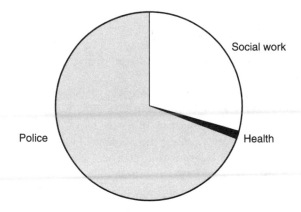

Figure 6.2 Distribution of estimated costs to other agencies of permanently excluded pupils, 1994/95

70 per cent of these additional costs, and reports and analyses from a number of forces suggest that the costs set out here are conservative.

Police and Social Services' costs for a small number of excludees continued at a high level into the following year. This included police officer time, court appearances, and residential education largely paid for by social services. One exceptional young person had costs to Social Services of £39,000, including the cost of residential school, and £22,000 to the police and criminal justice.

Extrapolating the total costs of permanent exclusion in all LEAs over a four year period

Using the 1994/95 figures calculated during the Commission for Racial Equality research it was found that:

- the mean cost to education (with wide variation) of a child excluded in 1994/95 was £1,892
- the mean cost of the continuing excluded child in 1995/96 was £5,134
- the mean cost to other services of a child excluded in 1994/95 was £1,024.

For the six LEAs in which those data were gathered, the total costs for the three year period in relation to the numbers excluded can be seen in row 1 of Table 6.5. Continuing exclusions from the previous year have been identified in row 2. These have been costed from the average rate derived from the research in the three unit costing local authorities and set out in Table 6.4.

Calculations have then been made to extrapolate the equivalent cost to all LEAs over those three years. The calculations have been made as follows. Numbers of permanently excluded pupils are known for England as a whole and for the six LEAs within which this work has been carried out. Working from the 1994/95 costs, the mean expenditure on permanently excluded pupils can be calculated and for the 46 per cent of cases continuing from the previous year. Taking account of average inflation at 2.7 per cent and the numbers excluded in the whole of England in 1993/94 and in 1995/96, estimates can be made of the total expenditure to all English LEAs that would arise during those periods.

Extrapolations can be made, in the same way as for education costs, to give total costs to other services for all LEAs in England. When these are added to the education costs a total expenditure of more than £71 million is arrived at for 1995/96. For 1996/97 estimates, the numbers of excluded pupils in that year are multiplied by the relevant unit costs to which an inflation factor of 2.7 per cent is also applied. Based on these calculations, the total cost, to education and other services, of permanently excluding pupils from school in England reaches £76 million. Carrying out the same operation using 1997/98 figures pushes the total expenditure just a little higher (Figure 6.3 and Table 6.8).

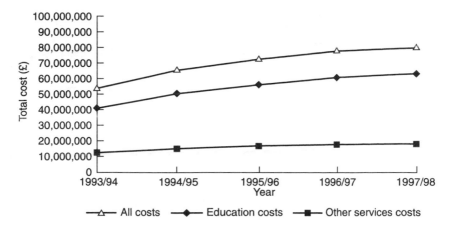

Figure 6.3 Costs to education and other services of permanent exclusions from schools in England, 1993–98

The rise in numbers and in expenditure is such as to make this group of pupils a significant cost to the public services. They are no longer a rare anomaly but a fixed part of the picture for which routine provision will need to be made – in mainstream school or elsewhere. Treating them as an aberration which may go away is a mistake in terms of the quality of provision for them, in terms of the likely outcomes for the individuals themselves and for their prospects of becoming contributing citizens.

The cost of inclusion

Costs were calculated for six pupils maintained in their schools. In most instances these pupils were in receipt of additional resources. The additional costs varied from £0 to £6,300, with a mean of £2,815. For these children were receiving full-time education. This was not without difficulty and personal costs to their teachers but the provision of education was approaching 100 per cent (at least in intended provision), the young person was not left without schooling and was not left unsupervised. The family stress was minimised and the difficulties of reintegration were avoided. The small number of cases that have been costed indicate that maintaining pupils in school by means of additional support is cost-effective expenditure.

The support required is sometimes specialist teaching for a small number of hours per week and, more often, the presence of a classroom assistant. The school will also often have special arrangements for monitoring the pupil's progress and behaviour; collaboration with parents is known to be important where it can be established.

Some of these pupils are maintained in school with little or no extra financial cost. Where specific problems or incidents are involved, this is feasible. External intervention of a substantial kind can 'turn around' some young

Table 6.8 Extrapolating the costs to the public purse of permanent exclusions, 1993–98

	1993/94	1994/95	1995/96	1996/97	1997/98
Permanent exclusions occurring in that year	11,181	12,458	13,581	13,453	13,041
Permanent exclusions continuing from the previous year	3,973	5,143	5,731	6,247	6,188
Education costs	£39,992,741	£49,770,028	£54,825,167	£59,779,166	£60,229,029
Other services costs	£12,769,530	£14,604,216	£16,352,956	£16,619,997	£16,546,003
All costs	£52,762,271	£64,374,244	£71,178,124	£76,399,163	£76,775,032

people experiencing (and posing) problems. With some of these pupils on the verge of permanent exclusion, even with the additional inputs made, their maintenance in school remains a strain on teaching staff and sometimes a distressing and disruptive experience for the other children. The estimated cost of maintaining in school pupils who might otherwise be excluded should be compared with the estimated costs that arise when pupils are permanently excluded with great caution. Inclusion policies need to be realistically resourced to avoid, in particular, detriment to the education of others.

Not only are the costs in the provision of replacement education high but also, in the first year of exclusion, it is likely that the receipt of education will be no greater than 10 per cent of the pupil's full entitlement. The costs to education of 'continuing' exclusion cases in the following year are much higher, partly because more education is actually provided. The costs to other agencies, though less well founded, are high with police and criminal justice bearing the larger part of the cost burden even though it is a minority of permanent excludees (in this study) for which costs are attributed to criminal activity.

It is evident that, in tackling what is a problem that extends beyond education, the sharing of information among the various agencies happens to only a limited degree and the ability to use collaborative strategies is greatly inhibited. This is despite an avowed, shared concern. While the costs to the other agencies are not directly attributable to the young person being permanently excluded from school, it is reasonable to assume that this group, particularly older excluded pupils, are vulnerable to temptations to be involved in illicit activities initiated by themselves or others. Being excluded is an alienating experience and is likely to push the young person further in that direction. Being excluded also provides time in unstructured and unsupervised environments where they may become involved in crime and, thereby, become a cost to the public purse. Maintaining pupils in school must reduce the likelihood of these developments.

The few cases of pupils maintained in school which we have costed indicate that this is cheaper than requirements for those in the 'continuing' exclusions category. This will not be possible for all troubled and troublesome children but is a preferred solution where costed support is actually provided and kept under review. Such pupils will also continue to receive *full-time* education.

Conclusion

Generalising from detailed costing data from a small number of local authorities has dangers yet, at present, provides the best basis for total cost estimates that we have. It assumes many regularities including the constancy and evenness of trends. However, other research would indicate that the numbers arrived at are reasonable. Even allowing for a 30 per cent margin of error either side of the figure given, the costs are very large. A sum, estimated at nearly £77 million, was spent in 1997/98 on all services to cater for permanently excluded children. The provision made for them is generally considered to be inadequate in quantity and quality. It is clear that the costs arising from permanent exclusion fall not just on education but also on Social Services and the criminal justice system. About 20 per cent of permanently excluded pupils are Social Services cases; 10 per cent are involved with the health services; a little over 25 per cent are involved with the police. The argument can be made by all the services that young people should be in school; it is the institutional arrangement set up for them. If they are not in school there are many opportunities for them to come to harm and to become involved in illegitimate activities.

The focus of effort and resourcing should be in the management of these young people to continue their education and development in structured environments to make the best of them and help them make the best of themselves. The allocation of funding to cope with exclusions that have occurred, the contradictory purposes of the agencies and the conflict among them, and the poor outcomes from exclusions point to a need to avoid this waste.

Two prominent factors are part of the context within which costs of permanent exclusion from school should be viewed. First, the costs to some of the services other than education may have arisen anyway and are not necessarily a consequence of a permanent exclusion. This should be balanced against the probability that our indicative costs are underestimates. Second, retaining some young people in school is extremely difficult. Strategies and resources would need to ensure that other children's education is not disrupted and teachers are not placed under unreasonable stress.

The most speculative of our estimates is on the cost of inclusion. Here the six cases described above were costed and averaged. The range is from no cost to £6,300. The average is £2,815. To then assume that this average cost applied to all 12,458 pupils in England excluded during 1994/95 and to a 46 per cent continuing group from the previous year gives a total remarkably similar to the costs of exclusion to education for that year at approximately £49.5 million. However, for this figure pupils would have been in receipt of ten times as much education, on average. It is likely also that the additional costs to the other services of around £14.6 million would not have applied.

The experience of permanent exclusion from school is deeply damaging to the pupils and very distressing for the parents and carers. In some cases these are families with a range of problems already and the exclusion from school is a further difficulty. There are dangers in increasing the burden on families that are not coping well, and the result may well be longer term calls on the public services. The financial costs which follow from exclusion are considerable yet they provide a vastly inferior, inadequate educational experience for the child and risks in terms of the development of a small section of the future citizenry.

Notes

1 Examples of sound costing studies exist for the Social Services (Knapp, 1986; Netten and Dennett, 1995; Cambridge and Knapp, 1997), the police (Chartered Institute of Public Finance and Accountancy (CIPFA), 1995) and the criminal justice system (Audit Commission, 1996b; Shapland *et al.*, 1995). Tsang (1994) has looked particularly at the costs of educational inclusion of marginalised populations.

2 Two from London; two metropolitan authorities; two county authorities. No LEA that was approached refused to co-operate.

3 Every effort was made to ensure that the sample was representative in terms of phase of schooling, gender, ethnicity and length of time excluded in so far as this was feasible with small numbers. The problems of getting parental agreement via the local authority for participation in a study of the costs and experiences (often painful) of events of the year before proved difficult. It required telephone calls from education officers and other staff (e.g. educational welfare officers) who knew the families to achieve the ten cases in each of the three LEAs.

4 Parents were asked to sign a form giving permission for agencies to give information to the research team on the time and costs of their involvement with the pupil following permanent exclusion. The permission was only for matters relevant to the exclusion and for a specific time period. Only one parent refused to sign. A copy of the permission form was sent ahead or shown before the interview with any of the professionals. Guarantees of confidentiality were given.

5 An inflation factor of 2.7 per cent was applied when calculating the costs for the following year.

6 A range of other costing studies were drawn upon to inform the calculations used in this research. From Netten and Dennett (1995) guidance was found for calculating GP costs and for adding an additional 20 per cent to gross costs to social work to cover administration. CIPFA (1995) indicated that 69 per cent of police expenditure is on officers' wages and that 20 per cent of officers' time is spent on documentation and recording.

7 There are also non-financial costs (not immediately quantifiable in finance terms) to the parents/carers as well as to the services. There is considerable distress to the children, their families and also the schools concerned, when exclusion takes place. Calculation should also include a measure of the quality/quantity of the substitute education and its appropriateness for the child, compared with mainstream school provision.

8 There are difficulties in estimating many of the costs that exclusion incurs. Estimating the costs within the education services alone posed some difficulties since LEAs had different arrangements and costing procedures. Estimates of total expenditure on permanent exclusions were consistently lower when arrived at through the unit costing approach as compared with the gross costing approach; this is in part due to the difficulties in the three gross costing LEAs of disentangling expenditure on the one cohort of excludees – 1994/95 – and the continuing excludees from previous years. In the three unit costing LEAs the reciprocal problem was to ensure that generic tasks related to the management of, and provision for, excludees were proportionately allocated to the individual cases costed. For these reasons the average and gross figures given are both likely to underestimate the total costs of permanent exclusion to education.

In costing police, health and Social Services expenditure there were additional problems. In the gross costing authorities, services were not able to identify a category of 'permanently excluded pupils' or the proportion of their school-age clients in that category. Indications were given about the numbers of cases which came to the attention of the health services, principally child and adolescent psychiatry, where behavioural difficulties in school were the presenting problem. Police had categories of young offenders covering 'truants and excluded pupils' but it is not always clear what the status of the exclusion was (fixed term, unofficial or permanent). It is likely that, particularly in the case of police and criminal justice, the numbers involved and the costs given are, again, an underestimate.

The allocation of expenditure between the services was, in a few cases, complex: accompanied transport to school may be paid by Social Services; Social Services may pay all or part of the residential therapeutic education fees. There are inconsistencies and unresolved contests over funding, particularly with some of the most profoundly troubled youngsters. In many cases it is difficult to say that the costs to the services other than education would not have arisen had there been no permanent exclusion; for this reason these costs have not been combined with education costs but are presented separately.

9 One of the thirty cases was costed out at over £60,000. This included secure accommodation, multiple court appearances, solicitors' costs and a 52 week placement in an out-of-authority residential school. Costs to the criminal justice system amounted to over £22,000 and to Social Services £39,000 including the residential schooling costs which fell to them.

7 The law, rights and excluded pupils

Richard Harris and Carl Parsons

Introduction

Since the end of the nineteenth century the state has taken upon itself the burden of schooling the whole population. In England and Wales local education authorities and funding authorities are now the vehicles for delivering this service (ss. 13, 14, 16 Education Act 1996). Surprisingly, children's rights to education are poorly protected in law. The legal duty to ensure that children are educated lies upon the parent of every child of compulsory school age, rather than upon the state (s. 7 Education Act 1996). The reality for nearly all children is that they will receive the education that the local education authority or grant maintained sector choose to provide for them; even in an 'education market' providers have decisive powers. It is in the difficult cases that the weak rights that children have to receive an education are most clearly revealed. These difficult cases involve children who have attended school but have been excluded by their headteachers. Exclusions were first regulated by the Education (No. 2) Act 1986. Acts of Parliament under Conservative administrations in 1993, 1996 and 1997 and in 1998, under the Labour government, have marked governments' responses to the increasing number of excluded pupils and to growing concern over what is happening to them.

Legislative activity in education since 1944 has been busy. The rate of legislative activity has increased decade by decade such that in the 1990s there have been ten Acts.[1] The claim appears well founded that there was irresponsible haste in the Education Reform Act 1988, which brought in the National Curriculum, and the Education (Schools) Act 1992, which provided the basis of the OFSTED school inspection system. It is no surprise that less important elements were drafted with less care, were based on minimal inquiry and responded to blatant political values. In the 1986 and 1993 Acts the exclusion sections are in the part of the Acts headed 'Miscellaneous'. Subsequent Acts have had sections headed 'Discipline'.

The argument is advanced that, from regulating a small problem that might have stayed small and even gone away, the disciplinary path was established in the Education (No. 2) Act 1986 and was reformed, amended and reamended in the twelve years that followed. The quantity of text in the Acts devoted to regulating the process of exclusion, and establishing judicial and ever more complex procedures for appeal, overshadowed any text relating to the needs of the child or the child's continued access to a full-time education. The legislation has continued to repair the framework founded upon fundamentally flawed premises.

The authoritarian popularism evident in the consistently negative labelling of these children, and the official response to them, matches official activity in other policy areas. Liberal social policy of individualising blame and limiting intervention provides the philosophical base. The problem of excluded children, still under 14,000 a year in England in 1997/98, nearly 0.1 per cent of the school population, was a problem which was 'made'. Professionals having to deal with these children and young people had their role shaped by the legislation and had a client group defined and hardened by quasi-legal procedures. Other countries, especially those with a social democratic welfare philosophy, have not found it necessary to define and respond to the problem of difficult children and young people in this way.

The Education Act 1993 and more recent legislation have not been helpful in providing for the education for permanently excluded pupils. The decisions of the courts have, if anything, limited the protection of individuals still further. This lack of protection needs to be understood in the context of the acute distress that results from exclusion for child and family and the possibility of long-term damage (Parsons, 1994; Cohen *et al.*, 1994).

Section 298 of the 1993 Act imposed a new duty on local education authorities. The duty rests with the local education authority even if a funding authority has responsibility for providing school places within the local education authority community (s. 27 Education Act 1996). They are obliged to make arrangements to educate pupils who are ill, excluded or otherwise unable to attend school. This chapter concentrates on the content and implications of this duty and its subsequent history. This is also an interesting area to test the continuing gravity of the situation reported by Mrs Thomas, Commissioner for Local Administration, that 'the area of Local Government activity in which it has proved most difficult to obtain justice for the citizen has been education' (Commission for Local Administration in England, 1989: 36).

The 'justice' that parents or pupils might wish to obtain in education arises clearly in the area of school exclusions. Justice or rights in this area involve two issues. First, under what conditions can a child be excluded from school? Second, what right has the child to continue to receive education provided by the state? The unsatisfactory truth is that the majority of excluded pupils receive a level of education from local education authorities which, were it to be provided by the children's own parents, would result in their criminal prosecution (Petrie, 1993).

Section 298, in imposing a duty on LEAs to make provision for the education of excluded pupils other than at school, was an advance upon a discretionary power given by section 56 of the Education Act 1944. The section has been re-enacted in the 1996 Act s. 19. It is set out in clear terms and appears to clarify the rights the excluded pupil had both to educational provision from the LEA and its quantity and quality. It is revealing to examine the meaning of key terms in the section and the requirements they do in fact make.

> 298 (1) Each local education authority *shall make* arrangements for the provision of suitable *full-time or part-time* education at school or otherwise for those children of compulsory school age who, by reason of illness, exclusion from school or otherwise, may not for any period receive suitable education unless such arrangements are made for them.
>
> (7) In this section '*suitable* education' . . . means *efficient* education suitable to his age, ability and aptitude . . . and any special educational need he may have.
>
> (Education Act 1993, emphases added)

Examining section 298 of the Education Act 1993

Shall make

'Shall make' is a common statutory formula that imposes a duty upon local education authorities (Foulkes, 1995: 178). By itself this phrase does not give a right to the pupil. If a pupil wished to claim before a court that the local education authority had failed to make provision under this section, whether by failing to provide suitable education contrary to subsection (7) or by failing to make arrangements at all contrary to (1), the pupil would have to point to some other legal rule that gave him the right to receive this provision. In England there is no jurisprudence that automatically builds a right from a duty (Wade, 1988: 749). Therefore, the duty to provide does not translate into a right to receive. A case that exemplifies this traditional principle is *R v. ILEA ex parte Ali* (in Wade),[2] a case on section 8 of the Education Act 1944, the duty on local education authorities to provide schools sufficient in

> number, character and equipment to afford all pupils opportunities for education

Mr Ali's son did not have a school place. The local education authority had failed to provide one. In refusing Mr Ali's claim, Woolf LJ said that the section was 'for the public in general . . . [it was] not intended to give the individual a cause of action'. A recent case, *Tandy*, also showed the difficulty by allowing (7) to be the other rule that generates a right to receive provision under (1).

Part-time

The phrase 'part-time' does not occur in the predecessor section 56 of the 1944 Act, the section that gave LEAs a discretion to educate excluded pupils. The drafters of the 1993 Act seem to have had a dual aim: to impose a duty upon LEAs, but eviscerate the duty of any content. How much time is 'part-time'? Full-time schooling is adequately defined in the Education Acts; part-time is not. If the section had been written to impose a duty upon LEAs to offer excluded children education at school or otherwise on a full-time basis, which could be differently defined for home-schooled children, the limbo state of most excluded pupils would disappear. This duty, together with the power of section 298(2) to establish Pupil Referral Units, would effectively deal with the issue of excluded pupils not being offered a suitable education. The drafters did not follow this course but left the statute ambiguous on this crucial point. Sacks (1982: 157) studied a number of cases of interpretative difficulty with statutes. He famously showed that 'unintelligible legislation was being added to the statute book because the government either lacked clear objectives, or, had *deliberately* intended to obfuscate in order to avoid controversy' (italics added). The enactment of a duty without content starkly revealed the government's lack of policy and objectives for dealing with excluded pupils. Signs of policy developing with a Labour government showed in the Social Exclusion Unit's (1998) report committing government to reductions in truancy and exclusion, and to full-time provision of education for those permanently excluded by 2002.

Where an excluded pupil is given three hours a week home tuition, this appears to fall squarely within the meaning of 'part-time'. Until the late 1990s it was difficult to see that a legal action contesting this against the LEA would succeed. What is clearly no longer an option is for the LEA, as a matter of policy, to offer no educational service at all to excluded pupils. A problem that did not exist was solved.

This duty was re-enacted in the same words in section 19(1) of the Education Act 1996. Section 47 of the Education Act 1997 removed the discretion to make suitable 'full-time or part-time' education for children who were excluded, etc., just leaving the phrase 'suitable education'. This change avoids litigation over interpretative problems but, probably, does not change the substance of the section. Another change in the 1997 Act is that a local education authority will have to 'have regard to any guidance given from time to time by the Secretary of State' (section 47(4), creating a new section 19(4A) in the 1996 Act). This is potentially exciting as DfEE guidance on the meaning of suitable provision will be a strong weapon for campaigners for worthwhile education for excluded children, as well as excluded children pursuing actions in the courts and complaints with the local government ombudsman. The new subsection, though, like its predecessors and linked provisions, is framed to encourage local education authorities to address the problem of exclusion, not to compel them to provide an adequate service. Crucially, no right is given to an excluded pupil to receive education for a specified time or with a specified content. Both would be simple to define. Content could be easily specified with respect to the National Curriculum or sections of it such as the core subjects. The 1996 Act Schedule 1 para. 6(2) defines in broad terms the curriculum required in a Pupil Referral Unit and sets forth a curriculum complaint system. This could have been the model for home-schooled children. The conclusion must be drawn that, despite these issues being discussed in the DfEE while the 1997 Act was being drafted, a deliberate decision must have been taken by senior officials not to give excluded pupils on home tuition even the minimal safeguards given to pupils in a Pupil Referral Unit.

Efficient and suitable education

'Efficient' and 'suitable' are found in section 36 of the 1944 Act, on which section 298 of the 1993 Act was modelled.

> 36. It shall be the duty of the parent of every child . . . to cause him to receive efficient full-time education suitable to his age, ability and aptitude.

Section 7 of the 1996 Act restates this duty.

Neville Harris (1995: 294) suggests that the words 'efficient' and 'suitable' would be construed together to mean receipt of the broad and balanced National Curriculum but this cannot be correct. The National Curriculum has not been imposed upon individual pupils but upon governing bodies and the headteachers of public sector schools. Part III of the Education Act 1993 made changes in the framework of the National Curriculum, but made no amendments to give individual pupils, let alone excluded pupils, a personal right to receive a National Curriculum centred education. Part V of the 1996 Act maintains this position, section 357 imposing a duty on local education authorities and schools to implement the National Curriculum. Pupils are not given a right or entitlement to receive it. Excluded pupils are closer to the situation of those in independent schools or home educated. What kind of curriculum would an independent school have to offer before a court would hold that a parent, in sending a child to the school, was failing to provide an efficient and suitable education?

Cases which have tested the meaning of efficient and suitable education

The Machzikei Hadass School Trust case

In the case of *R v. The Secretary of State for Education and Science ex parte Talmud Torah Machzikei Hadass School Trust* (1985) (*The Times*, 12 April), the school was challenging a decision of the Secretary of State. He had held that the school was unsuitable because its educational provision was solely narrowly fundamentalist religious instruction, based entirely on the Bible. Woolf J held that a school is 'suitable' if it primarily equips a child for life in a community of which the child is a member rather than the way of life of the country as a whole.

The case is exceptional in that a minority faith community was involved. The case also predates the National Curriculum, but as this binds only maintained schools it could hardly be relevant, even now, to the curriculum that would be acceptable outside the maintained school sector. It is worth noting that the court did not reason about the rights of the children taught in the school but around the supposed contraventions of the school's educational provision. The court found there were none. Neither has the secretary of state refought such a case since the Education Reform Act 1988.

There are a small number of cases on the meaning of the word 'efficient' in the Education Acts. The historical standard has been quite clear. In a criminal prosecution of parents for breach of an earlier version of the section 7 duty, *Bevan v. Shears* [1911] 2KB 936 at 939, the Chief Justice argued that:

> in the absence of anything . . . providing that a child of a given age shall receive instruction in given subjects, in my view it cannot be said that as to a particular child there is a standard of education by which the child must be taught . . . [the question is, is] the child being taught efficiently as far as that particular child is concerned?

Suitable education referred to the efficiency with which the education was provided, i.e. not the standards to which the child was being educated. This was made clear by section 19(6) of the 1996 Act.

'Suitable education', in relation to a child . . . means efficient education suitable to his age, ability and aptitude and to any special educational needs he may have.

Although efficient education is not independently defined, section 9 indicated its sense:

> [every provider] shall have regard to the general principle that pupils are to be educated in accordance with the wishes of their parents, so far as that is compatible with the provision of efficient instruction and the avoidance of unreasonable public expenditure.

See also s. 317 Schedule 27 para. 3.

The Tandy test

Efficiency has been tied to cost saving, not to standards to be achieved. In *R v. East Sussex County Council ex parte Tandy* [1997] Keene J was persuaded that 'suitable education' should reflect what was being provided in schools locally, and that the LEA should have regard to efficiency only in deciding between different forms of suitable provision. The Court of Appeal did not accept this argument nor did the House of Lords. So until *Tandy* was finally decided in the House of Lords on 20 May 1998 there continued to be a lack of clarity about the meaning of those key terms that all users of the statute needed to construe. What seems certain is that the Acts had been framed to avoid giving children private rights to receive the National Curriculum. Not surprisingly, the courts' unwillingness to set a standard of educational entitlement that Parliament has declined to set echoes through the cases.

Ambiguity concerning the meaning of a key phrase is not uncommon in local authority law. In housing law, local authorities were obliged to offer 'appropriate accommodation' to homeless families. This can be seen from *Pulhofer v. Hillingdon London Borough Council* [1986] AC 484. At the appeal before the House of Lords, Hillingdon Council were asked by their lordships to suggest accommodation that might not be 'appropriate'. The council suggested that a barrel would not be 'appropriate accommodation' as it was not capable of accommodating. The House of Lords decided that the meaning of the phrase 'appropriate accommodation' was not a matter of law but a question of fact to be determined by the council, the defendant in the action.

'Appropriate accommodation' suggestively parallels 'suitable education'. An underdetermined adjective is used to set the standard that is in dispute, a standard the local authority must minimally meet when dealing with the most disadvantaged. If the courts were asked to consider what would a local authority have to do to fail to provide 'suitable education' for an excluded pupil, would the answer be 'nothing'? And if it is a matter of fact, not law, is the local education authority alone to decide the meaning of suitable educational provision? In education cases, what stands out is the courts' reluctance to set a minimum standard for provision when the Education Acts have failed to set one. It is difficult to establish what educational provision for an excluded child would breach the 'efficient' and 'suitable' test. Home tuition by a non-qualified teacher? The cases seem not to support this (Petrie, 1993). An unpatterned and unstructured programme of tuition? This is more likely and happened in *R v. Gwent County Council ex parte Perry* 129 SJ 737: CA. This seems to touch the word 'efficient'. There must be strength in the argument that something imaginable must breach the statutory test else why have it? The protection offered by the law to the recipients of local authority services are too poorly defined and inadequately related to actual provision to provide a basis for challenge in law, except in a rare bad case. A pragmatic position is adopted by the courts when faced with the needs versus costs dilemma which pervades all local authority law. Lord Nicholls of Birkenhead, in *R v. Gloucester City Council ex parte Barry* [1997] 1 2 All ER at 11j, a social services act case, is clear. 'Who is to set the standard? To this there can be only one answer: the relevant local authority . . . the local authority sets the standards to be applied within its area . . . Cost is of more or less significance depending upon whether the authority currently has more or less money'. Of course, the local authority must take account of all relevant considerations, but in the last analysis, cost justifies cuts.

The law can be confusing in this area as, occasionally, litigants do win against a local authority. In *R v. East Sussex County Council ex parte T* (*The Times*, 29 March 1997) Beth Tandy was being educated at home as she had been diagnosed as suffering from ME (myalgic encephalomyelitis).[3] The LEA decided to reduce her home tuition from five hours a week to three in order to save money. This was part of an overall reduction in contact time for home-schooled children. Beth Tandy sought judicial review on s. 298 of the 1993 Act. Keene J's judgment contained interesting dicta, including that what amounted to 'suitable' must satisfy an objective test (which would include reference to the standard of education offered locally). An LEA could have regard to its resources because there might be more than one way of providing suitable education. As the LEA was not choosing between different suitable arrangements but simply curtailing one in order to save money, the LEA's decision was struck down. The court did not reason that three hours in itself could not be suitable education, nor in its judgment was a baseline set. However, this decision did not stand. In June 1997, the Court of Appeal allowed East Sussex's appeal, holding that the LEA could take into account the cost of home tuition and the impact it has on the financial resources available to fulfil that duty and other duties so long as proper consideration is given to the circumstances of a particular case (reported at [1997] 3 ELR 311). Provided an authority pays attention to all relevant considerations, including its own financial resources, it would still seem to be left to the local authority's judgement as to what 'sufficient education' might mean. This seems the more anomalous as the 1996 Act requires pupils in Pupil Referral Units to be educated in accordance with s. 351, a broad and balanced curriculum. Why are the excluded not offered a Pupil Referral Unit place?

Lord Browne-Wilkinson gave the leading speech in the House of Lords in *Tandy* [1998] 2 WLR 885. He said that the Court of Appeal decision was founded on the premise that s. 298 created a duty not to children individually but to children as a class. In the hearing before the House of Lords, East Sussex County Council withdrew this argument and conceded that the council owed an individual duty to each child who by reason of illness, exclusion or otherwise was not receiving a suitable education. The decision was based on the wording of s. 298(7) (see p. 109), Lord Browne-Wilkinson indicating that he thought this correct. Once agreed that East Sussex County Council owed a duty to Beth Tandy, what was the content of that duty, what did the LEA have to provide? Unfortunately, the House of Lords did not directly answer that. The question put to them was (p. 886 at F) did the LEA take an irrelevant consideration into account, its financial resources, in deciding to cut Beth Tandy's home tuition? The court said yes as suitable education (i.e. suited to . . . age, ability and aptitude and to any special educational needs) are, the court reasoned, solely educational considerations. Finance is not a factor on the list and thus an irrelevant condition. The section imposes a duty, not a discretion, and the LEA have no option but to comply with it.

A great victory? At the time of writing the scope of this decision seems unclear and, perhaps, will be rather narrow. At no point did the judges suggest that five or even the reduced three hours a week were unreasonable levels of provision. The decision is narrowly on the point that finance was an improper consideration in determining suitable and efficient provision for a particular child. So if East Sussex had reduced Beth Tandy's home tuition from five to three hours per week on the ground that she could be adequately educated, it appears they would not have acted illegally.

Lord Browne-Wilkinson argued, at one point, that just as the content of the duty upon parents under s. 37 of the Education Act 1944 (later s. 7 1996) to provide 'efficient . . . education suitable' etc. could not range according to the resources of the parent so the parallel duty under s. 298 could not vary according to the resources of the LEA. Although the comparison between a parent and an LEA is somewhat dubious, the judge's reasoning implies that an s. 298 child should receive the education that a parent is ordinarily obliged to provide for a child. This is usually full-time schooling. Is an LEA obliged to provide the equivalent of full-time schooling for s. 298 children? Frustratingly, the House of Lords did not say, simply declaring that in each case it will be a question of fact.

'That duty will not be fulfilled unless the arrangements do in fact provide suitable education for each child' (p. 890 at A). This points to more litigation being needed to settle the minimum threshold of provision that is reasonable (reasonableness is discussed later in this chapter). Earlier in his speech Lord Browne-Wilkinson said that 'what constitutes "suitable" or "efficient" education is [to be decided by] . . . the local authority and is [a matter of] . . .

opinion and degree'. This dictum is more distant from the parental duty. Litigation is bound to arise to settle it and, at present, children who are provided with five hours per week or less home tuition should be advised to seek judicial review of their LEA's decision.

X and others v. Bedfordshire County Council

If *Tandy* is not narrowly read it appears out of line with the traditional reasoning about local authorities' breaches of duty, as illustrated by *X and others v. Bedfordshire County Council* (1995) 3 All ER 353, a decision of the House of Lords. That decision was not a surprise, continuing the pattern of administrative law rules that local authorities are accustomed to in other spheres of their activity.

Five cases were heard together in the appeal, two child abuse and three special educational needs cases. The children in the education cases claimed that the local authorities had negligently, and/or in breach of statutory duty, failed to provide schooling appropriate to their special educational needs. At first instance (at the first hearing of the case before a judge) the claims were struck out as disclosing no reasonable cause of action, i.e. the judge held, for the kinds of reasons outlined above, that the children did not even have an arguable case so there was nothing to go to trial about. The appeals were against the judge's striking-out decision. The children aimed to try to get the cases heard at all. The local authorities argued that they had no case to answer. They did not have duties towards individual pupils, just general duties to provide a type of service. Lord Browne-Wilkinson, giving the leading speech of the House of Lords, argued that where a local authority is given a discretion 'the local authority cannot be liable in damages for doing that which Parliament has authorised. Therefore, if the decisions complained of fall within the ambit of such . . . discretion they cannot be actionable' (p. 368 h).

Liability can attach to a local authority only if its actions lie outside of the discretion given by statute. What are the boundaries of this discretion? His Lordship stated the position thus:

> Where Parliament has conferred a statutory discretion on a public authority, it is for that authority, not the courts, to exercise the discretion . . . if the factors relevant to the discretion include matters of policy, the court cannot adjudicate . . . and . . . cannot reach the conclusion that the decision was outside the ambit of the statutory discretion.
>
> (p. 317 b, c)

The judge gave an example of how policy might touch a local authority's discretion: 'notable examples are discretionary decisions on the allocation of scarce resources' (p. 370 j). This is the heart of the difficulty. Local authorities have limited financial resources. Increasing exclusions, homelessness, etc., put further pressure on these funds. In *X v. Bedfordshire* and in *R v. Gloucester*, courts have concluded that, unless Parliament expressly enacts that they must provide a service regardless of cost, the discretionary allocation of resources is to be left to the local authorities. In the world of public law these ideas are not new.

For example, in *R v. The Secretary of State for Social Services ex parte The Child Poverty Action Group* (1985) (*The Times*, 8 August), an action was taken by a claimant against the DSS. Staff had failed to pay claimants the benefits to which they were entitled. It was agreed that benefit staff were under a duty to best promote the welfare of claimants (this was the statutory duty that the case turned on). The court held that this duty did not mean that the Secretary of State had to search through the department's records to identify claimants who had been underpaid. The duty was a general duty, not a duty that gave rights to particular claimants.

The duty involved deciding how to best allocate resources so as to take *reasonable steps* to identify claimants who had been underpaid. The court would not intervene to tell the Secretary of State how to allocate resources – identical reasoning to that found in *X v. Bedfordshire*.

In the three education cases heard with *X*, one being *Keating v. Bromley London Borough Council*, it was claimed that from July 1977 to May 1979 and from September 1985 to November 1986 Bromley Council had failed to provide a place at any school for the plaintiff. The claim was based on the local authority's breach of its duty to provide school places under s. 8 of the 1944 Act. After a review of the relevant cases Lord Browne-Wilkinson concluded, denying Keating's claim: 'I find nothing . . . which demonstrates a parliamentary intention to give that class (pupils with special educational needs) a . . . right of action for damages' (p. 398 f).

All the appeals were dismissed as showing no reasonable cause of action, as a duty on an authority to provide a service (for children with special educational needs) does not generate a co-relative right of a child to receive the service. If Keating, who lost three years' schooling, has no private rights against his local education authority for its admitted breach of duty under section 8,[4] it is difficult to see that an excluded pupil would be in any better position if he or she sued because a local education authority failed to make a particular level of provision under s. 298 of the 1993 Act and its successors. The same is the position with respect to claims against school governors and head-teachers who exercise statutory administrative powers in the same manner as local authorities. Under these rules, the child has no personal right enforceable in damages to a state provided education. And this result is not a surprise, at least to the lawyer. Since *Dunlop v. Woollahra MC* [1982] AC 158 it appears to be the law in England that no damages (i.e. there are no private legal rights) are recoverable simply because a public body (the rule is much wider than local authorities) has negligently acted *ultra vires* (in breach of its duties and rules) and an individual has suffered loss. The reason for this is simple, an argument run time and again before the judges in public law actions. An individual who wins against a public authority will command more of the authority's resources than he currently receives (that is the point of the action). The resources are finite. So they will be taken from someone else whose needs the authority is meeting. Decisions about the allocation of resources must be left to the political arena, not to the judges. If Parliament had really intended to give homeless persons, excluded children and so on a real right to command the expenditure that their situations need, Acts of Parliament would directly say so. *Tandy* may mark a breakthrough with s. 298. The difficulty is, can a local authority be made to act in accordance with its duties? Keating and X had sued for damages, money to compensate them for the loss they had incurred by the authority omitting to provide its services to them. This suit was ineffective. A different approach is needed, not a claim based upon private rights. As Lord Browne-Wilkinson said (p. 397 h), 'There is . . . a long line of authority deciding that breaches of certain duties under the Education Acts can give rise to a successful claim . . . for an injunction'. An injunction is an order of the court which can be obtained through a procedure called a judicial review. This is an application to the High Court claiming that a local authority has acted *ultra vires*, outside of its legitimate power. This is the proceeding that lies behind *R v. East Sussex County Council ex parte Tandy.* An application needs to be brought by someone with a recognised interest in the outcome. In exclusion cases this is invariably the child or the child's parents. The application needs to be brought promptly, within three months of the last relevant event (usually, the local education authority appeal panel hearing). Judicial review can usually be used only once such appeal systems have been exhausted.

The judicial review procedure

In exclusion cases the judges are willing to hear cases before the exclusion appeal system is exhausted if there is a claim of procedural unfairness. This is the case even if it is only the penalty imposed by the headteacher which is said to be unfair (*R v. Governing Body of Rectory School* [1997] ELR 484).

Even if the applicant wins, the court still has discretion whether or not to grant the order asked for. If the court is so minded it will grant an order quashing the wrongful decision and ordering the decision taker to retake this decision in a proper manner. Note that even if a court can be persuaded that a local education authority is in breach of its duty to suitably educate excluded children, the court will tell the authority only to look at the matter again, to consider the relevant factors and not to be influenced by irrelevance. This is not what litigants want. They want a different decision or compensation. The courts have consistently held that if Parliament has placed a duty upon public bodies, for example, local education authorities, it is the local education authorities who have to take the decisions that the duty implies.

Exclusion-related judicial reviews have almost always been actions against schools rather than local authorities. There are three grounds for review which have been important in education cases.

1   *Procedural ultra vires:* failing to follow the correct procedure. In *R v. Governors of St Gregory's Roman Catholic Aided High School and Appeals Committee ex parte M* [1995] ELR 290, the hearing in front of the school governors was flawed as M, the child, was not permitted to be present, contrary to the Education (No. 2) Act 1986 (Amendment) Order 1993 and Statutory Instruments. However, procedural errors do not necessarily vitiate proceedings. It depends on the scale of the injustice generated. In this case, as M appeared before the appeals committee, the court held that the procedural error had been cured by this later adherence to correct form.

2   *Error of law:* this must appear on the record of the proceedings reviewed such as when an appeals committee makes an error about the rules that it should apply and this is obvious from its minutes. An example is an exclusion for a non-disciplinary reason contrary to s. 65 Education (No. 2) Act 1986.

3   *Breach of an implied limitation:* these limitations have been imposed by the courts on administrative bodies and are checks against unreasonableness, not considering relevant matters or considering the irrelevant, acting on no evidence, bias, the lack of a fair hearing. These are all aspects of fairness and natural justice. Exclusion judicial reviews are usually under this head as the complaint is typically of a lack of fairness or fair mindedness in the school which excluded the complainant. In *R v. The Board of Governors of Stoke Newington School ex parte M* [1994] ELR 131, M's head of year sat on the governors' exclusion panel which confirmed the headteacher's decision to permanently exclude. The head of year was a teacher governor, but as head of year had played a role in M's disciplinary history. Potts J held this to be an obvious failure to follow the rules of natural justice.

All who apply disciplinary sanctions must follow these rules. With respect to exclusions, these rules are given statutory force in the Education (No. 2) Act 1986 ss. 22–28 and re-enacted in the 1996 Act. The key difficulty with the judicial review process is again revealed by this case. If the decision maker has made a flawed decision, and the above examples concern preventable irregularities, the court will order the decision taker to take the decision again, applying the right test, procedure or whatever. What the excluded pupil wants, as does every applicant for judicial review, is a different decision from the decision that was originally taken. The court will not deliver this. Parliament has said that decisions about exclusions are those of the headteacher, backed by a system of confirmation and appeal. The courts will not usurp headteachers', governors' or LEAs' authority. The courts offer a review, an examination of decisions to check that the decision takers have acted within their legitimate area of discretion. In the end, the decision will be that of the statutory decision taker alone. In *Stoke Newington* the court refused to order the reinstatement of M to the school as M's admittance was a decision that the governors themselves ought to make. The judge also commented that M had had the benefit of home tuition since her exclusion some nine months earlier, implying that there was no urgency that M be placed in school. There is also a necessary implication that the part-time home tuition was not unlawful. The final result of the case is that the governors did reconsider admitting. They decided not to readmit. There were no further legal proceedings.

As long as a school does not stumble over procedural flaws, the only ground of attack upon an exclusion decision is in the area of reasonableness. Unreasonable decision taking is a type of *ultra vires* act. The established test for reasonableness in administrative law stems from the Court of Appeal's decision in *Associated Picture Houses v. Wednesbury Corporation* [1948] 1 KB 223. The case concerned a local authority's powers to license cinemas. Lord Greene MR thought it important that Parliament had entrusted the local authority with the power to take discretionary decisions and that courts should be slow to intervene, unless the decision was unreasonable. He said this meant that the decision would have to be so unreasonable that no reasonable local authority would have taken it. He added that to prove a claim of this kind would require very compelling evidence. This rule is particularly closely followed in local authority cases as the courts are duly impressed by the fact that local authorities are elected. Their policies reflect a political programme, democratically chosen by the electorate. An examination of two cases illustrates how the unreasonableness test operates.

In *R v. Governors of St Gregory's Roman Catholic Aided High School and Appeals Committee ex parte M* [1995] ELR 290, the child, M, was permanently excluded for muttering under his breath to another pupil, 'Why don't you just fuck off?' The comment was directed at a teacher who was within earshot (it is not clear what this means, but it is what the law report says). In the context of a strict school, the judge said that M had failed to show that the exclusion was unreasonable by a significant margin.

This is a predictable decision. So long as a school has a clear system of rules (now required by section 2 Education Act 1997) and the headteacher is fair in the investigation and not arbitrary in using exclusion as a punishment, the courts are very unlikely to intervene.

In contrast, and reflecting the lottery of 'reasonableness', is *R v. The London Borough of Newham ex parte X* [1995] ELR 303. A boy, X, stripped off the trousers and possibly the underpants of a younger boy who had taunted him. X was permanently excluded. Brooke J ordered X's reinstatement. The judge thought it critically important that X's schooling be not disrupted as he was in his GCSE year. The judge based this decision on procedural flaws and also on a claim that the penalty was disproportionate (a form of unreasonableness).

This is a case that must be on the borderline of the *Wednesbury* test. One could imagine the 'critical importance of every day' argument that so impressed Brooke J being used in other circumstances. What about the very young child, the child recently started in a new phase, the child who has a statement for special educational need, whom Circular 10/94 para. 22 suggests should not be readily excluded? The cases above illustrate that the courts are unlikely to generate a set of principles by which exclusion decisions can be tested. The courts are going to intervene only where there has been serious irregularity or irrationality. It might be difficult to predict what a particular judge will regard as irrational, and there is bound to be some unevenness in this back-stop intervention system. The best that an excluded child can obtain from the court is a quashing of the head's/governors' decision and an opportunity for the decision taker to decide again in a more fair-minded or procedurally correct way. Whether this will give the applicant what he or she really wants is another matter. This unsatisfactory situation persists even though the 1993, 1996 and 1997 Acts appear to make advances in the provision that should be made available to excluded children.

The 1998 Act continues the commitment to tightening already proven unsatisfactory law

Schools can now exclude a pupil for the full year's allocation in one term (s. 1). It is difficult to see how this can assist schools to succeed with their most difficult pupils. For those, either extra support at school (summoned through recognition of these pupils' behaviour as a special educational need) or in a Pupil Referral Unit is required. The Act does nothing significant to bring this real solution in to schools, trusting the old canards of blaming parents (s. 20 – parental contracts) for not supporting schools, or schools (s. 4 – publication of school discipline policy) for not laying clear standards and expectations.

Cosmetic changes are made (s. 6, s. 10), likely to have no significant effect in practice but revealing that the policy makers know exactly where the difficulties lie. What do we do with the most difficult children who will not conform to mainstream school (s. 6)? What level of educational support do we offer these (and others) while excluded (s. 10)? The questions remain. The answers needed are still avoided.

It is instructive to note the lack of congruence with the policy of the Children Act 1989. The welfare principle, Section 1: when a court determines any question with respect to '(a) the upbringing of a child . . . the child's welfare shall be the court's paramount consideration' enshrined in that Act has no parallel in the Education Acts. The drafters of the Education Acts 1993, 1996 and 1997 and the School Standards and Framework Act 1998 would have gone about their work in the full knowledge of the Children Act 1989, yet have made no endeavour to ensure similar levels of protection for the child. Some regard the Children Act as 'a bridge too far'. The Children Act welfare principle is binding upon local authorities in their role as Social Services departments, including the wide and general duty in section 17 (1) (a) 'to safeguard and promote the welfare of children within their area who are in need'. The courts will not extend the current restricted meaning of these duties to cover children covered by the Education Act 1996 s. 298 (1) rules. The reasons that justify the welfare principle in the law of families and Social Services departments are just as valid when one considers children and education departments.

The courts act as a control to ensure that random or arbitrary decisions are struck down. But the *Wednesbury* principle that underpins the courts' actions still gives local authorities and schools too wide discretion in this area. A number of writers argue that the best way forward is to sharply define children's rights (Eekelaar, 1994). Then they can be defended (Bainham and Cretney, 1993). Given the focus of the law upon remedies, especially remedies in cash terms, it is difficult to see how such rights could be established in a manner that the courts would give real effect to. This is a problem throughout all public sector law, that the citizen consumer of publicly provided services has no personal redress if the service is not provided. There does exist a framework of duties upon public authorities. A direct way forward is to strengthen the s. 298 duty so that local authorities have to provide suitable *full-time* education for excluded pupils in Pupil Referral Units or elsewhere. The 1997 Act has been a retrograde step in this, and other, respects.[5] Any demand that lacks clarity will have no impact on numbers excluded or provision for them. Such a demand is patently political, requiring the support and action of political groups.

Alternatives

If the courts are not a route to stemming the flow of exclusions, is it possible, as Lord Browne-Wilkinson suggested in *X v. Bedfordshire,* that the ombudsman might be able to remedy difficulties? The Local Government Act 1974, in establishing the Commissioners for Local Administration, excluded from their consideration by s. 26(8) and Schedule 5 para. 5(2) any action concerning the conduct, management or discipline in any school. This restriction has been repeatedly criticised (Hinds, 1995) but governments have not given any indication that it will be removed. The Commissioners have considered the procedure and operation of appeals panels even though they cannot consider the original decision to exclude. The Commissioners have been imaginative at times in attempting to bring exclusion cases within their remit. For example, in report no. 94/A/2147 re the London Borough of Newham, the Commissioner was able to review delays concerning an exclusion as the school which the child's parents would have wished to use was full at the time the parents were asked to express a preference. Criticism was made of a five months' delay before home tuition was offered and a recommendation made that compensation be paid and that the authority review the speed of its procedures. These recommendations were complied with. This seems a more successful outcome than litigation would deliver, although the reporting procedure of the Commissioners is necessarily slow. Local authorities are also reluctant to act upon the Commissioners' recommendations, to such an extent that the English Commission has taken the view that legislation should be enacted to enable citizens to seek court enforcement of their decisions (Foulkes, 1995).

Conclusion

The legislative situation pertaining in 1998 was most unsatisfactory. Pupils have few enforceable rights to protect them from exclusion and that will ensure that their education continues at an acceptable level if excluded. There has been recent legislation responding to the growing exclusion crisis but legislation that pulls both ways. LEAs now have the right to order reinstatement. More recently, following the 1997 Act, reinstatement by the appeal panel has been made possibly more difficult as it will consider the interests not only of other children but also of members of staff (s. 7). Will this not just encourage teachers to protest at an appeal of an individual pupil rather than engage in the longer and less focused process of demanding appropriate resources to allow them to manage and teach difficult pupils? There is also little legal control over the grounds for exclusion used within a school.

Section 2 of the 1997 Act provided a baseline of expectation in that schools are required to be explicit about standards of behaviour that will be accepted. Parents can also be required to agree to these standards before their child is admitted to a school. These provisions have the positive effect of reducing scope for arbitrary exclusion at the cost of creating a group of not educated children, children whose parents will not agree to abide by the class and cultural demands of the school.

Notes

1 **Education Acts since 1944:**
  Education Act 1944
  Education Act 1946
  Education (Miscellaneous Provisions) Act 1948
  Education (Miscellaneous Provisions) Act 1953
  Education Act 1959
  Education Act 1962
  Education Act 1964
  Education Act 1967
  Education Act 1968
  Education (Handicapped Children) Act 1970
  Education (Milk) Act 1971
  Education Act 1973
  Education (Work Experience) Act 1973

Education Act 1975
Education (School-leaving Dates) Act 1976
Education Act 1976
Education Act 1979
Education Act 1980
Education Act 1981
Education (Fees and Awards) Act 1983
Education (Grants and Awards) Act 1984
Further Education Act 1985
Education (Amendment) Act 1986
Education Act 1986
Education (No. 2) Act 1986
Education Reform Act 1988
Education (Student Loans) Act 1990
School Teachers' Pay and Conditions Act 1991
Further and Higher Education Act 1992
Education (Schools) Act 1992
Education Act 1993
Education Act 1994
Education (Student Loans) Act 1996
Education (Consolidation) Act 1996
Education Act 1997
School Standards and Framework Act 1998

Education Acts per decade
1940s – three
1950s – two
1960s – four
1970s – eight
1980s – nine
1990s – ten
Total: thirty-six

2 References to reports of legal cases use the standard conventions of law reporting.
3 Beth Tandy was 'child T' for a number of years until she reached the age of 16 and it was proper to name her. Her case continued over a five year period.
4 The appeal was on a point of law: at the hearing it was assumed that the factual claims made against the local authority were true as there had been no trial so, of course, the Keating's claim had never been tested.
5 **Education Act 1997 – Discipline and Exclusions Sections.** The main items from the discipline sections are set out below. Arguably seven of these items will lead to increased pressures to exclude (1, 2, 3, 4, 6, 7 and 8). Others will make no difference, and are largely in place (e.g. 4 and 5):

   1 Extending the permissible period of fixed term exclusions to forty-five days in one term (the whole year's allocation)
     (Part II, section 6)
   2 Contracts with parents
     (Part II, section 13)
   3 Detention of pupil without parental permission
     (Part II, section 5)

4 Published school discipline policy
   (Part II, sections 2 and 3)
5 LEA plans for supporting schools with disruptive pupils
   (Part II, section 9)
6 No requirement to admit children permanently excluded from two or more schools
   (Part II, section 11)
7 Increased school representation at pupil exclusion hearings
   (Part II, section 7 (3))
8 Appeals committees taking account of the interests of other pupils and staff at the school
   (Part II, section 7 (4))
9 Power to restrain pupils
   (Part II, section 4)
10 LEAs' responsibility *is to make arrangements for provision of suitable education, otherwise than at school (the expression 'part-time or full-time' has been removed)*
   (Part VIII, section 47)
11 Management Committees for Pupil Referral Units
   (Part VIII, section 48)

8 The media, schooling and exclusion

Introduction

The part played by the newspapers and television in creating, reinforcing and transmitting images of failing schools, poor teachers and disruptive pupils is public and pervasive. Considerable selection and shaping takes place in the presentation of 'stories'. 'Objective' reporting may be the aim of some media outlets, but editorial comment and an expression of the organ's own standpoint are also relevant aims. Additionally, newspapers and television provide a medium for the expression of views of 'experts', social commentators and professional or pressure groups.

A particular set of issues related to the presentation of educational stories is whether they set out to pander to an authoritarian minded audience, whether they are a reflection of the public view or whether there is the possibility of manipulation of news quite purposefully to support ideologically motivated positions and particular policy objectives. The interaction between news, public opinion and public policy is a theoretically and practically important focus. One needs to know about climate formation, climate change and climate manipulation. A moot point is whether politicians will struggle to change the law in the face of negative public opinion registered through the media. More accurately put, one needs to ask whether policy makers, policy advisers and politicians generally will be less motivated to change law, develop initiatives and redirect resources if, through the media, they are presented with inchoate, negative public reactions.

Television and newspaper stories, motivated to a greater or lesser extent by partisan views, coexist with a number of other news-making and communicative activities. There are pressure groups and small-scale projects which have sought to intervene in the area of exclusion: the National Children's Bureau, the Children's Society, the Advisory Centre for Education, the Association of Workers with Children with Emotional and Behavioural Difficulties and the Commission for Racial Equality have all pressed their cases directly with government departments, published letters and short articles in the press and run conferences. Special needs pressure groups, those concerned with criminal justice and teacher unions have all strongly expressed

and disseminated viewpoints in the area of school exclusions. The National Children's Bureau co-ordinated a consortium on children to challenge the discipline elements of the Education Bill 1997 – with a remarkable absence of success.

Though at some remove from the policy-setting forum, and though there is uncertainty about which significant voices are listened to by policy makers and politicians, one can hypothesise that any populariist government would want to be sure that any changes in legislation and resourcing could be legitimised before a wider public. Undoubtedly a climate of opinion is generated which is neither static nor without contradiction and conflict, but which constitutes part of the relevant context within which decisions are made.

The media, campaigns and more general communications are a manifestation of the value orientations in a country at one time. The examples discussed below show the largely authoritarian and punitive orientation which dominates. This resonates well with notions of self-reliance and individual responsibility. The stance taken appears to insulate itself from more elaborate representations of the problem and the longer term view. Kidd-Hewitt and Osborne write of 'the society of the image' (1995: ix) and suggest a degree to which our opinions are manufactured for us. As social scientists we may struggle to figure out whether the press is fired by the goal of manipulative power or commercial *laissez-faire*. Alvarado *et al.* (1987) claim that,

> dominant groupings are engaged advantageously in the struggle for ideological consent because their representations of those they contest can be circulated widely . . . class, gender, race, age.
>
> (Alvarado *et al.*, 1987: 7)

Stuart Hall and colleagues perceptively examine 'crisis' depiction and observe the limiting as well as creative role of the media.

> A 'public image' is a cluster of impressions, themes and quasi-explanations, gathered or fused together . . . the presence of such 'public images' in public and journalistic discourse feeds into and informs the treatment of a particular story. Since such 'public images', at one and the same time are graphically compelling, but also stop short of serious, searching analysis, they tend to appear in place of analysis – or analysis seems to collapse into image.
>
> (Hall *et al.*, 1978: 118)

Bingham (1997), as Lord Chief Justice of England, acknowledges that court sentences are affected by public opinion, however that is mediated. Why not law making also?

In the media representations analysed in the following sections, aggressive and simplified accounts may dominate, but they do not do so without challenge. The media has its own collection of allegiances, and personnel have

political and social commitments which are allowed to contribute to the diversity of media messages and interpretations. The five examples of media representations examined are the James Bulger killers, R excluded from Glaisdale Secondary School, M excluded from Manton Junior School, *Panorama/World in Action* transmissions and *Brookside* (the Tinhead exclusion story).[1]

The James Bulger killing

The killing of $2\frac{1}{2}$-year-old James Bulger on 2 February 1993 by two 10-year-old boys in Bootle (near Liverpool) staggered the nation and, subsequently, after the trial judgment, provided the content for the press and commentators through the press to galvanise moral outrage. The *Sun*, archbishops and government ministers contributed judgements and interpretations of the deed and offered 'meanings' which the murder held for society.

Responses to the killing can take place on a number of interesting levels. Individuals can have their personal reactions to such an event. Families and intimate groups can debate and agree on how the event can most satisfactorily be psychologically and socially presented. But, behind this, the media have powerful roles in informing and in shaping opinion and judgement. Legally sanctioned definitions and restrictions affect the power of the media in both roles.

Newspaper headlines at the time of the killing spoke of shock, horror, evil and incomprehension. Later, after the court's judgment was delivered on 23 November 1993 the boys' status as criminals and as evil was confirmed. The English judicial process had nearly run its course and the 'coding' or 'discourse' of the event was clearly established as 'moral' and 'legal'. The discourse was not couched in terms which were medical, or about (im)maturity or social disadvantage.

Michael King describes the outbreak of 'the demonisation of the two boys' (King, 1995: 172). The *Sun* discussing it said, 'The devil himself could not have made a better job of raising two fiends'. *The Times* too shared in this with a leader article on 25 November 1993 headed 'The Three Evils'. BBC's *The Moral Maze* dealt with it, also using 'evil', and the Archbishop of York sermonised in similar terms. The act was judged 'beyond comprehension', legitimising language and response which combined harsh punitive law, witchcraft and wickedness.

The media engaged in extensive expressions of horror. The judge was similarly shocked and referred to 'wicked and cunning boys' who had committed 'acts of unparalleled evil and barbarity', and yet in terms of causation, he had only to say

> It is not for me to pass judgement on their upbringing, but I expect that exposure to violent video films may in part be an explanation.
>
> (quoted in Smith, 1994: 227)

This comment was grossly simplistic, but odder still was the fact that no evidence had been presented on the video theme.

That this act was a matter of legal rather than medical or Social Services rendered it an enterprise of allocating blame, not identifying causes. Accepting that the two children were beyond the age of criminal responsibility and fit to plead channelled all efforts into the guilty/not guilty decision and then to their sentence

King (1997) makes the point that if the boys had been dealt with according to psychiatric coding, as mentally ill or disturbed children, this would have been inconsistent with the media presentation of them as the personification of corrupted innocence. He goes on,

> Indeed if mental health rather than law had been applied to the James Bulger killers, it is likely that society would have been presented with an expert diagnosis . . . a regime of therapy.
>
> (King, 1997: 118)

There was the possibility that the two boys may have been judged incapable of pleading – then there would have been no court case. In fact both children were subjected to much psychological testing. The final line on the statement in the assessment for one boy was paradoxical in that he 'presented as a capable young man, who would require treatment and support for some time to come' (Smith, 1994: 179). There were concerns expressed by psychiatrists at the absence of any therapeutic work with the children or the families in the period following the arrest.

The criminalisation (and demonisation) of these children was made possible by the legal decision to set the age of criminal responsibility at 10 by the 1963 revision of the Children and Young Persons Act. King points out that the case could have been dealt with outside the criminal law if the Labour government's legislation, passed by Parliament in 1969, raising the age of criminal responsibility to 14, had been implemented.

> A change of government and divisions within the Labour party throughout the 1970s on the issue of juvenile offending effectively made it possible for two ten year old boys to be found guilty of murder.
>
> (King, 1997: 113)

The age of criminal responsibility ranges from 18 in Belgium, Romania and Lithuania to 7 in Switzerland and Ireland. In Scandinavian countries it is 15 (King, 1995: 174). The possibilities for the attribution of blame and for dealing with illegal acts of young people are dependent on the national context.[2]

The sentencing process showed less than the usual regularity; Mr Justice Marland gave his recommendation for a minimum eight year sentence. The Lord Chief Justice raised this to ten years. The then Home Secretary, Michael Howard, six months later made the sentence fifteen years, citing public concern and the Bulger parents' 300,000 signature petition sponsored by the *Sun* newspaper.

On the matter of public concern and outrage which can be amplified by the media, Smith (1994) offers by way of a corrective to the view created by newspaper and television pictures. These showed that, as the boys were driven from the court, people did run forward to threaten, physically and verbally and, though there were six arrests, 'the tightly framed images of hatred on the television news seemed to exaggerate the scale of the incident' (Smith, 1994: 162).

The significance of the public and official reactions to the Bulger killers lies in the parallels to be found. These lie in a punitive legal framework, the individualising of blame and responsibility, justice winning out over welfare, and political voices speaking sternly of toughness rather than care. The complexity and paradox is also ever-present in the expression of horror at the deed, sympathy for the victim's family and pity for the perpetrators, and in the tension between retributive and restorative goals of the criminal justice system. Reactions of a similar kind are discussed in relation to R, a secondary pupil, M, a primary pupil, Tinhead (*Brookside*), and the presentations of *World in Action* and *Panorama* of these issues.

The case of R, excluded from Glaisdale Secondary School

The public contest over exclusions is said to have begun in April 1996 when the parents of 13-year-old R successfully appealed to an independent panel against his permanent exclusion from school (*Sunday Times*, 15 September 1996: 14). Cases followed with more high profile successful appeals and threatened union action. The *Sunday Times* article, reflecting back to events five months earlier, was temperate in tone: R 'was said to have attacked other pupils and threatened to butt a teacher'.

Articles on 23 April 1996 in a range of daily papers were less reserved. The *Independent* refers to R 'allegedly being involved in 30 incidents of violence and disruption since last September'. The *Daily Telegraph* writes of a 'violent 13 year old boy' and the *Guardian*, most illiberally, asks, beside a large head and shoulders photograph of R, 'Is he the worst pupil in Britain?'

The *Sun* headlines its piece 'Yob of the Form' and the *Daily Mirror* refers to R as 'a schoolboy thug', 'a classroom thug' and others like him as 'uncontrollable thugs' with 'pen-pushing yobs' supporting the child's return to the classroom. For the *Daily Express* it is 'hooligan' and 'violent pupil' and for the *Daily Mail* 'unruly teenager' and 'disturbed but streetwise teenager'.

The tabloids draw on evidence 'highlighted in a damning diary of violence and misconduct kept by teachers' (*Daily Mail*, 23 April 1996) or itemising the offences under the title '45 reasons why a head had to ban this thug' (*Daily Mirror*, 23 April 1996).

The story broadened and escalated with descriptions of the family. The *Daily Mail* reported that the father was 'tattooed and in his forties and had been an industrial cleaner before ill-health led him to give up work'. The mother '34, was also jobless and, like her husband, believed to be claiming income support'. She was educated at a special school and 'was known to have had behavioural difficulties' (*Daily Mail*, 23 April 1996).

The *Daily Mail* on 25 April 1996, through photographs and text, exposed the whole family and its day-to-day activities. They were having cable TV installed, and the younger brother waited for his school bus 'wearing brand new trainers'. 'Mr Wilding, 54 . . . has not earned his own living for years'. Their benefits were estimated at 'around a comforting £30,000 a year'. They had a caravan and a fishing expedition could be 'extended from a day out or two to a holiday'. The caravan was described as drawn by the elderly white Volvo estate.

The older brother was described going out 'slamming the gate of their family garden that has not a single flower in it'. The cost of his replacement education, were it to last for a year, was estimated at £14,940. The younger brother's home tuition was estimated to cost over £14,000 also.[3]

The *Sunday Times* (28 April 1996) puns a headline 'Running Wild', close to R's surname. It appears opposite an article on the fortunes of the Conservative Party, ironically titled 'Is Major Losing Control?' The page on unruly children gives several examples and police concerns are voiced. R is 'every mother's nightmare, except his own'. A section on 'Family fortunes' makes further revelations about the family; the mother, it claims, pushed a housing official down the stairs 'disabling him permanently'. 'The children enjoy the luxury of a video, CD [compact disc] player and cable television indoors, and play outside in £80 roller skates. The oldest received a £500 Amiga computer last Christmas.'

The *Independent* interview in the family house included in its description, 'the television is on, the dog is barking sporadically' (25 April 1996). Among the most stinging images is a cartoon in the *Daily Express* (25 April 1996) in which the Secretary of State for Education, Gillian Shephard, backed by John Major, holds a paper headlining 'Britain's place with "The Family from Hell"'. R's family is told by Mrs Shephard that she has arranged an educational tour for the whole family: 'two years in France, two years in Germany, two years . . .'.

A shockingly unforgiving piece appeared in the *Daily Mail* the following month. The much maligned 'in his forties', '54 year old', '56 year old' father, out of work for ten years because of ill-health, died. It was reported under the headline, 'Yob's father dies'.

The National Association of Schoolmasters/Union of Women Teachers (NAS/UWT) played a decisive role in this dispute, supporting teachers who went on strike rather than accept the teenager back in the school after the LEA reinstated him.

The case of M, excluded from Manton Junior School

M was excluded from Manton Junior School at the beginning of the autumn term 1996. Twice governors overturned the headteacher's decision to exclude M, 'a disruptive 10-year-old' (*Sunday Times*, 15 September 1996) 'said to be violent' (*Guardian,* 30 October 1996), 'allegedly "uncontrollable"' (*Guardian,* 31 October 1996). The result was first a strike threat by teachers and then a boycott by parents because the solution implemented was individual tuition in the school at what would have been an annual cost of £14,000, paid out of the school's budget.

M was excluded for a catalogue of thirty-eight alleged offences. Apparently assaults on other children brought things to a head. The refusal of the governors to agree the permanent exclusion, indeed the chairwoman's strong support for the child's attendance, led to a conflict with parents, teachers' unions, the LEA and the Secretary of State for Education all playing a public role along with M and his mother.

Eight staff voted to strike if M returned to lessons (*Guardian,* 29 October 1996) after a period of individual tuition. The chair of the governors accompanied M and his mother to the school and asserted:

> He has got a legal right to be in that school. The lad has done magnificently. It was a lot of money but it has been worthwhile. But I do not think it is a good idea to criminalise a 10 year old boy teaching him in isolation. Teachers have got powerful unions but children have nobody to speak up for them.
>
> (*Guardian,* 29 October 1996)

The chairman of the LEA Education Committee had been called on to intervene and helped broker the earlier settlement. The NAS/UWT had backed the decision of its members to strike if the child were readmitted to a class and was reported to be in direct confrontation with the chairwoman of the governors: 'If she wants to play power politics with the youngsters, she has picked the wrong union' (*Guardian,* 29 October 1996).

The headteacher closed the school because he would not guarantee the safety of the 194 pupils if staff were striking. A solicitor was called upon to act for the mother and threatened legal action against the headteacher and possibly against the local authority and other parties in the dispute (*Guardian,* 30 October 1996). Governors also voiced strong criticism of the teachers' union concerned.

At the beginning of November the mother and the governors gave in. The chairwoman of the governors resigned before a meeting with the parents. The mother was described as 'battle-weary' and bitterly disappointed that M had been made a scapegoat. She no longer felt able to continue when it resulted in the school being closed and other children's education being interrupted. She agreed to move M to another school.

As with R's experience at Glaisdale, the NAS/UWT played a decisive part. Accused of bully-boy tactics the union general secretary retorted, 'The bullies are the young thugs out there threatening teachers and terrorising their fellow pupils' (*Guardian*, 14 September 1996).

At the union's annual conference the following year he said, justifying the union's stance, 'We don't accept that we have social responsibilities, family responsibilities for these youngsters. Our job is to teach' (*TES*, 4 April 1997).

Widening the dispute brought in the Secretary of State for Education, who criticised governors, teachers and education officials 'for turning an unruly ten-year-old into a "notorious hero"' (*The Times*, 12 September 1996). Later she is reported as claiming 'This is entirely the responsibility of [Xshire] County Council' (*Daily Express*, 29 October 1997). The dispute extended to include more parties. An interesting postscript to the story is that this 'unruly pupil' (*Daily Mail*) and 'teeny yob' (*Sun*) was reportedly a model pupil in another school. From being 'Britain's most notorious school-boy', he is described as 'well-adjusted, highly motivated, polite, helpful' a year later (*Guardian*, 30 August 1997).

In conventional snapshot journalism, a historical dimension does not appear and the contemporary context is very narrow. Therefore, in the contribution that newspapers make to understanding, very little space is given to facts like the recent death of M's father, two other bereavements and the mother's diagnosed cancer.

Television documentaries on exclusions

The story of the Ridings School in Halifax, Calderdale, West Yorkshire, hit the news in the autumn of 1996. *Panorama* broadcast *The Ridings School* on 4 November 1996. It dealt remarkably sympathetically with the headteacher, who was interviewed in close up at some length. The programme's aim was to find out who was responsible and the key players interviewed included the Director of Education, the president of the NAS/UWT, Nigel De Gruchy, the Chief Inspector of Schools, Chris Woodhead, and the chair of governors.

Intriguing footage was also available, taken by long distance lens from a building overlooking the school, of misbehaviour on a grand scale. This filming took place at the time of the school inspection, which had been brought forward because of troubles at this school.

Exclusions figured in three respects in this story. First, the headteacher had found it necessary, early in her tenure at the school, to exclude thirteen children for a fixed period following a big fight. Second, there was dispute over a girl who had been in the news as a 13-year-old mother whose exclusion case was being bitterly fought. Third, the union had presented a list of sixty-one children who, if not to be excluded, were candidates for exclusion. The dispute was partly complicated by the fact that the union claimed that this was a confidential starting proposal and not a determined demand that 10 per cent of the school's population should be excluded.

Martin Bashir, the *Panorama* reporter, claimed that, 'The Ridings School in Halifax is now at the centre of a national debate about the collapse of moral standards and discipline'. Subsequent interviews and commentary acknowledge the history and complexity of the situation. The school had been established for four terms, the product of the amalgamation of two non-selective LEA schools. The school had to compete with grammar schools and a grant maintained school in the area. The coming together for both staff and pupils was troubled, the more so when £4 million promised for building and refurbishment was not forthcoming. Bashir commented on 'neglect, broken promises and a failure by all those responsible to act on clear signs that the school was in trouble'.

The children were shown at their worst throwing books across the room, not co-operating with teachers, misbehaving while sent to stand outside the room (a mobile classroom); there was even the wonderfully graphic picture of girls following the headteacher up the school steps making V signs at her back. The headteacher calmly presented the case, with little direct accusation, and was clearly near to tears.

Chris Woodhead suggested that pupils who were not taught well and stimulated would misbehave and that the fault did not lie with the children. Nigel De Gruchy was forthright in his judgement that some of the children should not be in this school and that his members had a right to see that the worst were excluded. The headteacher, recognising her failure to manage the school, resigned. The inspection of the school was damning and the school was closed for several days because it was judged to be unsafe. A new headteacher was brought in from a GM school to 'turn the school around' and a year later was rewarded with an OBE in the New Year's honours list.

The Unteachables, a *World in Action* documentary transmitted on 30 September 1996, focused on four children who had been excluded from school. This programme was unequivocally 'on the side of the children'. Though beginning with quotes from two reasonable teachers about the increase in problems of disruption and violence in school, followed by Mr De Gruchy on how children who misbehave 'forfeit their rights to education', the subsequent contributions showed understanding of how these children had come to behave in this way and the need for them to continue with their education.

In this documentary, M from Xshire (discussed earlier in this chapter) was pictured as a benign and lonely child out of school. A kindly governor explained movingly that M had suffered three bereavements in recent times, that his mother was unwell and that he needed support. A 13 year old from Manchester who had trouble reading 'but didn't want to go to the learning support unit' had been out of school for a long period with no education. The explanation here was given in terms of the lack of attention given to his special educational needs.

A third boy, whose case was given in this documentary, was not disruptive but had problems making relationships in school and had great difficulty in attending. After a period of education at home he was gradually integrated into lessons in a school in a way which he could tolerate. A fourth boy had been involved in criminal offences while excluded and was now enrolled at the Lennox Lewis College.

Significant contributors on the general problem of school exclusions were unanimously of the view that exclusion was something to be avoided. A head-teacher was explaining how he dealt with special educational needs and the resources he allocated to them. His fear was that with budgets becoming ever more limited, he would be unable to offer that level of support. In those circumstances it would be unsurprising if some children, unable to cope easily in the classroom, displayed behaviour which might lead to exclusion being considered.

An educational researcher, investigating school exclusions, who was interviewed located the causes with increased numbers of young children and young people having psycho-social difficulties and more families in poverty. He saw the elimination of exclusions as being a matter of changing the law and allocating resources to the small number of children who need support in managing their behaviour. A third contributor, a 'criminology researcher', reported on the large numbers of people she had interviewed in prison who have failed in education. Many had clear special educational needs which were not met, and it was reported that half the young men in prison had reading ages which put them below functional literacy levels.

Brookside: the exclusion of Tinhead story

Brookside is an English 'soap', broadcast three times a week in the mid-evening. The stories emerge from the lives of those living in Brookside Close on Merseyside. The series is produced by Ric Mellis. Merseyside Television, the company responsible, is owned by Phil Redmond, who had previously devised and written the young people's 'soap' *Grange Hill*, a story about a comprehensive school in London.

Among all the 'soaps' broadcast in the UK, *Brookside* is the most issue-centred. It has dealt with family disputes, abusive relationships, protection rackets, drugs, incest and euthanasia. The exclusion of Tinhead ran during January and February 1997. Tinhead (Timothy O'Leary) was introduced at the outset as a bully who picked on his friends as well as on a new boy and later on a black girl.

Mick is black and has recently become a school governor. The story hots up with Tinhead and his friends beating up the new boy, Tinhead getting drunk and ultimately, allegedly, with two other boys, jumping out on a black girl and hitting her, causing bruising and tipping her satchel out; the viewer sees only the aftermath of this last incident.

At the same time, Mick, on the governing body, is urging that something be done about bullying. He produces a revised bullying policy and robustly argues his corner as a parent governor, trying to override the agenda that has been set for the meeting. This story has all the ingredients one would associate

with exclusions and which were also evident in the documentaries: the badly
behaved boy, the headteacher trying to run his school in a disciplined yet
kindly way, parents upset at the disruption to their children's lives, angry
parents, virulent 'get them out' individuals and 'the middle-class intellectual'
(Ollie). Much of this is evident in the governors' meeting where the following
dialogue takes place:

Mick: My son doesn't want to go to school most days because he is so scared
          he is going to get a hammering. Now something has got to be done.
          We need to take action. If you ask me the ringleaders should be
          expelled immediately.
Ollie: Well actually Mick, I agree with you. Something does need to be
          done but, um, excluding the pupils isn't the answer.
Mick: Well, what is then?
Ollie: Well, I think we need to handle the situation very carefully. I mean,
          bullies often come from violent homes themselves. No, I think we
          should show them some understanding.
Mick: I am not going to get into all that trendy, liberal garbage, are you . . .
          I don't know why we are all pussyfooting around here. Let's just expel
          the lad responsible. Everybody knows who it is.

Tinhead's mother, Mrs O'Leary, is also on the governing body but Mick is
ignorant of this. In a subsequent governors' meeting there is an exchange
between the head and Ollie about mediation. Ollie then explains to Mick
that this involves a situation where

> the bullies and their victims are encouraged to get together and talk
> about what's been going on . . . It's about making bullies face up to
> what they have done, the hurt and damage they have caused other people.

Mick's view is that it is no good talking to some children because it makes no
difference and that a tough line is necessary. Mrs O'Leary refers to Mick's
'rambo style of school governor' and then raises the issue that 'all the
pupils excluded this year were black except for one'. This jolts Mick, who
wants to know more, much to the head's discomfort. Mick asks, dis-
believingly, 'Are you trying to tell me that all the trouble makers in this
school are black?' which leaves people looking more uneasy. Thus, one of
the most discomforting and unequal features of the real exclusions story is
raised.[4]

When the black girl, Tanya, goes back with Leo to Mick's house to clean up
after being assaulted, Tanya's mother Elaine is there with Mick and both are
extremely angry. Mick commits himself to 'going to that school tomorrow to
make sure he [Tinhead] is expelled'.

At a meeting with the head, the head suggests 'a personalised behaviour
programme'. Elaine rejects this as fudging the issue with 'a load of jargon'.

Ollie is also present at this meeting and makes the point that 'if the school simply puts him out on the street then we just shift the problem elsewhere. We do have a responsibility towards the boy. Well, he obviously has serious behaviour problems'. To this Mick replies, echoing the press stories of so many exclusion cases, 'but what about the other children in this school? Don't we have a responsibility towards them?' Mick also raises the matter of the black kids that were expelled not getting the same consideration.

Tinhead is expelled and Mrs O'Leary confronts Mick and Elaine tearfully and says, 'He has been chucked out of school, expelled . . . I know he can be a bit high spirited at times but he didn't deserve this. It's his GCSEs this year . . . what chance has he got of passing them if he can't go to school? This expulsion will follow him round for the rest of his life'. While Mick and Elaine retort with, 'He deserved everything he got', they are left looking sheepish.

Tinhead received practically no replacement education and gained no GCSE passes. He tried unsuccessfully to get into the army but his failure was due to a hearing problem rather than lack of qualifications. Sixteen months further on, Tinhead was still on the scene and had a job. He worked at a builders' merchant and had a wage. He was working 'scams', stole and went 'joyriding'. On the other hand he also bought a present for Bing, an older resident on 'The Close', and intervened when Julia was threatened with assault on the bus.

It is obvious that Tinhead is a worry still to his mother and to her partner, Sinbad. Sinbad remembers his turbulent youth and the difficulties he got into. There is also a sense of a community caring for a young person like Tinhead which helps to keep him 'included'. Tinhead is kept in touch with the family and community in 'The Close' and there is a sense of containment and surveillance.

Exclusions, parties and texts

Exclusion from school is a hotly contested area with individual incidents offering colourful personal stories and a limited range of clear, aggressive or defensive positions. Seen as a drama the blame can be located at the level of sets of individuals – the child, the parents, the teachers – or at the level of institutional arrangements and unequal distribution of resources and opportunities. It is important to note that the text media have tended to individualise and personalise the stories while the three examples from television programmes have projected a broader, more sophisticated 'social forces' review.

One can speculate about the political allegiances and social orientations of reporters in the two sorts of media. Certainly there have been accusations that *Panorama* and *World in Action* are peopled by left-wing journalists while *The Times* and the *Daily Mail* in particular have strong Conservative sympathies. The media inform, always incompletely, often with bias and frequently with 'a message'. Media allow us all to be 'informed'. Everyone is entitled to a view. Media amplify tensions and conflicts and often simplify to help people form these views. The views thus formed are those of voters and may influence what politicians think they can formulate by way of interventionist, supportive or punitive policy.

Lull and Hinerman (1997) refer to media scandals and the post-modern morality play where

> the scandal functions simultaneously as a moral anchor in a sea of conventionality, and a vigorous challenge to mainstream social values conditioned by the substantial forces of ideological and cultural hegemony.
>
> (Lull and Hinerman, 1997: 2)

By 'challenge' the authors mean that it tests and generally confirms what counts as 'proper' behaviour and 'proper' standards and reinforces ideological hegemony. Through media apparatus the comfortable and cultural elites together with economic elites 'establish and sustain relations of domination' (Thompson, 1990: 58). The way that difficult young people are to be defined is portrayed and simplified through the media which do not 'teach' nor emphasise the tensions, such as those mentioned in the Bulger case, between horror at the deed, sympathy for the victim's family and pity for the perpetrator. Media do not present the options between retributive and restorative approaches to the offenders. If not a 'scandal', the story is served up and packaged as voyeuristic, vicarious, shock-horror excitement for increasingly privatised lives. The newspapers reported the exclusions stories in a largely decontextualised (or a selectively contextualised) way with considerable use of emotive language while the *Panorama* anchorman portrayed the story as at the centre of a national debate about the collapse of moral standards and discipline. Slee (1998: 101) sees attitudes towards, and policies for, a whole range of 'disablement' as 'cultural politics'. The media play their part in shaping the discourse and defining the unacceptability and undeservingness of the excluded.

Notes

1 *Panorama* (made by BBC) and *World in Action* (made by ITV) have an established UK reputation for moderately radical documentary programmes on social issues.
2 Questions of a more general kind are raised by this variation in the age of criminal responsibility. In particular is there an embedded cultural commitment in some countries to seeing adolescents as dependent and subject to adult control and guidance such that transgressions on the part of the young are judged as failures on the part of adults? An affirmative answer would keep the age of criminal responsibility high. Where young children are ascribed autonomy and there are expectations of self-control, misdemeanours are *their* responsibility and the law will reflect this with low age of criminal responsibility. Or is it

the law which comes first in establishing the age of responsibility and public attitudes reflect this prior position?

3 These home tuition costs represent generous replacement education on the part of the local education authority. Chapter 6 gives figures for the cost of a year in mainstream education (approximately £2,500 for a secondary pupil) and for costs to the LEA following exclusion (approximately £4,600 for a full year equivalent).

4 Some months later an OFSTED inspection found Brookside Comprehensive to be below standard. Mick, feeling that a black child stands no chance in a below standard school, planned to move his daughter, Gemma, into the private sector.

9 Inter-agency work, schools and exclusions

Introduction

Tackling the school-level problems of exclusion, truancy, disaffection and, more generally, the alienation and difficulties of social adjustment of young people, is beyond the power of schools or the school system alone. Chapters 1 and 3 made plain the forces at work and the multiple deprivations often found in the domestic settings of those with challenging behaviour and 'self-inflicted' school failure. The agencies implicated in this are many, extending from mental health through social services to criminal justice as well as charities, some of which are contracted to carry out statutory work.

Regardless of causes, interventions can be designed which common-sense, theoretical reasoning and some empirical research evidence suggest will work. Powerful strategic and moral arguments support developments in which public and voluntary agencies work together to implement practical, social, economic and political plans for the prevention of school exclusions. Conceptual and management problems need to be addressed to reach agreement on whether these broad intervention plans are inter-agency, multi-agency, multi-professional or holistic. As ever, there are budgetary matters which are not divorced from value issues. The biggest barriers of all probably derived from the government policies introducing marketisation and managerialism which shaped all services from the late 1980s onwards. Services have been encouraged to set targets and performance indicators and allocate staff effort to the achievement of targets. Monitoring and appraisal were more and more related to targets, Performance Indicators (PIs) and the fulfilment of Service Level Agreements (SLAs). Competition, contracting and focused tasks militated against the co-operation and collaboration required to address social ills on a broad front.

It is realistic to begin pessimistically for, as van Veen *et al.* (1997: 10) state, 'in general the future for children and youth at risk is not, it seems, very hopeful'. This is not solely because of the contemporary problems which were listed above. Long experience of high investment projects has struggled to reveal sustained and systematic improvements in a way which is replicable and convincing to policy makers. Interrelationships between different services have not usually been durable despite voluminous, visionary support from various quarters. The school, however, remains the place where the largest concentrations of children are found. Here they can be accessible (if truancy and exclusion can be cut out) and here much of the attention of agencies can be focused. The 'full-service school initiatives' described by Furst *et al.* (1994) serve well as basic models for this. Here the school hosts the other child-focused services in purpose-built permanent accommodation. Lawson and Briar-Lawson (1997) and Lawson and Hooper-Briar (1994a) extend this to parent involvement.

There follows an examination of the different forms that the integration of services can take, discussion of the roles of the separate agencies themselves, the family, the individual and finally on the school. The final section is written with the intention of bringing it all together and deals with the further issues of 'projectitis' (Gardner, 1994: 189), and the absence of an official 'at risk' category of young people.

Focusing on the agencies

A definition of services integration, borrowed from the United States, is given in an OECD publication as:

> Ways of organising the delivery of services to people at the local level . . . a process aimed at developing an integrated framework within which on-going programmes can be rationalised and enriched to do a better job of making services available within existing commitments and resources. Its objectives must include such things as: (a) the co-ordinated delivery of services for the greatest benefit to people; (b) a holistic approach to the individual and the family unit; (c) the provision of a comprehensive range of services locally; and (d) the rational allocation of resources at the local level so as to be responsive to local needs.
>
> (OECD, 1996a: 35)

The key words which so often arise are co-operation, co-ordination and collaboration to describe processes and relationships. Inter-agency, inter-professional, multi-agency or multi-professional are terms related to structures. Integration needs to be at all four levels identified in the OECD (1996b) report – mandating, strategic, operational and field. Many examples are given of national schemes to address the problems of the variously identified groups of children and youth at risk. These examples come from Europe, North America and Australasia. Their diversity is striking.

In England in particular, but also across the other three countries of the UK, there is a lack of services and a lack of service co-ordination for disadvantaged children and families. It appears too that education is a thing apart; even where bad behaviour in the school and classroom is the issue it remains, for the most part, an educational problem. The Elton Report (DES, 1989), an admirably helpful and practical document in many ways, recognises 'the sheer variety of causes of, and cures for, bad behaviour in school' (p. 64) but refers to other agencies hardly at all. Police are mentioned and good relations between police and school are advocated but mainly in relation to dealing with intruders (DES, 1989: ch. 6). Parental involvement also has a place in this report.

In special educational needs policy other agencies – and parents – have a statutory part to play. The 1981, 1986 and 1993 Acts, the Code of Practice (DfE, 1994a), the Green Paper *Excellence for all Children* (DfEE, 1997c) and the *Guidance on LEA Behaviour Support Plans* (DfEE, 1998a) all make reference to multi-agency support. It receives *some* mention in the *Guidance on Social Inclusion* document for schools (DfEE, 1999). The call for inter-agency working has been widespread and strident. Requirements have been set for agencies to co-ordinate their work with others and link their 'plans' to demonstrate how they will co-ordinate and liaise. Paragraphs 39 to 45 of the *Guidance on LEA Behaviour Support Plans* proposed that the local authorities acknowledge that 'other local authority plans will interact in various ways with behaviour support plans' (DfEE, 1998a: 15). Children's Services Plans, Early Years Development Plans, LEA Educational Development Plans and New Start Strategy receive explicit mention. The Social Exclusion Unit (1998: 18) report was almost mocking the duplication and lack of co-ordination among these various plans.

In relation to young children more advocacy and more action in multi-agency working is found. The Children Act 1989, the Children (Scotland) Act 1995 and the Children (Northern Ireland) Order 1995 are all mandates expressing the need for co-ordination in the planning of local children's services. David's (1994) discussion of multi-professionalism underscores the reasons for this and its necessity for the protection of children from abuse. She also notes the barriers and difficulties – low morale, under-funded services, lack of time to develop working relationships, differences in status and pay, differing philosophies underpinning practice and different management structures (David, 1994: 3–4). These are surface manifestations of the 'New Professionalism' and its narrow targeting, efficiency requirements, within a history of separate government departments and separate training. However, services have long been unified in their competition over status and this works consistently against collaboration.

Hodgkin and Newell (1996: 6) report 'a new and exciting recognition in every continent that children must be given political priority and that doing so demands new structures'. Their report lists publications documenting policy failures (p. 27) and details ways in which failure is evident – invisibility of children, inadequate co-ordination between government departments, inefficient use of resources in central government and failure to promote children's responsible participation in society (Hodgkin and Newell, 1996: 26–38). In focusing on resources at national level and their waste the report states, 'Prevention, almost by definition, is a multi-agency affair. Unless children's or families' needs are addressed as a whole a preventive strategy can be sabotaged by one area of deficiency' (p. 35).

Clarke (1997) has questioned the extent to which coherent thinking, let alone planning, has gone into 'integration'. He pointed out that integration can vary in degree and level and refers to the annual report for 1997 of the Chief Inspector of Social Services (Department of Health, 1997a) in which integration can take a variety of forms: 'communication – consultation – collaboration – bilateral planning – joint planning' (M. Clarke, 1997: 24–25).

It is certainly the case that problems need to be faced in relation to strategic planning, funding, professional roles and goals, line management, training for inter-agency work and evaluation if the situation is to improve. Decisions need to be made about *what sort of integration or interrelationship is considered best*; the seamless robe of welfare may not be better than the garment which has clear seams which are very well stitched!

Magrab *et al.* (1997) identified the lack of training for professionals in implementing or working in an integrated service delivery system as a key problem. Magrab and colleagues go on to suggest that, from their research, efforts at training professionals for multi-disciplinary work 'are idiosyncratic and regional or local in nature' (1997: 100).

The problem in the UK for inter-agency working has been that, in the remodelling of the education system, the role of schools has become narrowed and, with the tightening and targeting of resources, attention to social problems in collaboration with other agencies appears to be beyond their legitimate brief. The case was made in Chapter 3 for viewing the education system in the UK as a competitive arena dispensing commodified life chances not as a nurturing, civilising community service.

Adler (1994) makes plain that the two major services where collaboration has been promoted, education and social services, 'have been parts of different institutionalised networks . . . have different norms, dialects, and missions . . . fertile ground for conflict, negotiations and coalition building' (1994: 2). Add to this the different training, hierarchies, pay scales, funding and physical locations and the challenges mount. Set this within a context of 'deprofessionalisation' (Dominelli, 1996; J. Clarke and Newman, 1997), 'New Public Management' (Ferlie *et al.*, 1996), targeted expenditure and quality measurement and the difficulties are compounded. And on the outer rim of this context is the ideological tussle between redistributive and allocative politics,[1] ably illustrated in the United States by Peterson (1981), or a distributional versus a relational conception of disadvantage, as discussed by Room (1995b) in Europe.[2] None the less, examples of good practice abound where agencies, focused on the needs of families and communities, have succeeded.

Hagen and Tibbitts (1994) describe child-centred policy in action in Norway with its egalitarianism and welfarist approaches demonstrating 'a particular concern for vulnerable populations' (1994: 3). There are home-school counsellors, medical professionals based in schools and generally the sense that school is a community resource. In 1991 the Ministry of Children and Families was formed in Norway.

Great theoretical support exists for an ecological approach to family support, as Mawhinney (1994) discussed in relation to Ontario, Canada. In Canada there has been a call for a Ministry of the Child (Mawhinney, 1994: 35), as indeed there has been in the UK (Barnard, 1997). A position of Minister Responsible for Children's Issues and a Children's Bureau was established in the Canadian federal government while the State of Ontario had a very active Advisory Committee on Children's Services. Hodgkin and Newell (1996) provide further examples of government structures for children with different names and different degrees of integration. They also recommend a Cabinet Office Children's Unit (1996: 69) with a Minister for Children taking charge and the establishment of a statutory independent Office of Children's Rights Commissioner (1996: 101).

Adler (1994: 4) presents the complexity of the education network for a typical city and acknowledges that the various constituents may not be aligned: professional associations, universities, parents, local government are by no means natural political allies. There is often the need for a 'third party' to promote partnership – a 'provocateur of collaboration', in Adler's terms (1994: 3).

Mawhinney reasserts a point made by others that

> successful interventions depend upon the capacity for a flexible response by professionals who share an understanding of the ecological context of the child. Current research on collaborative efforts has confirmed that there is no single model for restructuring services that best enhances the capacity for flexible responses.
>
> (Mawhinney, 1994: 37)

Unfortunately, fragmentation of effort, often by design as much as neglect, has characterised work with disadvantaged families and children at risk. Koppich (1994) ably describes this in the particular context of California and, by implication, in the United States as a whole. The Audit Commission in examining the situation in England and Wales concluded: 'progress towards an inter-agency strategic approach to the full range of children's services has been disappointing except where it is mandatory' (Audit Commission, 1994: 18).

Numerous Acts and official guidance documents over the years have urged collaboration between services. The constant need for reiteration reflects enduring concerns arising from experience, and much of the research conducted into inter-agency working, showing the apparent failure of such collaboration to work out in practice. Lloyd (1995) and Kendrick (1995) have recorded continuing impediments to collaboration in projects and policies in England and Scotland respectively.

There is a view that the community and the families must be major partners in inter-professional work and not simply clients. This in itself is radical, and Evans (1997) describes the several forms which such participation can take. Whatever form community participation should take there are obviously big struggles ahead and revolutionary changes needed. The professionals cannot work regularly in an integrated fashion and can get caught up in 'turf issues' (Evans, 1997: 12) so the prospects of giving up jealously guarded power and status to 'the community' is hard to envisage. Moves to develop practice in this direction continue to develop and, even if most struggle, they appear to offer significant advantages.

Focus on schools

It is startling for a visitor from the UK to see schools in Denmark with fitted-out dentists' and doctors' surgeries, or experience in Sweden the sense of integration between village centre, library and school with its nuclear fall-out shelter doubling as a weight training room, or peek into an Illinois high school and see the labelled doors of one, two or three full-time counsellors. None can visit the UK unperturbed by education's relative segregation there. Parsons (1996b) has argued, in relation to the UK, that the teaching workforce can powerfully remodel its role and increase its professional stature by taking on a broader social role.[3] Furst *et al.* write convincingly that, 'As the needs of students continue to increase, schools will need to come into a leadership role in service provision for students and their families' (Furst *et al.*, 1994: 71).

The OECD project on *Integrating Services for Children at Risk* (OECD, 1996a) reports the nature of the problem:

> Many industrialised countries are experiencing unacceptably low levels of educational attainment and high levels of school drop-out among youth who are not disabled and who appear to have the capacity to follow a normal curriculum. Thus many youths do not acquire the capabilities needed to adapt to employment opportunities. Educational reform measures to address these problems are being taken in some countries. However, the characteristics of the children and youth who are at risk suggest that stronger links between the education, health and social service sectors might be needed in order to address complex, underlying contributing factors that reside outside the education system itself.
>
> (OECD, 1996a: 7)

Interesting reports are given on the Nordic experience where, for instance, health visitors are based in Danish schools and, if children show signs of low achievement or repeated, unexcused absences from school, it is the health visitor who is judged to be the most appropriate person to visit the home (OECD, 1996a: 17).

France has its ZEPs (Zones d'Education Prioritaires), the Netherlands has its OVB (Educational Priority Policy). The UK, an originator of Educational Priority Areas (EPAs) in the 1970s, has done little from 1979 onwards, within education or across agencies, to address disadvantage. Following the Education Reform Act (ERA) 1988, there is greater competition, a more defined curriculum, more testing, and finance being on a pupil unit basis. 'The ERA does not specifically address the needs of educationally disadvantaged children and youth' (OECD, 1996a: 50). The UK arrangements for educational disadvantage changed with the Education Act 1998 which introduced Education Action Zones, a compensatory education move reminiscent of the EPAs of the 1970s.

Local authority budgets were significantly diminished, restricting the ability of agencies to play a reallocative or preventive role. Gipps (1990) predicted the negative effects of the marketisation of education and, in particular, of the national assessment programme which 'will be to control what is taught and how it is taught; possibly at all levels, while also increasing and emphasising inequalities in educational attainment that reflect social inequalities' (1990: 157).

In the OECD reports, the Single Regeneration Grant (SRG) was cited as the most powerful funding mechanism for unifying policy in the UK. About the Children Act 1989, a seemingly comprehensive law that aimed to accomplish service integration, it was admitted that 'this Act relates almost exclusively to the social service jurisdiction. Neither this Act nor ERA [Education Reform Act 1988] are truly focused upon service integration linkages between the social service and education sectors' (OECD, 1996a: 68).

The implementation of the Education Act 1997 was supported by a number of guidance documents which encourage coordination of services at the strategic level but whether this will work at school level (and 'street level') is doubtful. As education has become (at the levels of mandate and strategy) more targeted and accountable for more narrowly assessed achievements so there was a reduction in the space and legitimation for taking on the broader social and socialisation roles with young people and co-ordinating work with others who had this goal. Prime Minister James Callaghan can be credited with beginning a government drive 'back to basics' and in his Ruskin College speech of 1976 (full report in *Times Educational Supplement*, 22 October 1976) he asserted that: 'There is no virtue in producing socially well adjusted members of society who are unemployed because they do not have the skills.'

This resonated with public opinion at that time when public spending cuts were forced on the Exchequer by the oil crisis and its consequences. The quote represented a simplistic view.[4] As Welton (1985) stated:

> The idea that schools are an integral part of the welfare network for children and young people is not easily accepted either by teachers, or other professionals working with children and their families.
>
> (Welton, 1985: 62)

Callaghan's comment, based as it was on civil service briefing, showed that this acceptance did not exist among highly placed politicians or their closest public servants. The National Curriculum, in its original 1988 form and as revised by Dearing, still emphasised a narrow diet of traditional knowledge. *Curriculum Guidance 5* (NCC, 1990e) contained some pointers to activities in personal, social and health education in schools but it clearly had a subservient place. The inspection framework for schools (OFSTED, 1993, 1995a) also made plain where importance was to be attached, and 'breadth and balance' did not relate to addressing a holistic notion of the young person. These were notions applied to 'the curriculum' but not to spiritual, moral or social aspects of education. The pastoral curriculum has been squeezed. While the adoption by teachers of too explicit a welfare role would stretch their workload and their talents, the narrowness with which many teachers and writers interpreted the pastoral role runs counter to the needs of the situation. Ribbins reports the widespread view that pastoral care must be related primarily to the academic needs of the school and that it is principally about supporting learning (Ribbins, 1985: 3). There are more children in the late 1990s for whom, at least for a period, something distinctly therapeutic and nurturing is required. For younger children Hayden demonstrated clearly the complex problems which lay behind the pupil behaviour problems which confronted teachers (Hayden, 1994, 1997).[5]

Focus on the family

As a general intercultural finding, children with difficulties come from families with difficulties. Lawson and Briar-Lawson (1997) state that nineteen of the twenty-six risk factors for children are also ones for the family. 'The children's crisis is also a family crisis which is a teacher's crisis and a school crisis' (Lawson and Briar-Lawson, 1997).

While children may spend 15,000 hours in school during the compulsory years of education, they spend over 49,000 waking hours in the care of parents and community. Furthermore, the experience is more intense. As stated in Chapter 3, around 30 per cent of children in the UK were living below the poverty line in 1992, 1,840,000 in lone-parent families and 1,850,000 in two-parent families. In 1997 numbers were again in excess of 3 million.

Underachievement by children in education is often related to economic and social disadvantage, and poor families are subject to 'savage inequalities' (Kozol, 1991). In the United States 25 per cent of children younger than 6 were poor (US National Center for Health Statistics, 1993, reported in Corrigan and Bishop, 1997: 150). African American and Hispanic children are two to three times more likely to live in poverty than white children, but in the latter group the proportion rose from 9.7 per cent in 1973 to 15.6 per cent in 1992. Thus, to put families at the centre makes for credible practical policy initiatives. Figure 9.1 maps the range of agents and agencies.

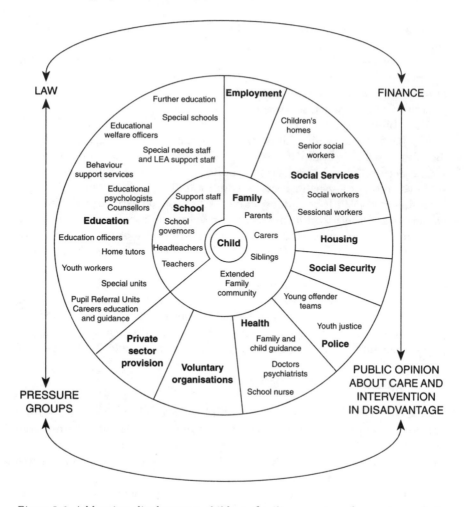

Figure 9.1 Addressing disadvantage: children, families, agents and agencies, and the wider context

By tradition or legislation, or both, the roles of professional personnel are described, if not prescribed, and their funding allocated separately for their personnel and targets. Co-operation among them in England and Wales is promoted by the Children Act 1989 (Scotland and Ireland passed parallel legislation later). A core focus for Social Services, the lead agency for the Children Act, has been on child abuse and, within this, sexual abuse. The 'Children at Risk' category, later the 'Child Protection Register', was a particularly narrow area of concern.

Local authorities, and this means their Social Services departments, have been required to produce Children's Services Plans. Guidance on this has been revised (Department of Health/DfEE, 1996) because the Social Services

Inspectorate's report (Department of Health, 1995) indicated that few of the published plans contained either strategic statements or action plans for the future.

Particular concern about co-operation between agencies is raised by the judgement that:

> There is not a uniform approach to co-operative planning between different agencies with roles relevant to children's services. Furthermore, relationships between agencies vary with time as inter-agency co-operation develops and the priorities and pre-occupations of the individual participant agencies change.
>
> (Department of Health, 1995: 6)

Linking with other agencies has very often appeared a secondary activity and indicates changes needed in management, culture, training and funding. The Inspectorate also reported, equally worryingly, on how plans were short on information about how services were to be delivered.

> There was a tendency to express the mapping of supply in terms of policies, objectives and strategies [rather than] stating exactly what plant, human resources, and programmes of provision were at their disposal.
>
> (Department of Health, 1995: 8)

Services in England may be further advanced at the levels of mandate and strategy than at operational or field levels. There are examples of ambitious schemes from the United States which combine inter-agency work, a family focus and radically new professional training. Corrigan and Bishop (1997) report on work:

> to prepare a new generation of inter-professionally oriented service providers who possess the knowledge, skills and values to create family-centred, community-based, integrated education, social services, and health systems.
>
> (Corrigan and Bishop, 1997: 149)

The challenge is evident in the descriptions given, and wariness has to be expressed at any expectation that the transfer across cultures of radical, categorically funded, charisma-led schemes will be easy. Yet to persist with only minor repairs to fundamentally flawed existing approaches holds more dangers. Corrigan and Bishop write of 'the re-imaging and re-inventing of schools' (1997: 151). The school is described as the site for a huge list of child-oriented professionals — so there are building as well as cultural implications. The family-focus is more challenging still in the way that both Corrigan and Bishop (1997) and Lawson and Hooper-Briar (1994b) see it. Not only is there an inter-professional approach but the family is 'involved' and 'trusted'. Other projects have urged that community representatives are engaged in decisions about local services. A prime goal is not to undermine the family but to empower it. *Project Unity* and *The Healthy and Ready to Learn Center* work in this way, as discussed in Corrigan and Bishop (1997: 154–155). A further element in the scheme for the delivery of such services is the training in 'community based care, co-ordinated care and family centred care' (Corrigan and Bishop, 1997).

The seven major conclusions presented by Peter Evans and Philippa Hurrell in the OECD study on services for children and families at risk deserve brief consideration, if only to see how far short practice currently falls. These proposals are seen as having validity across cultures, systems and economies:

1   there needs to be a holistic view of the child and balanced support systems which are nurturing and preventative in nature
2   the narrow categorical organisation of services is inadequate and new integrated and preventative systems are required
3   integrating services and co-ordinating agencies is the most promising comprehensive system
4   decentralisation is a key condition for effective services integration
5   evaluation will need to be developed to take account of complex systems change and serve accountability, and cost-effectiveness analyses
6   equitable funding across client types
7   trans-disciplinary training.

(OECD, 1996b: 99–103)

The four-level analysis offered by the OECD studies is helpful. The mandating level of legislation and policy is clearly important as it legitimises, calls up resourcing and focuses attention. The mandate is a civic expression of care (or its absence) and a statement about the location of responsibility or blame, or how responsibility is to be shared between government agencies and the family.

The strategic level is territory of the senior managers who, in many ways, often have a responsibility also for the operational level. While good communication and willingness to co-operate are important at the strategic and operational levels the field personnel need to be equipped, in terms of training, information, time and resources to function in a way which is inter-agency, multi-professional and cross-services. The street-level practitioners interacting with children, families and communities are the processes by which the interventions are carried out. At best these workers are trained and managed in an inter-professional manner.

Focus on the individual

To atomise the problem down to the body and psyche of the perpetrator of the problem is the ultimate reductionist and libertarian move. Some young people do have very specific diagnosable disabilities which need expert one-to-one attention or an individualised education (or development) plan. Arguably, even where the major focus is in changing the environment – such as the provision of a classroom assistant to help with a 'difficult' 8 year old or a youth facility for 14 year olds – there is also need for inputs and guidance *for the individual* to adjust to new goals and new opportunities. Equally, where work has been done with an individual to develop, say, anger management skills, teachers and families need 'adjusting' to recognise, build upon and respond positively to observed improvements. What is to be avoided in this is the grudging comment from adults, 'There, it isn't that hard to behave yourself, is it?'

The fast tracks to individualising the problem and the treatment are through 'medicalising' the problem or moralising the 'choices' a child has made. A medical label is attached to many challenging young people, most commonly Attention Deficit and Hyperactivity Disorder (ADHD). Dyslexia had been a common label sought and applied with the argument that the reading difficulty, undiagnosed and untreated, had led to frustration and difficult behaviour. There are societies for families with children who have or claim these disabilities and arguments over appropriate provision:[6] the debate over Ritalin for ADHD children rages in the UK at the time of writing.

With more obvious medical conditions (a broken leg or asthma) attention cannot be given only to the environment (no stairs, clean air) or to prevention (flat pavements, testing before birth). There are steps to be taken with the individual. There are professionals who do this. Invariably there is a need for action at other levels.

The moralising position is one where blame is individualised and the fault lies with the perpetrator. The phenomenological self has made choices to behave in this way. This is very much the view which comes through in Chapter 7 with the media treatment given to children who kill or are excluded from school. The tension and compromise in managing young people making 'wrong', certainly oppositional, subcultural, choices leads to more heated debate on at least two counts. The first is that making the choices they do, be it disruptive behaviour or drug use, they are deemed undeserving of intervention and the expenditure of resources. They should face only punishment and containment: no goodies for baddies. The second count is the need to acknowledge the decision-making role of the young person and induce and empower alternative ways of behaving – one of the ways may well be pointing out the strong possibility of exclusion from school, or from society by imprisonment, if current behaviours continue. If a professional takes full responsibility for a young person's moral choices, or explains them away totally by reference to poor background or awful family experiences the individual has no agency in their own reform. To be rescued is to be disempowered.

Focus on criminal justice

A major worry in relation to excluded pupils and behaviourally difficult or disaffected youngsters is that they could turn to crime. Three consultative documents and a White Paper were produced in the autumn of 1997 by the Home Office. Intervention and preventive strategies found a minority place in all four documents. In *New National and Local Focus on Crime* (Home Office, 1997b), two of the thrusts, common in other welfare areas, were the publication of a plan (p. 10) and the collaboration among professionals. This collaboration appeared to be mostly in relation to the exchange of information. There was mention of the Youth Offender Teams' involvement in safety and crime reduction schemes and the suggestion that 'They could also help in providing supervised leisure activities' (1997b: 12). This was a remarkably slight intervention in preventive work. The role of the Youth Service was stated in a similar fashion apparently ignorant of the work they do and can do; to say that 'staff are often experienced' and 'might be able to make a significant contribution' (1997b: 13) appeared to downgrade personnel and activities which, at the least, fill young people's time, when they might get involved in wrongdoing, and at best underrated the positive changes that can result from young people being led in challenging and developmental activities which lead to personal growth and fulfilment.

The tenor of all three consultation papers was punitive. There was much more on 'tough on youth crime' than on 'its causes'. There was little on how resources, attention and statutory personnel might be directed at working with young people, families and communities to establish conditions and activities which would draw young people away from crime. *Tackling Delays in the Youth Justice System* (Home Office, 1997a) was entirely about speeding up the wasteful procedures reported by the Audit Commission (1996b). Tackling this easily defined and quantifiable problem was not going to address fundamental needs in relation to youth offending.

In *Tackling Youth Crime* (Home Office, 1997c) it was stated, 'The Government believes that more should be done to help protect young children from being drawn into crime'. The child safety order and the local child curfew were restrictive and punitive measures aimed, what is more, only at the under-tens. These were minor and partial interventions. All this went unchanged into the White Paper, aggressively entitled *No More Excuses* (Home Office, 1997d), a signal maybe that the Home Office felt in no way that it needed to excuse ineffective policies.

However, the White Paper contained a very useful evidence-based discussion of the facts about youth crime, including the causes. Despite Part II being entitled *Preventing Youth Crime* and the occurrence of phrases like 'nipping offending in the bud' (Home Office, 1997d: 2) and 'preventing offending by young people is a key aim' (pp. 9–10), it had more on addressing 'an excuse culture' (p. 2) and 'we must stop making excuses for youth crime'

(p. 3), and on links between crime and social disadvantage and poverty. The White Paper stated 'a simplistic, deterministic view of the causes of crime is not supported by the facts and risks both insulting those in deprived circum-stances who do not commit offences and making excuses for those who do' (1997d: 7–8). Subsections on *the duty on youth justice agencies* and how to *reinforce the duty on youth justice agencies* were about focusing the work of the various professional groups – but mostly after offending had taken place. Under 'tackling causes' broader policies were listed including support for families (getting single parents off benefit and back to work and helping to prevent marriage breakdown), 'a determined assault on social exclusion', help-ing children achieve at school, 'real opportunities for jobs' and 'action to tackle drugs' (1997d: 11–12). Money was to be allocated and there were to be 'statutory partnerships to prevent and reduce crime and disorder'. There was nothing on the provision of youth clubs, more workers with young people, raising living conditions or the concerted policies in the United States on early intervention to prevent crime reported by Greenfield *et al.* (1996).

As in the UK, crime is listed as a major concern among citizens of the United States. Most money is devoted to a narrow range of solutions, most notably the imprisonment of those who have already committed crimes. As in the UK much less attention and funding has been directed at diverting youths from crime before they begin offending. Greenfield and colleagues (1996) compared four different sorts of intervention and preventive approaches with California's 'three-strikes' law guaranteeing extended sentences for repeat offenders. The four approaches focused on different phases of young people's development. They were

- home visits by childcare professionals for two years to young dis-advantaged mothers and four years of day care
- training for parents and therapy for families with young school-age children who have shown aggressive behaviour in school
- four years of cash and other incentives to induce disadvantaged high school students to graduate
- supervision of delinquents.

Three of the four sorts of programmes proved more cost-effective in reducing crime (as measured in these pilot projects) as compared with imprisonment of recidivists. Early home visit and day care intervention with high risk youth and their families compared less well. It required very large expenditures involving large numbers of youths and the crime reduction benefits did not appear until many years later. Graduation incentives worked best; 'the cost of preventing serious crimes with this program is somewhere around $4,000 per crime (or around 250 serious crimes prevented per million program dollars)' (Greenfield *et al.*, 1996: 37). It has to be acknowledged that the early childhood intervention may serve other welfare goals. The

Greenfield research referenced studies which indicated reductions in child abuse, savings on medical and social services costs associated with fostering and improved performance in school (1996: 39). This points again to necessities for integrated approaches to welfare to address multiple disadvantages and the avoidance of several types of negative outcome.

The Audit Commission's *Misspent Youth* (1996b) calculated the wastefulness and delays in dealing with youth crime. It noted the limited attention given to prevention and diversion. The Northampton Diversion Unit and the Scottish Children's Hearing System were described approvingly. McGuire's (1995) compilation of articles on reducing reoffending offered powerful evidence on the feasibility and effectiveness of preventive strategies with those who had already offended. The National Association for the Care and Resettlement of Offenders (NACRO, 1997) Young Offenders Committee report likewise looked for restorative and reintegrative approaches towards young people who offend. 'A virtuous cycle of less crime, less spending on criminal justice, more spending on prevention and less crime must be the overall objective of public policy in this area' (p. 26). Again NACRO's call for inter-agency working was strong: 'Intensive programmes also need to involve parents and schools very much more centrally than has been the case in the past' (p. 27). The Rainer Foundation report (Johnson and Parker, 1996: 24) concluded that 'the young people in our survey are, in the main, "children in need". Before punitive measures are imposed other options and opportunities should be given the highest priority'.

Exclusions, truancy and involvement in crime are known to affect some groups to a far greater extent than others. Even where this is largely accepted and the predictability of misfortune known, services (Social Services as well as criminal justice) react after the 'crisis'. Prevention is not a prime goal. Thus disadvantaged families, ethnic minorities (especially African Caribbean), and young people in care or leaving care are caught up disproportionately in punitive action. Young people who have been 'looked after' are a poignantly vulnerable group. The Department of Health's (1997a) Social Services Inspectorate made plain the educational failure experienced by this group: 75 per cent have no academic qualifications; 23 per cent of adult prisoners and 38 per cent of young prisoners have been in care. Devlin's (1995) popularist accounts of prisoners' poor skills and low levels of educational attainment attested, by their number and consistency, the preparation that these ultimate outcasts received for their role.

Crime and its costs occur, in part at least, not through the ignorance or oversight of policy makers but because of purposely pursued individualism of neglect which is passed off as liberalism, and authoritarian popularism which prefers and understands punishment better than prevention.

Bringing it all together: schools, agencies and voluntary organisations working together to reduce disaffection and exclusion

To bring agencies to work together is an enormous challenge. But the shared tasks they face with children, youth and families at risk would appear to make the collaboration essential. If solutions are intended by politicians and sought by professionals certainly the aims of the health service cannot be achieved alone;[7] *Health of the Nation* targets for young people on, for example, sex and HIV/AIDS education, drug prevention and exercise, require education to play a part. In relation to youth offending there is a part to be played by education, social services and the youth service. Social workers, in cases involving families and young children, can be supported by mental health services and education. Exclusions from school, and the other problems with which that is so often connected, clearly demand multi-agency involvement. Blinkered pursuit of highly managerialist goals of any one service can burden another, lead to cost-shunting, inefficiency and ineffectiveness and to an overall greater cost to the public purse.

The Education Reform Act, Single Regeneration Grants and the Children Act are monumental. They are monumental in being large, high profile and casting their long, individual shadows over all children. Service integration is promoted by none in a sense which is relevant to disadvantaged or at-risk young people. SRGs are classic categorical funding initiatives, long shown to be intellectually and practically limited in their capacity to address deep-seated and long-standing social problems.

While the public agencies have been ever more targeted in their work, areas which they have not covered well have found funding through 'projects' sometimes 'pilot projects'. Gardner's (1994) criticism of 'projectitis' was precisely because it denied the enduring and recognised character of the problem the project addressed. Projects were short term, unstable and generally not attractive to workers trying to make a career. Projects are often the product of crisis concern and not the outcome of considered strategic planning. Disaffection, exclusion and behaviour problems have been slowly moving from attention by 'projects' to being addressed by secure funding.[8]

Therefore, the direction taken by proposals to address disaffection and exclusion is unsurprising, but why the UK does this is partly because the UK does not have an official category of 'at risk' which covers children and young people who may be drawn into anti-social, self-damaging and criminal activity. If there were an 'at risk' category in the UK, as there is in some countries in mainland Europe,[9] then legislation, resources and action may be valuably co-ordinated and directed to that group.

These are 'joined-up problems' (Social Exclusion Unit, 1998) and demand 'joined-up solutions'. Resources, political mandate and the commitment of professionals at every level will be needed to address school disaffection and its consequences. The wider context of employment, facilities for the young and relationships with mainstream institutions need addressing equally. Otherwise the problem is sustained by the context yet welfare agents are expected to tackle it.

Much of the above is couched in terms of 'policy *science*' – focusing upon the clarification and improvement in the organisation and functioning of societal agencies. Policy *scholarship* has a different role to play in disinterestedly applying analytical techniques to the emergence of policy issues, policy options and communicating judgement, research findings and cautions. Policy scholarship or policy science, one must never forget that decision makers are influenced by much more than humanistic debate.[10]

Notes

1 Redistribution is about contests over inequality. If wealth and income were more evenly spread and welfare payments were at a level which reduced the incidence of poverty then the redistributive policy, it is argued, would address the problems. Allocative politics is about ensuring sufficient access to and use of education, welfare services and cultural goods that the society has available. The first is about how much inequality a society can tolerate while the second is mindful about how citizens are to engage with the wider society.

2 Room sees the distributional approach (like the 'redistributional') as distinctly Anglo-Saxon and common more to the UK and US systems. The relational approach, like the 'allocative', is dynamic and seeks to ensure, not just that the poor have more money but that they are able to engage with society's mainstream institutions.

3 The teaching profession in the UK has lost the control it had over the curriculum, and over examining and assessment. It may appeal to the less acknowledged but none the less powerful self-serving and ambitious motives of professionalism to take on a more holistic responsibility for the child. This may involve alliances with social and health service groups. Government proposals certainly call for the integration of the service plans drawn up by different professional groups. Strategic self-advancement possibilities may move the teaching profession more effectively than the moral arguments about better and fuller care for children.

4 Some professionals working with challenging youngsters respond to a reminder about Callaghan's 1996 stricture that they would be *so* happy if they could produce 'socially well adjusted members of society'. They see great virtue in this and unemployment is *not* judged to result from pupils' lack of skills; there just are not the jobs. Arguably Callaghan's speech was politically well judged and intentionally sociologically (and economically) naive. The same sort of speech could invite that same judgement at the end of the millennium.

5 As primary school children make up only 14 per cent of permanent exclusions and their background problems are so frequently so severe, there may be a good case to have different legislation and regulations for these cases. It is an indication of governmental unwillingness to develop welfare policy in this area that so little is *known* 'officially' about this group of young children. Acquiring and interrogating information on the social and domestic needs of

young behaviourally difficult pupils would signal the potential for action. Public awareness of the extreme disadvantage of many of these pupils open the government to pressures for action, pressures to which the government does not want to be exposed.

6 For example, for dyslexia in the UK there are the British Dyslexia Association and the Dyslexia Institute. For Autism and Asperger's Syndrome there are the National Autistic Society and, world-wide, OASIS (On-line Asperger's Syndrome Information Support) and Autism Network International. For Attention Deficit and Hyperactivity Disorder, there are the ADD/ADHD Family Support Group and the Hyperactive Children's Support Group.

7 There is no reason to assume a common agenda for politicians and professionals. Managerialist approaches imposed by a controlling central government have damaged some professional groups badly. Central government has been keen to emasculate them as centres of power and possible resistance. Literature on professionals suggests that their goals are often not the publicly expressed service ideals but have much to do with maintaining their status, income and conditions of work (Etzioni, 1969; Friedson, 1970). In Special Education the ideology of 'expertism' (Troyna and Vincent, 1996) and the conflicts and fragmentation of professional groups (Tomlinson, 1996) raise important questions about, not just the competence of professional groups to achieve welfare goals, but also their motivation to do so.

8 The movement towards the acceptance that exclusions and disaffection are not transitory phenomena has been slow to arrive. While government money must be bid for for projects, LEA Behaviour Plans and Children's Services Plans may ensure local diagnosis of the dimensions of the problems and coordination in addressing them. The interrelation of the agencies may support a more enduring policy stance and a monitoring of impact.

9 In Denmark the ombudsman for children is one of the co-authors of an influential report, *Risikobørn: Hvem er de, hvad gør vi?* (Jorgensen *et al.*, 1993). In the Netherlands, the Ministry of Education, Culture and Welfare commissioned a report on *The Education of Children at Risk in the Netherlands* (Kloprogge and Walraven, 1996).

10 There should never be surprise that evidence coupled with ethical argument serve as limited inputs into political decision making. Ideologies and authoritarian popularism can motivate decisions even where there are calculable short- and long-term costs.

10 Political values, welfare and educational policy

Introduction

A number of issues have been reserved until this chapter, though they should resonate with and amplify points of theory and history in Chapters 1 and 3. Chapters 4 to 8 reported data and interpretations on school exclusions and Chapter 9 dealt with a particular set of policy proposals currently popular. Education is a public institution and any perceived failure in its functioning needs to be examined within a socio-political context, a historical context and an economic context – not that these are in any way independent of each other. To that end this chapter examines the political values which have informed education and welfare policy, the language through which it is expressed, the construction of youth, their transitions to full citizenship,[1] the limitations placed on their social rights and the place of education and other agencies in these transitions. The topography and causality of disadvantage which this language entails and the policy architecture within which the values and language are contained are discussed. Consideration is given to education and welfare futures informed by another set of values and with a different set of strategic and practical responses to 'difficult' and vulnerable young people; in this final section, social exclusion and school exclusion are drawn together.

In sociological theorising and in policy making there is an enduring struggle along the structure–agency continuum; the extent to which we view human action as a consequence of the structural conditions of a person's life – unemployment, poor housing, marginalised involvement with social institutions – or a consequence of individual choice. This is of profound theoretical relevance, as discussed in Chapter 1; it is about the extent to which we view humans as 'free' or as 'determined'. The conclusion reached also informs policy making in moral and practical senses. If 'society' is deemed to bear a responsibility for individual deviant behaviour it is reasonable to assume that a supportive, interventionist role is motivated among education policy makers. If individual agency is considered the prime source of deviant behaviour, that behaviour may be medicalised or criminalised and call up intervention or punishment, or the perpetrator may be denied resources and access. The complexity grows with the acknowledgement that some people play a greater part in creating and controlling their biographies and life experiences than others.

Political values and the practices of education and welfare

The UK has a divisive and competitive school system. Goals articulated for it were increasingly narrowed up to the end of Conservative rule in 1997, and standards and school improvement have been about external tests and examinations. The schools of the UK have never been less about democracy, equity, empowerment, community or joy. Harold Silver writes:

> A good school was . . . one which matched its work closely to nationally set goals. The dominant definitions of good schools in Britain, particularly since the late 1980s, have not only been a long way from considerations of warmth, kindliness and humanity, however hard the schools might work to keep these alive.
>
> (Harold Silver, 1994: 101)

The education systems in both the UK and United States appear to have gone down narrow, prescriptive routes where atomised, measurable achievements have become the set goals. Wider societal goals or a focus on the full, learning person appear to have been relegated. Distrust of these social engineering goals is evident in their displacement by a view that the bigger problems in society will be solved if we can concentrate on solving the smaller problems in school. Barry Holtz reviewed with sadness *Fifteen Thousand Hours* at the start of this period; he reminded us that

> we once hoped that schools would create new models of community, encourage new commitments toward meaningful vocations, end racial discrimination, and open up new avenues out of poverty and unhappiness. Right now, it seems, we rejoice if children can be taught to read.
>
> (Holtz, 1981: 300)

The policy discourse of schooling moved from optimistic and enabling in the 1960s to restricting and controlling in the 1990s. This position was reached more by the winning battle positions taken up by central government against other lesser centres of power, namely LEAs and teacher unions, rather than by a commitment to any industry or employment lobby. Chapter 3 argued that for all of the six functions of schooling there had been a move to the controlling end of the continua, and away from the personally empowering pole. Furthermore, the custodial and credentialling dimensions appeared dominant. There clearly is no sustainable or coherent rationale which links changes in school content and processes (or those in higher education) with the world of work. There is more quantifiable evidence that levels of investment in industry affect productivity than that standards of reading affect national output. Attempts to show how education should meet the needs of industry have been poorly founded on data, practically simplistic and intellectually flawed. This is no surprise when employment opportunities for young people have been structurally limited yet it is young people's deficiencies which are blamed for their unemployment. In an altogether disconnected fashion parental choice is the force identified to produce 'the schools we need'. Therefore, completing the loop means that the responsibility for producing the schooling system, its content, processes and purposes, is best left to parents exerting their wishes through the market mechanism. It is hardly likely that the ever changing body of parents has the improvement of gross national product in the forefront of its collective mind.

As the millennium approaches, the school has fewer 'family' characteristics — notions of nurture and care as the young grow. Indeed the market relationship is a distancing and non-collusive one, the counter of commerce dividing customer and provider, underpinning antipathy to welfare and special measures to address disadvantage. A system which allocates to market competition the role of driving up standards is bound to have casualties. Ranson (1993) rightly points to the choice made between markets and democracy. In the market of education, choice (the vote) is choosing a school place and each unit, the family, is expected to operate according principles of possessive individualism. Ranson sees the outcome as being 'to erode local democracy and to reinforce a segmented society' (1993: 334). Schools are less than ever a community resource responding to a local, collective, democratic will. Their response to a national will has been enforced through curriculum stipulations, assessment and inspection, which have focused on separate attainment within individualised, 'marketised' schools. As collective choice is the aggregate of private choice, 'the market as a result places public policy and collective welfare beyond the reach of public deliberation, choice and action: in other words, democracy' (Ranson, 1993: 339).

The casualties referred to above are institutional and individual. Some schools close, and some individuals are unwelcome in conventional mainstream schools and are excluded. Until 1998 there was only vestigial political will to provide alternative education provision for these excluded pupils.[2] There were children and young people in school judged to be failing, struggling or difficult, who constituted 'unsaleable goods' (Bennett, 1993), 'damaged goods' (John, 1996) or 'scoundrels' (Garner, 1995) and were blamed for their own plight: see Blyth and Milner (1994) on 'victim blaming'. As Slee puts it,

> Individual student pathology deflects from the harder questions about the exclusionary imperatives of educational markets expressed through league tables, test scores and 'failing schools' that are unable to

simultaneously exhibit the preconditions for the 'effective' containment of difficult children and the raising of GCSE scores.

(Slee, 1998: 103)

The responsibility for the 'pathology' of these children was individualised and the additional resources required to make appropriate educational provision could be righteously withheld. Only where the problem was 'medicalised' or an SEN statement had been applied were additional funds forthcoming. 'Behaviour' problems brought little support when the problem was actually evident and still less to groups which were vulnerable or 'at risk'.

Chapter 2 set out the numbers of pupils excluded and the provision made for them. The size of the problem is known but there is not good information, either nationally or within most LEAs about the nature of the excluded population and still less about those vulnerable to exclusion. The UK has not had an official 'at risk' category. One struggles to see the term associated with anything other than children 'at risk' of exposure to harm or abuse or of engagement in delinquent activity. It does not broaden to encompass children inhibited from normal social, intellectual or emotional development. Educationists are happier with the term 'special educational needs'. Social Services use the term 'children in need'. In disseminating the conclusions of the OECD (1996b) study on *Successful Services for our Children and Families at Risk*, the conference held at the London Institute was entitled 'Making Services Work for Disadvantaged Children and Young People' (16 September 1997). To have put the phrase 'at risk' in the conference title would have been confusing for welfare professionals in the UK, who would probably have associated this with the narrower concern of child abuse. A much more limited range of professionals would have been attracted to the conference. The absence of an 'at risk' category means that, in education, policy makers are not inclined to target personnel to intervene early. Social Services are equally unlikely to intervene in a broadly preventive way. They have indeed become a reluctant, underfunded crisis operation. Offe (1996) relates government stances on welfare to its perceived success in its 'steering' role. Across Europe governments have experienced disappointments in accruing the resources to fulfil responsibilities.

The result is a professedly 'realistic' reduction in the scope of the state's steering claims, competences and responsibilities, and of the agenda of what can and should be the object of public policy.

(Offe, 1996: 107)

Esping-Anderson's (1990) now classic typology of welfare systems appears to place the UK ever more squarely in the 'liberal' category (rather than the 'corporate' or 'social democratic'). The professional ideology, indeed that required for secure professional status, is of a social democratic and inclusive kind but that has been sidelined by efficiency drives and judgements by UK conservative policy makers about the ineffectiveness of generic social work. Langan's (1993) summary of the diminished power of social work expressed the situation well and there are few signs that the situation has altered under a new government:

> The dominant trends in social work are moves away from the professional and political optimism embodied in the Seebohm Report. It is no longer assumed that the state will support welfare needs: they must now be sought in the mixed economy. It is no longer assumed that the ambition of social work is to provide universal services . . . services must be 'targeted' . . . social work's claims to professional expertise lie in ruins.
>
> (Langan, 1993: 164)

The similarities between education and social services are to be found not in their market orientation, though Social Services and the health services do have purchaser–provider arrangements, nor simply in the depressed morale of their staff, but in their narrowly defined professionalism. The managerialism is about targets and their achievement. The 'here-and-now' practicality, the efficiency emphasis, bureaucratically disciplined and logged tasks all serve to minimise attention outside the narrowly defined current time frame and to focus efforts on achievable goals with existing client groups. In part this is legitimised by the language and labelling which is in use.

The language of disadvantage

Where the causes of disadvantage, social exclusion or alienation are located is an ideological and political choice. Even the linguistic form locates causes and blame in one place rather than another. 'I am disadvantaged', 'I am disabled', 'I am excluded', 'I am alienated', in English – in the UK – conveys an internal state, a personalised experience. The past participle allied to the verb 'to be' is staticly descriptive, inert and leaves responsibility with the subject. Yet 'to disadvantage', 'to disable', 'to exclude' and 'to alienate' are active verbs which can be used with subject and object: society disadvantages me or disables me; the school excludes me; the world of youth training for jobs that don't exist alienates me.[3]

Campbell and Oliver (1996: 36) discuss the medical model of disability and the excluding and limiting definitions of disabled people which follow from this. Indeed their whole book is about the organised struggle to change labels and attitudes and ultimately policies and provision. It is the language in which discussion of some groups is bound up that restricts thinking about solutions and commitment to action to take account of their needs. The language is not an accident of evolution or a value-free functional device; it is a social creation serving social group purposes.

The term 'at risk' takes us beyond these static notions into the future and hypothetical. Such a term applied to groups is at the mercy of anti-intellectualism and empiricist outcomes orientations. Carr and Hartnett (1996) refer to the deintellectualisation of educational policy and short-termism. Acceptance of the category, 'at risk', is to be speculative, though speculation may be based on and borne out of past experience, research and sound theorising. It is to consider intervention and to have a longer term of view: action now to avoid bad outcomes later.

Clegg and Megson (1973) had a view on the education of what they termed 'children in distress'. In the agency versus structure debate they are firmly of the view that behaviour problems in children are 'created'.

> Children who are criminal or vicious or ill-adjusted to the society in which they move, or even where children are merely badly behaved, have often served a long apprenticeship of distress.
>
> (Clegg and Megson, 1973: 11)

Smith (1987) reports the demise of Educational Priority Areas in England and offers explanations for their fall from favour; loss of legitimised definition of target group was among the reasons. Identifying a group as 'at risk', the 'vulnerable', defines a welfare target group. Intrinsically it sets an inter-ventionist, preventive agenda. It demands resources, monitoring and action. To lose the official definition on identity means the target and resources disappear.

Thus society's less fortunate, including children excluded from education, can be construed as culprits, victims or a threat – or a combination of these. The child's behaviour may be acknowledged as disruptive, even dangerous, and it may be accepted that there are clear causes in the child's history or environment – yet exclusion is still judged necessary. There may be clear causes that excuse or explain the behaviour, but the child still loses most of his or her educational entitlement. The choice of where responsibility for dis-advantage lies is articulated by the powerful voices and legitimised through the communication media as suggested in Chapter 7.

Messages which challenge this position are silenced, blunted or deflected. The New Right has expertly broadcast the messages of personal responsi-bility, the effectiveness of the market, the drawbacks associated with inter-vention and welfare and, ultimately, the inevitability and justice of inequality. Human experiences of poverty, poor housing and exclusion from school are construed as private woes rather than public ills, to rephrase Wright Mills (1970). The legacy from the policies of the New Right for the incoming Labour government in the UK has been precisely that government does not have to take responsibility; the market, and the efficiency and discipline it demands, are established as key mechanisms. The new govern-ment can cautiously retreat from this minimalistic welfare position at will and at leisure. Global economic uncertainties do not encourage governments to extend and strengthen the welfare net.

Youth and 'transition'

Young people in the late twentieth century face an ever lengthening period of insecurity and dependence. Children are spending more, having sex younger, drinking younger. They are hedonistic consumers and targeted aggressively through advertising. For many, the disparity between their freedom and opportunities outside school and the limitations and subservience within school jars. It is interesting, even paradoxical, that the packaging of education as a consumer product has not addressed young people themselves as the customers. Arguably young people need something quite different from education for a period of their lives which is less and less a predictable transition to 'adult' economic and domestic status. Indeed the period 14–25 is probably best seen as a stage or phase in its own right and not merely as a transition.

During children's period of growing up, the family is decreasing as a source of stability and guidance. In the years of the Conservative government, interventions to make communities more supportive of young people were lacking, with local authorities rate capped and the youth service a regular victim of 'savings', with the result that it was left to the market to cater for children's leisure needs. There has existed a remarkably unsupervised and neglected terrain between home and school. School has become narrowed and competitive and diminished over the period as a focus for leisure activities. Indeed the loss of many extra-curricular clubs and activities can be directly traced to the Thatcher/Baker imposition of a contract that specified 1,265 hours of directed time per year. No longer treated as 'professionals', teachers in large numbers withdrew their goodwill.

As young people approach school leaving at 16, few move into work and most will go on to continue their education. Allowances for young people (17 year olds) were withdrawn in 1995. And from 1998 young people moving on to higher education pay towards tuition fees as well as bear the accumulated brunt of pegged student grants. Young people's economic dependence continues to increase. Families are *less* likely to be able to bear the burden of this extended financial support (Jones, 1995). Sixth form studies, further education college, vocational education and training are the regular expectations of 16–18 year olds. Higher education is also a 'mass' experience. A career, with the continuity and stability which that implies, is an uncertain prospect towards the end of this long period of youth 'transition' and this extended period is certain to continue.

Young people make what Coles (1995) sees as the traditional, interrelated transitions from school to work, the domestic transition from family of origin to family of destination and the housing transition in moving from the parental residence. While these may be the main transitions and they take place over a longer period and with less predictability, there are others which relate to their status as citizens. They become voters (more disillusioned than in the past), car drivers, members of organisations, protesters and supporters, owners and debtors and, in some cases, parents. Policy has not acknowledged the long and uncertain youth period or catered for it outside of opportunities for education and training. All this is seen as a problem by most commentators. Few examples exist in the literature where benefits of such a period are cited. Young (1987) from the Australian context, Ainley (1991) in Britain, and Baumier and Léotard (1998) in France, offer optimistic and constructive perspectives on young people having a less forced and more supported 'transition' in a turbulent period of personal identity formation. Ironically, in the so-called period of high modernity, it may be the youth period that offers most opportunity for freedom, agency and Giddens's (1991a) reflexive 'making of one's own biography'; but this will not be so if insecurities are great, resources small and it adds up to an experience of disempowerment or alienation.

It is youth's continued marginalisation and the compromised and partial entry to citizenship status which are sources of concern. It is the social exclusion, with associated possibilities of crime, lack of participation, unemployment or unemployability, and long-term dependency which the state apparatuses need to address. There continue to be groups which are predictably marginalised in contexts of competition and uncertainty. As Jones and Wallace correctly perceive, 'paths to adulthood, far from being individualised, can still be predicated from social class origins to a great extent in both Britain and West Germany' (Jones and Wallace, 1990: 37).

Citizenship

Citizenship is a potentially useful concept in understanding responses to youth, disadvantage, delinquency and school exclusions. Marshall's (1950) delineation of citizenship is outdated and does not relate well to conditions of late modernity. For Marshall citizenship conferred civil rights, political rights and social rights to a populace conceived in fairly passive terms; individuals did not have to demand their rights and those denied the first two would be only the imprisoned and the insane while the young would be expected to achieve them through maturity and socialisation. Half a century ago, this provided a credible rhetoric in the context of near full employment, a sexual division of labour, stable nuclear families and considerable control in internal affairs held by nation-state governments. Citizenship has been seen as sets of reciprocal rights and duties supporting the stability and development of political, economic, social and cultural life.

In the late 1990s citizens express their responsibilities by working and economically supporting themselves and their children, upholding the law – paying taxes and abstaining from crime – and participating as voters. Their social rights are met through the welfare state with schooling, healthcare, Social Services support, pensions, police and unemployment benefit. Citizenship in this form is a safety net, a way of redistributing resources generally and a way of providing for those who for some reason cannot provide for their own needs. Citizenship was a matter of universal membership transcending class,

youth were seen as meeting the criteria, if indeed an underclass could be said to exist.

John Hills (1997b) writes of the sudden intrusion into British political discourse of the term 'social exclusion'. Even the attempted use of the term 'underclass' signals the need to recast the ideas of citizenship, belonging and social solidarity. Citizenship is not unconditionally given. Civil and political aspects of citizenship are about freedom, opportunities to engage in the democratic process; in these aspects citizenship is about the absence of hindrance. Salter (1998), writing in the context of recent developments in the National Health Service, contrasts civil and political rights with social rights:

> Social rights are formulated in a positive way requiring an interventionist state to achieve them. Furthermore, they are given an absolute status and their fulfilment is not seen as conditional upon the ability of the state, primarily its economic ability, to provide them.
>
> (Salter, 1998: 210)

Salter overstates this absolute duty to deliver the welfare component. In law and in practice in the areas of housing, Social Services, health and education, local authorities, health trusts and local education authorities have been exonerated in cases of non-provision of services (mainly by reason of lack of resources), providing systems are in place to fulfil what had once been taken as their statutory duties. By barely perceptible drift, social rights have had limits placed on them. The limitations on social rights are becoming more explicit with welfare to work policies demanding the exercise of duties in return for the right to welfare payments.

The pressures grow stronger for the withdrawal of welfare where groups can be construed as undeserving. Dean (1997) sums up the way partially contrived conditions have redefined youth.

> In the 1980s and 1990s . . . the ascendancy of the Radical Right has largely succeeded in recasting the welfare state as an encumbrance from the past and in reconstituting youth in terms of its threatening qualities rather than its promise for the future.
>
> (Dean, 1997: 57)

The 'underclass', unhelpful as a sociological category, is helpful as a political myth and covers the mass of undeserving poor. Thus a malleable situation develops where manipulators of ideology can legitimise the reduction in expenditure on welfare. To label the 'mass of undeserving poor' as a class, albeit, an underclass, vests them with a cohesion, organisation, culture and intentionality sufficient to justify fear and negative sanctions. Murray (1990), transferring his sad vision from the United States, and publishing out of the right-wing Institute of Economic Affairs, sees underclass formation evidenced by rises in unemployment, crime and illegitimacy. Baggulay and Mann (1992) satirised Murray's underclass as 'idle, thieving bastards' and Murray's (1994) attempt at consolidation with the publication, *The Crisis Deepens*, has not established the 'underclass' with academics or the public.

On the other side even the employed, house-owning, law-abiding, 'full' citizens experience a degree of instability that they find disturbing. Sennett (1997) writes of the widening moral distance between the mass and elites that has accompanied this experience of instability.

> The masses, now comprising people in suits and ties as well as those in overalls, appear peripheral to the elite productive core; the emerging economy profits by shrinking its labour base. The economy's emphasis on personal agency helps explain why welfare dependency and parasitism are such sensitive issues for people whose fortunes are now troubled in the world.
>
> (Sennett, 1997: 167)

We may view this transformation as inevitable, as in Beck's (1992) *Risikogesellschaft* (*Risk Society*),[4] a post-modernity where previous securities are removed for many and the drive to privately insure for health and unemployment is considerable. Beck himself acknowledges that risks are unequally distributed and may follow existing class inequalities. That these are changing and being accentuated at the lower end is argued by Westergaard:

> The divide between this underclass and the majority is increasingly the most salient and challenging line of social division for the future, by contrast with the older divisions of class now said to be in eclipse.
>
> (Westergaard, 1992: 576)

The moral distance between the 'comfortable classes' and the so-called underclass has been reinforced from unexpected quarters. Halsey (1993), outraged at single parent families, condemned the situation 'where the man never arrives never mind leaves . . . never participated as a father but only as a genital'. Dennis (1993), a fellow 'ethical socialist', rails against the irresponsibility of single motherhood. Dahrendorf locates the origins of the 'underclass' in the economic sphere though 'not at fault for its own condition', then discusses those thus labelled in pejorative terms – 'a cumulation of social pathologies . . . laid back sloppiness' (Dahrendorf, 1987: 4–5). It is, indeed, easy for structural analysts to individualise causality and culpability.

At the extreme end of the underclass grouping are the criminals. Among the most severe exclusion responses is imprisonment which, at its most extreme, is without education, restorative policies or rehabilitation. Indeed, despite efforts by such bodies as the Howard League for Penal Reform and radical criminologists, Rutherford sees 'the resurgence of elimination as an ideal of criminal policy' (1997: 133). Certainly, as external forces have driven up the number of disadvantaged, opinion is managed to reduce their deservingness.

The topography and causality of disadvantage

Increasingly the poor are socially and geographically separate. Their housing and schools, even their shops and healthcare resources, are different. This physical separation emphasises their 'otherness'. It also distances us further from a shared responsibility. The concentration of disadvantage gives effect to the 'underclass' thesis but is a particular manifestation of block partial social citizenship.

The numbers living in poverty grew from 5 million in 1979 to just under 14 million in 1993/94 – from 9 per cent to 25 per cent of the population. For children the numbers in poverty in the same period rose from 1.4 million (10 per cent) to 4.2 million (32 per cent) (Hills, 1997). Some of these figures are contested (Green, 1998) but 'the poor' form a larger proportion of the population in the UK than in most other European countries; in the OECD listing only Ireland, Spain, Portugal and Greece are below the UK. In terms of welfare spending the UK is also well down the league.

Housing quality has improved over the years since 1971, while overcrowding persists disproportionately in houses of ethnic minority families. Those registering *no* housing deprivation rose from 75 per cent in 1971 to over 94 per cent in 1991 (Office for National Statistics (ONS), 1996). The poverty concentrations in inner cities, and out-of-city council estates, provide the solid visual evidence referred to by writers on the underclass.

Working upstream: education and welfare futures

To understand any social issue it must be seen in the context of the historical, cultural, economic and political conditions of the period. This is important for intellectual and sociological soundness as well as for strategic planning. As late modern times become more uncertain and social scientists predict even less reliably, paradoxically the importance of such sociological understanding may grow. Through 'policy scholarship' a social–historical approach to research 'can illuminate the cultural and ideological struggles' (Grace, 1995: 3). In the context of services for children and families at risk it is essential to analyse the social structural focuses which foster the creation (or do nothing to prevent) poverty, social exclusion and childhood disadvantage. Economic choices are made – even within the restraints of global economic movements – about how wealth, income, expenditure and social goods are to be distributed. However it is done is then legitimated either by resort to arguments of 'inevitability' or 'deservingness'. The poor, the at risk and the disadvantaged are created, defined, *judged and controlled.*

There are numerous contradictions to be perceived in the management of the economy, welfare and schooling. The schooling system, as discussed in

Chapter 1, has a key status-giving function. It is a competitive arena, to a greater or lesser extent, and changes over time in all countries. It reinforces and legitimises social and, with it, economic inequality. The economy has already established inequalities which correspond to, and contribute to, children's unequal performance in education.

Welfare, especially where more ambitiously conceived as a preventive function, has to work against a state of affairs *designed into the system.* The 'underclass', exclusions, youth crime and premature death in the lowest social classes are likewise designed into the system.

The 'war on poverty' has been fought with more vigour in the United States than anywhere else and resonates with righteous values, yet Gans begins his book by stating, 'For much of its history, America has been waging war against many of its poor people' (Gans, 1995: ii). He gives thirteen functions of labelling the poor. These functions include the creation of jobs for the better-off population 'to modify, police, control or guard them' (1995: 93), moral legitimisation, value reinforcement, popular culture villains and the reproduction of stigma. Indeed, Gans suggests that 'Undeservingness has enabled agencies that are established for helping the poor to evade their responsibilities' (1995: 100). Exclusions from school, disruption, disaffection and youth crime can be seen as evoking similar responses among the public, fuelled to a degree by media representations, and experiencing oversight, neglect and punishment.

The solutions are sought in several quarters. The market, with the hope/ expectation of trickle-down has been and, in part, remains within the policies implemented by the Labour government. Strict fiscal controls to keep productivity and wealth creation high and stable lead to continued inward investment or a reduction in out-flows of money, higher levels of employment and consumption, and higher tax revenues to fund the inevitably growing welfare sector. Even if unemployment benefit, single parent benefit and housing benefits are reduced, education, healthcare and pensions will grow. The market is undeniably a focus for working upstream.

The major problem with the market as a mechanism for income redistribution, safety netting and allocating resources to the needy ('deserving' or 'undeserving') is that it does not. Its main strength is its requirement that everyone join the market. Its reliance on forcing people's participation by benefit reductions means greater poverty for those not succumbing to the incentives of the market to work or not being able to work through unavailability of jobs. The market can operate as a market only if there is competition, if individuals pursue selfish interests and there have to be losers.

Emerging policy is to maintain general levels of funding, seek some redistribution within budget sectors and target those who, in many senses, are the greatest losers. Education Action Zones (DfEE, 1997b), Health Action Zones (Department of Health, 1997c) and targeting of the 'worst estates' are necessary crisis responses to alleviate the worst aspects of the market failure to include all in its benefits. This is the strained liberal solution.

To tackle exclusions funding has been increased marginally (DfEE, 1998c) but it is coupled with exhortation, graduated target-setting and the demand for plans – LEA Behaviour Support Plans (DfEE, 1998a) and Pastoral Support Plans (DfEE, 1999). The approach is warily interventionist.

Welfare is seen here as an adjunct to, and dependently responsive to, the economy. Its role remains confused as both safety net and punitive experience. Its clients are individual failures. School exclusion, as currently legislated and practised, fits well within this scenario.

Communitarianism is presented as the way forward by idealists, conservatives, those with religious convictions and socialist in a bewildering variety of forms. The fullest expression is to be found in Etzioni (1995) which does bewilder and combine moral and practical arguments from the most diverse quarters. At root, the book is an entreaty to define, disseminate and adhere to shared values. He believes that the extension of rights has gone too far and that the place of responsibilities has been underplayed. The goal is moral reconstruction through the family, education and, of course, the community with the community occupying the middle ground between individual and state. Communitarianism is proposed as the basis for recreating social solidarity and an emphasis on 'the politics of the common good' rather than the politics of rights (Sandel, 1992:16). The weakness of the communitarian positions lies in both its plurality and the dispersed nature of its constituency. Unlike the market position with its economic incentives and penalties this approach is a moral crusade – the first is pressure without legitimation, the second is legitimation without content.

The 'stakeholder society', as seen by Hutton (1996), is a moral call but rooted in the politics and economic management of capitalism. Looking back on eighteen years of Conservative government he sees both economic mismanagement and that

> Altruism and the civilising values of an inclusive society have been sacrificed on the altar of self-interest, of choice, of opting out and of individualism.
>
> (Hutton, 1996: 15)

Of course, self-interest, choice, opting out and individualism are all the safe values for the well-off. The stakeholder capitalism proposed by Hutton is, as one would expect from an economist, a largely economic blueprint to 'extend the area of stake-holding in companies and institutions . . .; extend the supply of cheap long term debt; and to decentralise decision-making' (Hutton, 1996: 298). He is strongest with his recasting of Keynesian economics. He argues against excessive inequality, records the under-funding of public services and allocates important minority space to the democratisation of welfare (Hutton, 1996: 306). He recognises the necessity of income transfers between classes and generations within wider political and economic structures.

Acknowledging the requirement of the state to legitimise welfare expenditure, and especially *increased* welfare expenditure, he writes perceptively of financial and moral sources of that legitimation:

> the hard, political requirement that the middle class and the top third of the income parade must have good reason for accepting progressive taxation upon which welfare depends. They need to get enough out of the system directly in terms of provision and indirectly in terms of social cohesion to make them support the principle of universal welfare to which they are disproportionately heavy contributors. That requires well-designed and high quality welfare services that meet their needs as well. On the other hand, acceptance of such a settlement assumes that there is a wider public morality which insists that universal participation is the only moral basis upon which the welfare system and society as a whole can be constructed.
>
> (Hutton, 1996: 306–307)

Hutton has not been satisfied with New Labour's response in power, claiming 'it lacks an idea of what it wants to do with power, whose interests it is serving and what kind of economy and society it wants to build' (Hutton, 1997b). He accuses the new government of 'political transvestism' and of having 'a genuinely conservative programme'.

The policies of the first year of Labour government contained much to reassure Hutton's 'top third of the income parade' by refusing to raise income taxes for the better off, reinforcing the standards and effectiveness measures in education, 'safeguarding' the National Health Service and getting tough on youth crime.

Citizenship provides a further, related set of rationales by which a government can choose to manage its economy (in so far as a government can manage the economy) and welfare provision. As discussed earlier in this chapter, however, it offers a weak and outdated rationale for intervention, indeed, a rationale which could exclude non-stakeholders more resolutely.

The focus upon social exclusion or inclusion holds more promise, has a recent and Europe-wide pedigree and excites academics and policy makers alike. A necessary element in this is to reconfigure the European poverty discussion in which Room (1995b) contrasts the Anglo-Saxon tradition, which is focused on distributional issues, with that now established in the European Union, which focuses primarily upon relational issues. Poverty research was about what level of income a person needed to function in the society; social exclusion is about income and resources only in so far as it affects social participation, social integration and access to power. While this second approach brings us back nearer debates about 'rights', it goes further in raising questions about what is needed to enable citizens to function in specific ways, to participate in different levels and institutions of society, and to experience belonging rather than alienation – economic, social, political or criminal.

Social exclusion theorising acknowledges the complexity and rapidity of change of modern life. It is still a confused concept, subject to definitions of convenience. 'Les exclus' meant for René Lenoir in 1974, 'the mentally and physically handicapped, suicidal people, aged invalids, abused children, drug addicts, delinquents, single parents, multi-problem households, marginal, asocial persons, and other "social misfits"' (quoted by Hilary Silver, 1994: 532). Underclass theorising, though having a similar focus to social exclusion theorising, prompts different policy responses.

The problem of school exclusions affects some parts of the community disproportionately and raises, as a result, class, culture and competition issues and tensions. This problem as a whole, and the over-representation of African Caribbean and looked-after pupils within the problem, continues to require specific and general measures which may also deal with the loss of education and the diminished life chances which may accompany it.

Appropriate full-time educational provision needs to be assured for young people if they are to be enabled to develop personally and be equipped to join the citizenry. A denial of rights to education, through the act of exclusion and inadequate replacement education, will be individually damaging to those on the receiving end, and will reinforce disaffection in those sections of society most affected.

It is important to bear in mind constantly when considering the proposed policy solutions that they are not simply technical or resource allocation matters. Decisions on these levels rest on ideologies and discourses which are deeply rooted and sustained in our society. Hutton may decry at a general level that 'we do live in a fundamentally unfair society and a run-down democracy. There must be change' (Hutton, 1997a: x). The OFSTED report on *Exclusions from Secondary School* may end with the assertion that 'no democracy can afford to write off thousands of young people' (OFSTED, 1996b: 31). Sad to say, there does not have to be change and we can afford to write off thousands more. Understanding the forces which legitimate current legislation, expenditure and practice in school exclusions is vital if the problem, some would say tragedy, is to be addressed at a fundamental level.

Notes

1 It can be argued that it is mistaken, in theoretical and policy terms, to view 'youth' as a transition, a movement out of childhood and compulsory education and into work, independence and 'adulthood'. It is now best seen as a lengthy period during which patterned conditions and behaviours pertain. These are, as with other stages of life, affected by socio-economic factors.

2 Though numbers of permanently excluded pupils are small, the small amount of replacement education supplied is a 'marker' for the role of education and whom

it serves. Home tuition provision has settled to around three hours a week and is seldom more than five, unless group tuition is arranged. Pupil Referral Units are usually part-time placement, the number of sessions per week for an excluded pupil often being dependent upon the numbers that have to be catered for. It is not until 2002 that LEAs must provide full-time education for all permanently excluded pupils in England.

3 Arguably this is a key, hidden foundation to policy debates about where on the structure–agency continuum a position is established. Foucault's (1972) discourses allow and disallow, in deeply embedded ways, conceptualisations and language. There can be an absolute and genuine incomprehension on the part of a person with an individualist, agency, freedom and personal responsibility orientation when it is suggested by a structuralist that background and environmental forces may have greatly increased an individual's likelihood of engaging in disruptive behaviour or crime. The individualist's response can be a wide-eyed, 'But they were exercising choice'. The same mechanisms which operate at the level of individual exchanges operate at the level of groups and ideologies.

4 It is uncertain how significant the concepts of risk and 'manufactured uncertainty' are, but it is clear that at the individual level there is less security and at national government level there are increasing forces and centres of power beyond their prediction and control.

Postscript

Failing to stop the permanent exclusion of a 6 year old

While writing this book, I was focused on theoretical perspectives on school exclusion – the adverse effects and the compromised rights of the child-citizen to education. Then, the reality of permanently excluding a 6 year old unfolded before me and I was unable to stop it. I was a governor at a local primary school, T, situated on an estate of mainly local authority housing with a roll of around 200 children.

The child LS started school in January 1996 and, following a catalogue of difficulties, he received a four day fixed term exclusion at the end of the spring term 1998. He returned for the summer term and two days later, on 23 April, was permanently excluded. I first heard about the child on 12 May at 9.10 a.m., when I received a telephone call asking if I would be one of the school governors to consider the head's decision to permanently exclude LS. This meeting was due to begin at 9.30 a.m. (in 20 minutes' time) and I was due to teach at 10.00 a.m. I had to refuse.

At the end of that week I contacted the chair of the governors and discovered that three governors reviewing the head's decision, with guidance from the Exclusions Officer, had upheld the permanent exclusion. The mother, it was reported, was not inclined to appeal.

LS is 6 years old. His parents had been separated for some time and the governors' subcommittee reviewing the exclusion were made aware that LS was distressed by infrequent and unpredictable contact with his father. The mother had already made a written request that the assessment procedures for statementing should begin and LS was at Stage 3 of the code of practice.

On the evening of Monday 18 May I contacted the Exclusions Officer. I discussed the case with him and he judged that the headteacher had presented and documented a strong case. As Exclusions Officer he had given guidance to the governors who had upheld the headteacher's decision. He acknowledged that the Behaviour Support Service, although contacted, had not been brought in to help address LS's problems.

I wrote hurriedly to the chair of governors, one of those on the review panel, and communicated my unhappiness with the decision. My letter would have been received on Tuesday 19 May. On Wednesday 20 May I completed a more considered letter to the chair of governors setting out my reservations about the exclusion and delivered it by hand prior to the full governors' meeting that evening. The head and other members of the governing body were aware that I intended to challenge the decision. They were given a copy of my letter (Letter A) giving eight reasons for reversing the decision. The agenda item on exclusions was reached at 6.00 p.m., two hours after the start of the meeting.

Letter A

20th May, 1998

Copies for the members of the Governing Body and Head Teacher of [T] School

Dear [chair of governors]

Permanent exclusion of LS

This is a follow up to my earlier hurried letter to you. Below are a set of reasons for my judgement that the head teacher's decision to permanently exclude LS was wrong and the sub-group of governors' decision to uphold the permanent exclusion was made in error.

1   The exclusion of a 6 year old, who has a troubled life anyway, is not appropriate to a school with a moral and community commitment.
2   Not all possible steps were taken in this case to marshal support from outside before excluding; specifically the Behaviour Support Team was not brought in to offer support and advice which they would do fairly speedily for a child on Stage 3 of the Code of Practice.
3   Governors were not kept informed about the problem as it developed, a problem about which they would have views, may have been able to offer support or may have been able to add weight to the head teacher's requests for assistance.
4   The Governors' Guidance on Exclusions (School Governors: A Guide to the Law) page 62 attached (para 6, line 3) states that the decision should be taken 'taking account of the consequences'. The governors will know of likely consequences from an earlier exclusion and could have been further informed, however speculatively, before reaching their decision.

5 The act of exclusion – except in dire circumstances and as a last resort (which this was not) – is an act where a school repudiates its responsibility, expects another school to take up the problem (eventually) and has made the problem worse by the rejection and expulsion from education.

6 The protests of other parents are not sufficient to warrant this action; it is not a matter about 'what of the other 29?'. It is a matter of all 30! We do not give up.

7 The effect on the other children and the stress to the teacher have to be kept in check but ways to do this are available and have to be fully explored first.

8 A school which excludes such a young child lays itself open to press mockery and the charge that it is a school in trouble.

Yours sincerely

Carl Parsons

I had copied Letter A and a piece from the *Governors' Legal Guide* and distributed these among the governors. Those present included the chair of governors and the two others who had been on the exclusion subcommittee, a parent governor who was also a helper in the classroom and one other governor. The head, deputy headteacher and clerk to the governors were also present.

The approach I took in the meeting was to build on the letter and argue on two fronts: first, that it is morally unacceptable for a school with a community-wide responsibility to exclude a child, particularly one so young; second, that the Behaviour Support Team had not been involved before the decision to exclude was taken. The governors stated that they had questioned the headteacher at length about the incidents which led up to the exclusion, the school's strategy in trying to tackle the problems and discussed whether the school had the capacity to manage this child. They had decided to back the headteacher. Principal among the offences committed by LS, and the one which precipitated the permanent exclusion, was that he was 'strangling' a little girl in front of her mother, herself a classroom assistant in the school. When the two children were separated, another boy in the class comforted the girl and LS had lashed out and hit him in the face.

The school staff expressed the opinion that children such as this should be in special schools, and could not be managed in mainstream. It was argued that it was the *system* that was letting the child down, not this school, and that this school did well by children such as this; indeed the school had managed to work successfully with children who had been excluded from other schools. My criticisms, it was said, should be directed at these other schools. Children with problems who moved onto secondary education from T school, where staff have managed capably with them, were often subsequently excluded from school. The governor who had been least involved with the whole business did wonder if everything had been done and particularly whether, as indicated by the wording of the passage in the *Governors' Legal Guide*, the consequences of exclusion on the child have been taken into account. Apparently the Exclusions Officer had advised them to make their decision *without* taking the consequences into account and told them only afterwards that LS would receive only three hours' home tuition a week.

In spite of my rational argument for a full hour against the permanent exclusion I was unable to sway opinion at the meeting. Had there been a vote among all those in the room it would probably have been eight to one against (possibly seven to one with one abstention). I finished by saying that the LEA might not uphold this decision.

On Friday 22 May I sent material to the Exclusions Officer which indicated that the exclusion rates in the LEA were higher than in other similar LEAs and that the proportion of exclusions from primary school were higher still. At the same time I faxed a letter (Letter B) to the Education Officer, asking that the LEA reconsider this permanent exclusion decision with a view to reinstating.

Letter B

22nd May, 1998

[Mr A]
Education Officer
Area Education Office

Dear [Mr A]

Permanent exclusion of LS from [T] Primary School

I am an LEA governor at [T] Primary School [Z town]. LS, aged 6, was permanently excluded on 23rd April. Three governors, with [Mr Y] in attendance as Exclusions Officer, upheld the decision at a meeting on 12th May. At a governors' meeting on 20th May I made the case during a one hour discussion that the decision was wrong on several counts but could not move the five other governors present or the head and deputy. I read in Circular 10/94 para 19 that the LEA has a duty to consider whether to uphold the exclusion. I am formally asking that the LEA does that without delay.

Very briefly some of the reasons for considering the permanent exclusion wrong are:

the age of the child;
only one period of fixed term exclusion had been applied (4 days before Easter);
further periods of fixed term exclusion could have been used giving time for assessments;
the Behaviour Support Service had not been involved (apparently attempts had been made – to my mind not forcefully enough bearing in mind the consequences of the action);
Page 11 of the Circular (para 24) states that if the school does not feel it has the resources to cope 'the head teacher should discuss . . . with the governing body'. This did not happen. I only knew of the exclusion on the morning of the governors' sub-committee meeting to consider the head's decision.

There are further reasons. I believe that the younger the child the more demanding should be the conditions that should be met before exclusion. If the requirements are that all reasonable action should be taken before the decision to permanently exclude is taken then my judgement is that that requirement has not been met.

You may know of my work on exclusions and that I am evaluating a Local Education Authority's Behaviour Support Service. [X] LEA appears to exclude at a rate greater than the average for LEAs of its type and the difference is greater at the primary level. This area of [X] LEA shows up particularly badly in this respect. I have faxed the Exclusions Officer a copy of the brief report which demonstrates this. Therefore, I think (back to the governor role) that the LEA must disabuse heads of the availability of permanent exclusion except as a LAST resort. I believe the case of LS is one where this stand could most usefully be made.

I am faxing this because of the urgency of the case. I will try to speak with you later today. I am usually contactable at work on [xxxxxxx], but will be moving about a good deal today, and am away Mon–Wed inclusive next week.

Yours sincerely

Dr Carl Parsons

Prior to the governors' meeting I had telephoned LS's mother and on Thursday 21 May visited the mother and LS. She was not willing to consider an appeal and hoped to find another school for LS. She had written letters to the Exclusions Officer and had made approaches to other schools. She appeared unaware that she had approached exceedingly popular schools and would be unlikely to find a place for her son there. She had also told them that she was unhappy with the school LS was attending, not that he had been excluded.

LS and I spoke briefly on my first visit. He was playing on his video games. He appeared shy but displayed signs of being unsettled. His writing and reading appeared below average but I told him how nice I thought some of the letters of the alphabet he had written were.

I phoned the mother back on Friday 22nd having spoken in the mean time to the Exclusions Officer. He had already put the case of LS to the EOTAS (Education Otherwise Than At School) Management Group and arranged home tuition for him to begin as soon as possible. Shortly after this the reply from the LEA arrived (Letter C). The LEA stood firmly behind the exclusion decision.

I waited until 4 June before concluding that I could no longer continue as a governor at the school. I communicated to the chair of governors and the headteacher that 'my anger and disgust at the decision has not subsided'.

Letter C

26th May, 1998

Dear Dr Parsons

Thank you for your fax of 22 May, in which you express your concerns about the permanent exclusion of LS from [T] County Primary School.

I understand the issues that you are raising, and have taken the opportunity to discuss the case, and your points, with [Mr Y], the Exclusions Officer. I must advise you that the process has already moved several stages beyond the decision of the disciplinary sub-committee of [T] CP governors. As we understand it, Circular 10/94, when requiring that 'all reasonable steps' be taken by a school before permanently excluding, does not indicate 'reasonable steps' in the form of a tariff. Rather, we believe that those steps which are reasonable are particular to the circumstances of each individual case.

In this instance, your colleague governors, the Exclusions Officer and the parent felt that the school had met this criterion. I note your concerns about the partial involvement of the Behaviour Support Service but, as I expect you are already aware, there is a difference of view concerning the school's attempt to involve the service. I also understand that, in lieu of the service, the school sought, and implemented, advice on behaviour strategies from the Special Needs Support Service.

The LEA is of the view that, on balance, LS did behave as described by the school; the school had taken all reasonable steps, and that if the LEA overturned the unanimous decision of the sub-committee of governors to exclude, and directed his reinstatement, it was likely that his pattern of disruptive behaviour would continue. In consequence, the LEA upheld the governors' decision and informed the school and Ms S of this. I have no further discretion to revisit that LEA decision. Further, Ms S has also notified us in writing that she does not intend to appeal the exclusion, and we have actioned the provision of some home tuition as part of the first phase of reintegration back into mainstream school, when LS is ready for that move.

It is clear from your letter that you are deeply troubled by the governors' decision. I think, however, that you, as a governor, are bound by a collective responsibility for the decision and, as such, it would be very difficult for the LEA to accede to your individual request to overturn a decision that otherwise was properly taken. May I suggest that, given your interest and expertise in exclusions matters, you consider offering yourself as a member of the Disciplinary Sub-Committee of the [T] governors where you can influence initial decisions of governors.

I am sure that you will be aware that from 1 September there will be a legislative requirement for schools to involve the Behaviour Support Service before excluding – although, as yet, we do not have a definition of what constitutes 'involve'. This should prevent the reoccurrence of concern over behaviour support input, which occurred in LS's case.

Thank you for sharing your anxieties about this case with me.

Yours sincerely

Education Officer

For the remainder of the summer term I provided some input until the home tuition started (two one-and-a-half-hour sessions per week) and have taken LS out to establish a relationship with him. He is small, confused, obviously troubled, and a great strain for his mother. He is also interested, wants to please and values a structured and predictable activity. He continues to receive weekly counselling and is now on Ritalin. At the start of the autumn term, when he became a Year 2 pupil, he remained at home with very little happening that will lead to 'reintegration back into mainstream school'. In the spring term of 1999 LS was continuing on three hours of home tuition.

The current exclusion system has worked as intended. It has failed LS, as it will fail other needy children who deserve and, one would have thought, have a right to full-time education. The Education Act 1997, the Children Act 1989, the United Nations Convention on the Rights of the Child, the European Court of Human Rights, common sense and humanity are not enough to ensure that a 6 year old continues in full-time education in England.

References

Adler, L. (1994) 'Introduction and overview', in Adler, L. and Gardner, S. (eds) *The Politics of Linking Schools and Social Services*, London: Falmer.

Ainley, P. (1991) *Young People Leaving Home*, London: Cassell.

Alvarado, M., Gutch, R. and Wallen, T. (1987) *Learning the Media: An Introduction to Media Teaching*, London: Macmillan.

Apple, M. (1986) *Teachers and Tests*, London: Routledge.

Arblaster, A. (1974) *Academic Freedom*, Harmondsworth: Penguin.

Archard, D. (1993) *Children: Rights and Childhood*, London: Routledge.

Archer, M. (1979) *Social Origins of Educational Systems*, London: Sage.

Audit Commission (1994) *Seen But Not Heard: Coordinating Community Child Health and Social Services for Children in Need*, London: Audit Commission.

Audit Commission (1996a) *Local Authority Performance Indicators 1994/95*, London: Audit Commission.

Audit Commission (1996b) *Misspent Youth . . . Young People and Crime*, London: Audit Commission.

Baggulay, P. and Mann, K. (1992) 'Idle, thieving bastards? Scholarly representations of the underclass', *Work, Employment and Society*, 6.1: 113–126.

Bailey, S. and Gunn, M. (1991) *Smith and Bailey on the Modern English Legal System*, London: Sweet and Maxwell.

Bainham, A. and Cretney, S. (1993) *Children: The Modern Law*, Bristol: Family Law.

Baker, K. (1993) *The Turbulent Years*, London: Faber and Faber.

Ball, S. J. (1994) *Education Reform: A Critical and Post-Structural Approach*, Buckingham: Open University Press.

Barbalet, J. M. (1988) *Citizenship Rights, Struggle and Class Inequality*, Milton Keynes: Open University Press.

Barber, M. (1996) *The Learning Game: Arguments for an Education Revolution*, London: Cassell.

Barber, M. (1998) 'Creating a world class education service', keynote address to the North of England Education Conference, Bradford, 6 January.

Barnard, N. (1997) 'Ministry for children believed overdue', *Times Educational Supplement*, 20 June: 4.

Barnett, C. (1986) *The Audit of War*, London: Macmillan.

Baumier, A. and Léotard, M.-L. (1998) 'Génération Kangourou', *L'Express*, 8 January: 26–34.

Beck, J. (1996) 'Nation, curriculum and identity in Conservative cultural analysis: a critical commentary', *Cambridge Journal of Education*, 26.2: 171–198.

Beck, U. (1992) *Risk Society: Towards a New Modernity*, London: Sage.

Bennett, P. L. (1993) 'Stockpiling the unsaleable goods', *Education*, 182.7: 126–127.

Benzeval, M. and Webb, S. (1995) 'Family poverty and poor health', in Benzeval, M., Judge, K. and Whitehead, M. (eds) *Tackling Inequalities in Health: An Agenda for Action*, London: Kings Fund.

Benzeval, M., Judge, K. and Whitehead, M. (1995) *Tackling Inequalities in Health: An Agenda for Action*, London: Kings Fund.

Berg, I. (1973) *Training and Jobs: The Great Training Robbery*, Harmondsworth: Penguin.

Bernstein, B. (1975) *Class, Codes and Control*, London: Routledge and Kegan Paul.

Bernstein, B. (1990) *The Structuring of Pedagogic Discourse: Volume IV, Class, Codes and Control*, London: Routledge.

Best, R., Ribbins, P. and Jarvis, C. with Oddy, D. (1983) *Education and Care: The Study of a School and its Pastoral Organisation*, London: Heinemann.

Bingham, Right Hon. Lord (1997) Speech given to the Police Foundation, 10 July 1997 by the Lord Chief Justice of England.

Blackman, S. (1995) *Youth: Positions and Oppositions*, Aldershot: Avebury Press.

Blishen, E. (1969) *The School that I'd Like*, Harmondsworth: Penguin.

Bloom, B. S. with others (1956) *Taxonomy of Educational Objectives*, New York: McKay.

Blyth, E. and Milner, J. (1994) 'Exclusion from school and victim blaming', *Oxford Review of Education*, 20.3: 293–306.

Blyth, E. and Milner, J. (1996a) 'Unsaleable goods and the education market', in C. Pole and R. Chawla-Duggan (eds) *Reshaping Education in the 1990s: Perspective on Secondary Schooling*, London: Falmer.

Blyth, E. and Milner, J. (1996b) 'Black boys excluded from school: race or masculinity issues?' in Blyth, E. and Milner, J. (eds) *Exclusion from School: Inter-Professional Issues for Policy and Practice*, London: Routledge.

Board of Education (1927) *Report on Consultative Committee on the Education of the Adolescent* (Hadow Report), London: HMSO.

Bourdieu, P. (1990) *The Logic of Practice*, Cambridge: Polity Press.

Bourdieu, P. and Passeron, J. (1977) *Reproduction in Education, Society and Culture*, London: Sage.

Bourne, J., Bridges, L. and Searle, C. (1994) *Outcast England: How Schools Exclude Black Children*, London: Institute of Race Relations.

Bowles, S. and Gintis, H. (1976) *Schooling in Capitalist America*, London: Routledge.

Briar-Lawson, K. (1997) Address given to the Children and Youth at Risk Network, European Conference on Education, Frankfurt, September.

Brown, P. (1997) 'Cultural capital and social exclusion: some observations on recent trends in education, employment and the labour market', in Halsey, A. H., Lauder, H., Brown, P. and Wells, A. S. (eds) *Education: Culture, Economy and Society*, Oxford: Oxford University Press.

Brown, P. and Lauder, H. (1995) 'Post-Fordist possibilities: education, training and national development', in Bush, L. and Green, A. (eds) *World Year Book of Education: Youth Education and Work*, London: Kogan Page.

Brown, P. and Lauder, H. (1997) 'Education, globalisation, and economic development', in Halsey, A. H., Lauder, H., Brown, P. and Wells, A. S., *Education: Culture, Economy and Society*, Oxford: Oxford University Press.

Bynner, J. (1998) 'Youth in the information society; problems, prospects and research directions', *Journal of Education Policy*, 13.3: 433–442.

Cambridge, P. and Knapp, M. (1997) 'At what cost? Using cost information for purchasing and providing community care for people with learning disabilities', *British Journal of Learning Disabilities*, 25.1: 7–12.

Campbell, J. and Oliver, M. (1996) *Disability Politics*, London: Routledge.

Carlen, P., Gleeson, D. and Wardhaugh, J. (1992) *Truancy: The Politics of Compulsory Schooling*, Buckingham. Open University Press.

Carr, W. and Hartnett, A. (1996) *Education and the Struggle for Democracy*, Buckingham: Open University Press.

Central Advisory Council on Education (1963) *Half Our Future* (Newsom Report), London: HMSO.

Cerny, P. (1990) *The Changing Architecture of Politics: Structure, Agency and the Future of the State*, London: Sage.

Chadwyck Healey (1994) *The 1991 Census CD Rom*, Cambridge: Chadwyck Healey.

CIPFA (1995) *Police Statistics: 1995–96 Estimates and 1993–94 Actuals*, London: Chartered Institute of Public Finance and Accountancy.

Clarke, J. and Newman, J. (1997) *The Managerial State*, London: Sage.

Clarke, M. (1997) 'Is this integration? Using a coupling framework to explore systemic change', paper given at the European Conference on Educational Research, Frankfurt, September.

Clegg, A. and Megson, B. (1973) *Children in Distress*, Harmondsworth: Penguin.

Cockett, M. and Tripp, J. (1994) *The Exeter Family Study: Family Breakdown and its Impact on Children*, Exeter: University of Exeter Press.

Cohen, R., Hughes, M., Ashworth, L. and Blair, M. (1994) *School's Out*, London: Barnados and Family Service Units.

Coldman, D. (1995) 'Truancy and the curriculum', in O'Keefe, D. and Stoll, P. (eds) *Issues in School Attendance and Truancy*, London, Pitman.

Coles, B. (1995) *Youth and Social Policy*, London: UCL Press.

Collins, R. (1978) *The Credential Society*, New York: Academic Press.

Commission for Local Administration in England (1989) *1988–1989 Annual Report*, London: HMSO.

Commission for Racial Equality (CRE) (1996) *Exclusion from School: The Public Cost*, London: CRE.

Commission on Social Justice/Institute for Public Policy Research (1994) *Social Justice: Strategies for National Renewal*, London: Vintage.

Corrigan, D. and Bishop, K. K. (1997) 'Creating family-centered integrated service systems and interprofessional educational programs to implement them', *Social Work in Education*, 19.3: 149–163.

Corrigan, P. (1979) *Schooling the Smash Street Kids*, London: Macmillan.

Dahrendorf, J. (1987) 'The erosion of citizenship and its consequences for all of us', *New Statesman* 113 (12 June): 12–15.

David, T. (1994) 'Introduction: multiprofessionalism – challenge and issues', in David, T. (ed.) *Protecting Children from Abuse under the Children Act 1989*, Stoke-on-Trent: Trentham.

Dawson, P. (1981) *Making a Comprehensive Work*, Oxford: Blackwell.

Dean, H. (1997) 'Underclassed or undermined? Young people and social citizenship', in MacDonald, R. (ed.) *Youth and the 'Underclass' and Social Exclusion*, London: Routledge.

Dennis, N. (1993) *Rising Crime and the Dismembered Family: How Conformist Intellectuals have Campaigned against Common Sense*, London: Institute of Economic Affairs.

Department of Health (1995) *Children's Services Plans: An Analysis of Children's Services Plans, 1993/94 – Summary Report*, London: Department of Health.

Department of Health (1997a) *Better Management, Better Care*, Sixth Annual Report of the Chief Inspector, Social Services Inspectorate, London: HMSO.

Department of Health (1997b) *When Leaving Home is Also Leaving Care: An Inspection of Services for Young People Leaving Care*, London: Department of Health Social Services Inspectorate.

Department of Health (1997c) *The New NHS: Modern, Dependable*, London: The Stationery Office.

Department of Health (1998) *Our Healthier Nation*, London: The Stationery Office.

Department of Health/Department for Education and Employment (1996) *Children's Services Planning: Guidance*, London: Department of Health.

Department of the Environment (1991) *Deprivation Index: A Review of Approaches and a Matrix of Results*, London: HMSO.

DES (1977) *Curriculum 11–16: Working Papers by HM Inspectorate*, London: HMSO.

DES (1980) *A View of the Curriculum*, London: HMSO.

DES (1981) *Curriculum 11–16: A Review of Progress*, London: HMSO.

DES (1989) *Discipline in Schools (Report of the Committee of Enquiry chaired by Lord Elton)*, London: HMSO.

DES/Welsh Office (1981) *The School Curriculum*, London: HMSO.

Devlin, A. (1995) *Criminal Classes: Offenders at School*, Winchester: Waterside.

Dewey, J. (1966 [1916]) *Democracy and Education: An Introduction to the Philosophy of Education*, London: Collier Macmillan.

DfE (1992) *Exclusion: A Discussion Paper*, London: Department for Education.

DfE (1993) *Press Release on National Exclusions Reporting System*, London: Department for Education.

DfE (1994a) *Code of Practice on the Identification and Assessment of Special Educational Needs*, London: Department for Education.

DfE (1994b) *Pupils with Problems*, London: Department for Education.

DfE (1995a) *National Survey of Local Education Authorities' Policies and Procedures for the Identification of, and Provision for, Children who are out of School by Reason of Exclusion or Otherwise*, London: Department for Education.

DfE (1995b) *Grants for Education Support and Training (GEST) Scheme: Truancy and Disaffected Pupils Category – Directory of Approved Projects – 1994–95*, London: Department for Education.

DfE/Welsh Office (1992) *Choice and Diversity: A New Framework for Schools*, London: HMSO.

DfEE (1995a) 'Discipline at the heart of schools' standards drive – Shephard', DfEE Press Release, 27 September.

DfEE (1995b) *More Willing to School: An Independent Evaluation of the Truancy and Disaffected Pupils GEST Programme*, London: Department for Education and Employment.

DfEE (1995c) *Truancy and Disaffected Pupils Category: Directory of Approved Projects 1995–96*, London: Department for Education and Employment.

DfEE (1996a) *Truancy and Disaffected Pupils Category: Directory of Approved Projects 1996–97*, London: Department for Education and Employment.

DfEE (1996b) 'Squire announces £4M to tackle pupil behaviour', DfEE Press Release, 4 March.

DfEE (1997a) *Compendium of Reports on Truancy and Disaffected Pupils Projects 1995–96 (Volumes 1–3)*, London: Department for Education and Employment.

DfEE (1997b) *Excellence in Schools*, London: HMSO.

DfEE (1997c) *Excellence for All Children*, London: HMSO.

DfEE (1997d) 'Permanent exclusions from schools in England 1995/96', DfEE Press Release 342/97, 30 October.

DfEE (1998a) *Guidance on LEA Behaviour Support Plans*, Circular 1/98, London: Department for Education and Employment.

DfEE (1998b) *The Requirements and Guidance for Careers Services 1998*, London: DfEE.

DfEE (1998c) 'Morris reveals ambitious new plan to cut truancy and exclusion from school', DfEE Press Release 386/98, 29 July.

DfEE (1999) *Draft Guidance on Social Inclusion: Pupil Support*, London: Department for Education and Employment.

Dominelli, L. (1996) 'Deprofessionalising social work: anti-oppressive practice, competences and post modernism', *British Journal of Social Work*, 26: 153–175.

Dore, R. (1976) *The Diploma Disease*, London: Allen and Unwin.

Douglas, J. W. B. (1964) *The Home and the School*, London: MacGibbon and Kee.

Duffy, K. (1995) *Social Exclusion and Human Dignity in Europe*, Strasbourg: Council of Europe.

Eekelaar, J. (1994) 'The importance of thinking children have rights', in Eekelaar, J. and MacLean, M. (eds) *Family Law*, Oxford: Oxford University Press.

Eggleston, J. (1984) 'School examinations: some sociological issues', in Broadfoot, P. (ed.) *Selection, Certification and Control*, Lewes: Falmer.

Elliott, J. (1996) 'School effectiveness research and its critics', *Cambridge Journal of Education*, 26.2: 199–224.

Esping-Anderson, G. (1990) *The Three Worlds of Welfare Capitalism*, Cambridge: Polity Press.

Etzioni, A. (1995) *The Spirit of Community*, London: Fontana.

Etzioni, A. (1969) *The Semi-Professions and their Organization: Teachers, Nurses, Social Workers*, New York: Free Press.

Evans, J. (1997) 'Community participation in developing integrated services: a community building perspective on service integration', paper given at the European Conference on Educational Research, Frankfurt, September.

Farrington, D. P. (1996) *Understanding and Preventing Youth Crime*, York: Joseph Rowntree Foundation.

Featherstone, M. (1990) *Global Culture: Nationalism, Globalisation, and Modernity*, London: Sage.

Ferlie, E., Pettigrew, A., Ashburner, L. and Fitzgerald, L. (1996) *The New Public Management in Action*, Oxford: Oxford University Press.

Foucault, M. (1972) *The Archaeology of Knowledge*, London: Tavistock.

Foulkes, D. (1995) *Administrative Law*, London: Butterworths.

Franklin, B. and Parton, N. (eds) (1991) *Social Work, the Media and Public Relations*, London: Routledge.

Friedman, M. and Friedman, R. (1980) *Free to Choose: A Personal Statement*, London: Secker and Warburg.

Friedman, M. and Schwartz, A. (1982) *Monetary Trends in the United States and the UK*, Chicago: University of Chicago Press.

Friedson, E. (1970) *Profession of Medicine*, New York: Dodd Mead.

Fulcher, G. (1989) *Disabling Policies? A Comparative Approach for Education Policy and Disability*, Lewes: Falmer.

Fulcher, G. (1993) 'Schools and contests: a reframing of the effective schools debate?' in Slee, R. (ed.) *Is There a Desk with My Name on It?*, London: Falmer.

Furlong, V. J. (1985) *The Deviant Pupil: Sociological Perspectives*, Milton Keynes: Open University Press.

Furst, F., Curcio, J. L. and Young, D. L. (1994) 'State full-service school initiatives: new notions of policy development', in Adler, L. and Gardner, S. (eds) *The Politics of Linking Schools and Social Services*, London: Falmer.

Gans, H. J. (1995) *The War against the Poor: The Underclass and Antipoverty Policy*, New York: Basic Books.

Gardner, S. (1994) 'Afterword', in Adler, L. and Gardner, S. (eds) *The Politics of Linking Schools and Social Services*, London: Falmer.

Garner, P. (1995) 'Schools by scoundrels: the views of "disruptive" pupils in mainstream schools in England and the United States', in Lloyd-Smith, M. and Davies, J. D. (eds) *On the Margins*, Stoke-on-Trent: Trentham.

Garner, P. (1997) 'Staying out . . . wanting in? Tales of young people excluded from school', paper presented at the European Conference on Educational Research, Frankfurt, September.

George, V. and Miller, S. (1994) *Social Policy towards 2000: Squaring the Welfare Circle*, London: Routledge.

Giddens, A. (1984) *The Constitution of Society*, Cambridge: Polity Press.

Giddens, A. (1991a) *Modernity and Self Identity: Society and Self in the Late Modern Age*, Oxford: Polity Press.

Giddens, A. (1991b) *The Consequences of Modernity*, Cambridge: Polity Press.

Giddens, A. (1998) 'Risk society: the context of British Politics', in Franklin, J. (ed.) *The Politics of Risk Society*, Cambridge: Polity Press.

Gilbertson, D. (1998) 'Exclusion and crime', in Donovan, N. (ed.) *Second Chances: Exclusion from School and Equality of Opportunity*, London: New Policy Institute.

Gipps, C. (1990) 'The social implications of national assessment', *Urban Review*, 22.2: 145–159.

Goldstein, H. (1995) *Multilevel Statistical Models*, 2nd edn, London: Edward Arnold.

Goodson, I. F. (1985) *Social Histories of the Secondary Curriculum*, Lewes: Falmer.

Goodson, I. F. (1995) *The Making of Curriculum: Collected Essays*, London: Falmer.

Grace, G. (1995) *School Leadership: Beyond Education Management – An Essay in Policy Scholarship*, London: Falmer.

Graham, J. and Bowling, B. (1995) *Young People and Crime Research Study 145*, London: Home Office.

Gray, J., Reynolds, D., Fitz-Gibbon, C. and Jesson, D. (eds) (1996) *Merging Traditions: The Future of Research on School Effectiveness and School Improvement*, London: Cassell.

Green, D. G. (1998) 'The great poverty myth', *Sunday Times*, 4 January, News Review: 9.

Greenfield, P. W., Model, K. E., Rydell, C. P. and Chiesa, J. (1996) *Diverting Children from a Life of Crime: Measuring Costs and Benefits*, Santa Monica, CA: Rand Corporation.

Hagen, U. and Tibbitts, F. (1994) 'The Norwegian case: child-centred policy in action?' in Adler, L. and Gardner, S. (eds) *The Politics of Linking Schools and Social Services*, London: Falmer.

Hall, S. (1988) 'New ethnicities', in Donald, J. and Rattansi, A. (eds) *Race, Culture and Difference*, London: Sage.

Hall, S., Critcher, C., Jefferson, T., Clarke, J. and Roberts, B. (1978) *Policing the Crisis: Mugging, the State and Law and Order*, London: Macmillan.

Hallam, S. (1997) 'Truancy: can schools improve attendance?', *Viewpoint* 6.

Halsey, A. H. (1993) quoted in Melanie Phillips, 'The head of the family', *Guardian*, 23 February, p. 19.

Hargreaves, D. (1967) *Social Relations in a Secondary School*, London: Routledge and Kegan Paul.

Hargreaves, D. (1994) *The Mosaic of Learning*, London: Demos.

Harris, N. (1995) *The Law Relating to Schools,* Croydon: Tolley.

Hayden, C. (1994) 'Primary age children excluded from school: a multi-agency focus of concern', *Children and Society*, 8.3: 257–273.

Hayden, C. (1997) *Children Excluded from Primary School*, Buckingham: Open University Press.

Hayek, F. A. (1976) *The Constitution of Liberty*, London: Routledge.

Hayek, F. A. (1988) *The Fatal Conceit*, London: Routledge.

Heater, D. (1990) *Citizenship: The Civic Ideal in World History, Politics and Education*, London: Longman.

Hills, J. (1997a) *The Future of the Welfare State: A Guide to the Debate*, York: Joseph Rowntree Foundation.

Hills, J. (1997b) 'A case for investigation', *LSE Magazine*, winter: 7–9.

Hinds, W. (1995) 'Supervising the education system: the work of the local ombudsman', *Education and the Law,* 6.2: 91–102.

Hirst, P. H. and Peters, R. S. (1970) *The Logic of Education*, London: Routledge and Kegan Paul.

Hobsbawm, E. (1995) *The Age of Extremes: The Short Twentieth Century 1914–1991*, London: Abacus.

Hodgkin, R. and Newell, P. (1996) *Effective Government Structures for Children*, London: Calouste Gulbenkian Foundation.

Hoggart, R. (1958) *The Uses of Literacy*, Harmondsworth: Penguin.

Holtz, B. W. (1981) 'Can schools make a difference?' (review of Rutter *et al.*, *Fifteen Thousand Hours*), *Teachers College Record*, 83.2: 300–307.

Home Office (1997a) *Tackling Delays in the Youth Justice System: A Consultation Paper*, London: Home Office.

Home Office (1997b) *New National and Local Focus on Crime: A Consultation Paper*, London: Home Office.

Home Office (1997c) *Tackling Youth Crime: A Consultation Paper*, London: Home Office.

Home Office (1997d) *No More Excuses: A New Approach to Tackling Youth Crime*, London: Home Office.

Hopkins, D. (1990) *TVEI at the Change of Life*, Clevedon, PA: Multilingual Matters.

Hopper, E. I. (1977) 'A typology for the classification of education systems', in Karabel, J. and Halsey, A. H. (eds) *Power and Ideology in Education*, New York: Oxford University Press.

House of Commons (1998a) *Disaffected Children – Fifth Report of the Education and Employment Committee, Volume 1. Report and Proceedings of the Committee*, London: The Stationery Office.

House of Commons (1998b) *Disaffected Children – Fifth Report of the Education and Employment Committee, Volume 2. Minutes of Evidence and Appendices*, London: The Stationery Office.

House of Commons (1998c) *Government's Response to the Fifth Report from the Committee Session 1997–98: Disaffected Children*, London: The Stationery Office.

Howarth, C., Kenway, P., Palmer, G. and Street, C. (1998) *Monitoring Poverty and Social Exclusion: Labour's Inheritance*, York: Joseph Rowntree Foundation.

Hutton, W. (1996) *The State We're In*, London: Vintage.

Hutton, W. (1997a) *The State to Come*, London: Vintage.

Hutton, W. (1997b) 'Blair's big tent is now blowing in the wind', *Observer*, 26 October.

Hutton, W. (1997c) 'Lack of welfare state causes poverty', *Observer*, 26 October.

Imich, I. (1994) 'Exclusions from school: current trends and issues', *Educational Research*, 36.1: 3–11.

Jamieson, I. (1996) 'Education and business: converging models', in Pole, C. J. and Chawla-Duggan, R. (eds) *Reshaping Education in the 1990s: Perspectives on Secondary Schooling*, London: Falmer.

Jencks, C. (1972) *Inequality: A Reassessment of the Effects of Family and Schooling in America*, New York: Basic Books.

John, P. (1996) 'Damaged goods? An interpretation of excluded pupils' perceptions of schooling', in Blyth, E. and Milner, J. (eds) *Exclusion from School: Inter-Professional Issues for Policy and Practice*, London: Routledge.

Johnson, T. and Parker, V. (1996) *Is a Persistent Young Offender a 'Child in Need'?*, London: Rainer Foundation.

Jones, G. (1995) *Leaving Home*, Buckingham: Open University Press.

Jones, G. and Wallace, C. (1990) 'Beyond individualisation: what sort of social change', in Chisholm, L., Buchner, P., Kruger, H. and Brown, P. (eds) *Childhood, Youth and Social Change: A Comparative Perspective*, London: Falmer.

Jørgensen, P. S., Ertmann, B., Egelund, N. and Hermann, D. (1993) *Risikobørn: Hvem er de, hvad gør vi?*, Copenhagen: Social Ministry.

Joseph Rowntree Foundation (1995) *Inquiry into Income and Wealth, Volumes 1 and 2*, York: Joseph Rowntree Foundation.

Karabel, J. and Halsey, A. H. (1977) *Power and Ideology in Education*, New York: Oxford University Press.

Kelly, A. V. (1995) *Education and Democracy: Principles and Practice*, London: Paul Chapman.

Kendrick, A. (1995) 'Supporting families through inter-agency work: youth strategies in Scotland', in Hill, M., Kirk, R. H. and Part, D. (eds) *Supporting Families*, Edinburgh: HMSO.

Kidd-Hewitt, D. and Osborne, R. (1995) *Crime and the Media: The Post-Modern Spectacle*, London: Pluto.

Kinder, K., Wakefield, A. and Wilkin, A. (1996) *Talking Back: Pupil Views on Disaffection*, Slough: NFER.

King, M. (1995) 'The James Bulger murder trial: moral dilemmas and social solution', *International Journal of Children's Rights*, 3: 167–187.

King, M. (1997) *A Better World for Children: Explorations in Morality and Authority*, London: Routledge.

King, R. (1980) 'Weberian perspectives and the study of education', *British Journal of Sociology of Education*, 1.1: 7–23.

Kloprogge, J. and Walraven, G. (1996) *The Education of Children at Risk in the Netherlands*, Amsterdam: Ministry of Education, Culture and Social Welfare.

Knapp, M. (1986) 'The relative cost-effectiveness of public, voluntary and private providers of residential child care', in Culyer, A. J. and Johnson, B. (eds) *Public and Private Health Services*, Oxford: Blackwell.

Koppich, J. E. (1994) 'The politics of policy making for children', in Adler, L. and Gardner, S. (eds) *The Politics of Linking Schools and Social Services*, London: Falmer.

Kozol, J. (1991) *Savage Inequalities: Children in America's Schools*, New York: Harper and Row.

Lacey, C. (1970) *Hightown Grammar*, Manchester: Manchester University Press.

Lane, D. A. (1990) *The Impossible Child*, Stoke-on-Trent, Trentham.

Langan, M. (1993) 'New directions in social work', in Clarke, J. (ed.) *A Crisis in Care? Challenges to Social Work*, London: Sage.

Lawson, H. and Briar-Lawson, K. (1997) *Connecting the Dots: Progress toward the Integration of School Reform, School-linked Services, Parent Involvement and Community Schools*, Oxford, OH: Danforth Foundation and the Institute for Educational Renewal at Miami University.

Lawson, H. A. and Hooper-Briar, K. (1994a) *Expanding Partnerships: Involving Colleagues and Universities in Inter-professional Collaboration and Service Integration*, Oxford, OH: Danforth Foundation and the Institute for Educational Renewal at Miami University.

Lawson, H. A. and Hooper-Briar, K. (1994b) 'Issues of vision, innovation, mission outcomes and competent practice', in Adler, L. and Gardner, S. (eds) *The Politics of Linking Schools and Social Services*, London: Falmer.

Layder, D. (1993) *New Strategies in Social Research*, Cambridge: Polity Press.

Layton, D. (1973) *Science for the People*, London: Allen and Unwin.

Lewis, E. J. (1995) *Truancy: The Partnership Approach*, London: Home Office.

Lindsey, J. K. (1995) *Modelling Frequency and Count Data*, London: Oxford University Press.

Lister, R. (1990) *The Exclusive Society: Citizenship and the Poor,* London: Child Poverty Action Group.

Lloyd, C. (1995) *The Welfare Network: How Well Does the Net Work?*, Oxford: School of Education, Oxford Brookes University.

Lloyd-Smith, M. (1993) 'Problem behaviour, exclusions and the policy vacuum', *Pastoral Care in Education*, 11.4: 19–24.

Lloyd-Smith, M. and Davies, J. D. (1995) 'Introduction: issues in the educational careers of "problem" pupils', in Lloyd-Smith, M. and Davies, J. D. (eds) *On the Margins*, Stoke-on-Trent: Trentham.

Lull, J. and Hinerman, S. (1997) 'The search for scandal', in Lull, J. and Hinerman, S., *Media Scandals*, Cambridge: Polity Press.

Mac an Ghaill, M. (1996) 'Sociology, state schooling and social class: beyond critiques of the New Right hegemony' *British Journal of Sociology of Education*, 17.2: 163–176.

MacDonald, R. (1997) 'Youth, social exclusion and the millennium', in MacDonald, R. (ed.) *Youth, the 'Underclass' and Social Exclusion*, London: Routledge.

McGuire, J. (1995) *What Works: Reducing Re-offending*, Chicester: Wiley.

MacIntyre, A. (1985) *After Virtue*, 2nd edn, London: Duckworth.

MacIntyre, D. (1987) 'The idea of an educated public', in Haydon, G. (ed.) *Education and Values: The Richard Peters Lectures*, London: Institute of Education, University of London.

192   *References*

Mackereth, N. (1997) 'The Prince's Trust Educational Programme', in Martin, C. and Hayman, S. (eds) *Absent from School: Truancy and Exclusion*, London: Institute for the Study and Treatment of Delinquency.

McLaren, T. (1993) *Schooling as a Ritual Performance: Towards a Political Economy of Educational Symbols and Gestures*, London: Routledge.

McManus, M. (1987) 'Suspension and exclusion from high schools: the association with catchment and school variables', *School Organisation*, 7.3: 261–271.

Magrab, P. R., Evans, P. and Murrell, P. (1997) 'Integrated services for children and youth at risk: an international study of multi-disciplinary training', *Journal of International Care*, 11.1: 99–108.

Malcolm, H., Thorpe, G. and Lawden, K. (1996) *Understanding Truancy: Links between Attendance, Truancy and Performance*, Edinburgh: Scottish Council for Educational Research.

Marshall, T. H. (1950) *Citizenship and Social Class*, Cambridge: Cambridge University Press.

Mawhinney, H. B. (1994) 'Discovering shared values: ecological models to support inter-agency collaboration', in Adler, L. and Gardner, S. (eds) *The Politics of Linking Schools and Social Services*, London: Falmer.

Mead, M. and Wolfenstein, M. (1955) *Childhood in Contemporary Societies*, Chicago: University of Chicago Press.

Merton, R. K. (1968) *Social Theory and Social Structure*, New York: Free Press.

Midwinter, E. (1970) *Nineteenth Century Education*, Harlow: Longman.

Mills, C. W. (1970) *The Sociological Imagination*, Harmondsworth: Penguin.

Mortimore, P. (1996) 'High performing schools and school improvement', paper presented to the Schools of the Third Millennium Conference, Melbourne, Australia, February.

Mortimore, P. and Whitty, G. (1997) *Can School Improvement Overcome the Effects of Disadvantage?*, London: Institute of Education, University of London.

Murray, C. (1990) *The Emerging British Underclass*, London: Institute of Economic Affairs.

Murray, C. (1994) *The Underclass: The Crisis Deepens*, London: Institute of Economic Affairs.

NACRO (1997) *A New Three Rs for Young Offenders: Responsibility, Restoration and Reintegration*, London: National Association for the Care and Resettlement of Offenders.

National Commission on Education (1993) *Learning to Succeed*, London: Heinemann.

National Commission on Education (1996) *Success against the Odds*, London: Routledge.

NCC (1990a) *Careers Education and Guidance: Curriculum Guidance 6*, York: National Curriculum Council.

NCC (1990b) *Education for Citizenship: Curriculum Guidance 8*, York: National Curriculum Council.

NCC (1990c) *Education for Economic and Industrial Understanding: Curriculum Guidance 4*, York: National Curriculum Council.

NCC (1990d) *Environmental Education: Curriculum Guidance 7*, York: National Curriculum Council.

NCC (1990e) *Health Education: Curriculum Guidance 5*, York: National Curriculum Council.

Netten, A. (1994) *Unit Costs of Community Care*, Canterbury: Personal Social Services Research Unit, University of Kent.

Netten, A. and Dennett, J. (1995) *Unit Costs of Community Care*, Canterbury: Personal Social Services Research Unit, University of Kent.

Newburn, T. (1996) 'Back to the future? Youth crime, youth justice and the rediscovery of "authoritarian popularism"', in Pilcher, J. and Wagg, S. (eds) *Thatcher's Children? Politics, Childhood and Society in the 1980s and 1990s*, London: Falmer.

Oakeshott, M. (1989) 'Education: the engagement and the frustration', in Fuller, T. (ed.) *The Voice of Liberal Learning: Michael Oakeshott on Education*, London: Yale University Press.

OECD (1996a) *Integrating Services for Children at Risk*, Paris: Organisation for Economic Co-operation and Development.

OECD (1996b) *Successful Services for our Children and Families at Risk*, Paris: Organisation for Economic Co-operation and Development.

OECD (1997) *Implementing Inclusive Education*, Paris: Organisation for Economic Co-operation and Development.

Offe, C. (1996) *Modernity and the State*, Cambridge: Polity Press.

Office for National Statistics (1996) *Housing Deprivation and Social Change*, London: HMSO.

OFSTED (1993a) *Access and Achievement in Urban Education*, London: HMSO.

OFSTED (1993b) *Handbook for the Inspection of Schools*, London: HMSO.

OFSTED (1995a) *Guidance on the Inspection of Nursery and Primary Education*, London: HMSO.

OFSTED (1995b) *Pupil Referral Units: The First Twelve Inspections*, London: OFSTED.

OFSTED (1996a) *Recent Research on the Achievements of Ethnic Minority Pupils*, London: OFSTED.

OFSTED (1996b) *Exclusions from Secondary Schools 1995/96*, London: OFSTED.

O'Keefe, D. (1994) *Truancy in English Secondary School*, London: DfE/HMSO.

O'Keefe, D. and Stoll, P. (1995a) 'Understanding the problem: truancy and curriculum', in O'Keefe, D. and Stoll, P. (eds) *Issues in School Attendance and Truancy*, London: Pitman.

O'Keefe, D. and Stoll, P. (1995b) *Issues in School Attendance and Truancy*, London: Pitman.

OPCS (1995) *The Health of Our Children*, London: Office of Population and Census Studies.

Oppenheim, C. and Harker, L. (1996) *Poverty: The Facts*, London: Child Poverty Action Group.

Parsons, C. (1987) *The Curriculum Change Game*, Lewes: Falmer.

Parsons, C. (1994) *Excluding Primary School Children*, London: Family Policy Studies Centre.

Parsons, C. (1996a) 'Exclusions from schools in England in the 1990s: trends, causes and responses', *Children and Society*, 10: 177–186.

Parsons, C. (1996b) 'Developing new skills in teachers', in McClelland, V. A. and Varma, V. (eds) *The Needs of Teachers*, London: Cassell.

Parsons, C. and Howlett, K. (1996) 'Permanent exclusion from school: a case where society is failing its children', *Support for Learning*, 11.3: 109–112.

Peters, R. S. (1973) *The Concept of Education*, London: Routledge

Peterson, P. (1981) *City Limits*, Chicago: University of Chicago Press.

Petrie, A. (1993) 'Education at home and the law', *Education and the Law*, 5.3: 139–144.

Pilling, D. (1990) *Escape from Disadvantage*, Basingstoke: Falmer.

Plaskow, M. (1985) *The Death of the Schools Council*, Lewes: Falmer.

QCA (1998) *Education for Citizenship and the Teaching of Democracy in Schools*, London: Qualifications and Curriculum Authority.

Ranson, S. (1993) 'Markets or democracy for education', *British Journal of Educational Studies*, 41.4: 333–352.

Raven, J. (1975) 'School rejection and its amelioration', *British Educational Research Journal*, 1.2: 22–24.

Raven, J. (1976) 'User perceptions of, and reactions to, the education system and their implications for policy', *British Educational Research Journal*, 1: 14–16.

Reid, K. (1987) *Combating School Absenteeism*, London: Hodder and Stoughton.

Reiman, J. (1990) *The Rich Get Rich and the Poor Get Prison*, London: Macmillan.

Reynolds, D. (1996) *Making Good Schools: Linking School Effectiveness and School Improvement*, London: Routledge.

Ribbins, P. (1985) 'Editorial: three reasons for thinking more about schooling and welfare', in Ribbins, P. (ed.) *Schooling and Welfare*, Lewes: Falmer.

Riley, K. (1994) *Quality and Equality: Promoting Opportunities in Schools*, London: Cassell.

Roberts, K. (1997) 'Is there an emerging British "underclass"? The evidence from youth research', in MacDonald, R. (ed.) *Youth, the 'Underclass' and Social Exclusion*, London: Routledge.

Robinson, F. and Gregson, N. (1992) 'The "underclass": a class apart?', *Critical Social Policy*, 34: 38–51.

Room, G. (1995a) 'Poverty and social exclusion: the new European agenda for policy and research', in Room, G. (ed.) *Beyond the Threshold: The Measurement and Analysis of Social Exclusion*, Cambridge: Polity Press.

Room, G. (1995b) 'Poverty in Europe: competing paradigms of analysis', *Policy and Politics*, 23.2: 103–113.

Room, G. *et al.* (1991) *National Policies to Combat Social Exclusion*, Brussels: European Commission.

Rutherford, A. (1996) *Transforming Criminal Policy*, Winchester: Waterside.

Rutherford, A. (1997) 'Criminal policy and the eliminative ideal', *Social Policy and Administration*, 31.5: 116–135.

Rutter, M. (1984) 'Continuities and discontinuities in socioemotional development', in Emde, R. and Harmon, R. (eds) *Continuities and Discontinuities in Development*, New York: Plenum.

Rutter, M. (1991) 'Services for children with emotional disorders', *Young Minds Newsletter*, 9 October.

Rutter, M. and Smith, D. J. (eds) (1995) *Psychosocial Disorders in Young People: Time Trends and their Causes*, published for Academia Europaea, Chichester: Wiley.

Sacks, V. (1982) 'Towards discovering parliamentary intent' [1982] Stat. LR 143, 157.

Salter, B. (1998) *The Politics of Change in the Health Service*, London: Macmillan.

Sammons, P. and Reynolds, D. (1997) 'A partisan evaluation – John Elliott on school effectiveness', *Cambridge Journal of Education*, 27.1: 123–136.

Sammons, P., Hillman, J. and Mortimore, P. (1995) *Key Characteristics of Effective Schools: A Review of the School Effectiveness Research*, London: Institute of Education/OFSTED.

Sandel, M. (1992) 'The procedural republic and the unencumbered self', in Avineri, S. and De-Shelit, A. (eds) *Communitarianism and Individualism*, Oxford: Oxford University Press.

SCAA (1994) *The National Curriculum and its Assessment: Final Report (Dearing Report)*, London: School Curriculum and Assessment Authority.

SCAA (1996) *Desirable Learning Outcomes*, London: School Curriculum and Assessment Authority.

Schools Council (1965) *Raising the School Leaving Age* (Working Paper 2), London: HMSO.

Schools Council (1968) *Young School Leavers (Schools Council Enquiry 1)*, London: HMSO.

Schools Council (1971) *Choosing a Curriculum for the Young School Leaver*, London: Evans/ Methuen Educational.

Schutz, A. (1970) *Phenomenology and Social Relations*, Chicago: University of Chicago Press.

Scottish Office (1997) *Sharing Good Practice*, Edinburgh: Moray House.

Selznick, P. (1949) *TVA and the Grass Roots*, Berkeley, CA: University of California Press.

Sennett, R. (1997) 'The new capitalism', *Social Research*, 64.2: 161–180.

Sewell, T. (1997) *Black Masculinities and Schooling*, Stoke-on-Trent: Trentham.

Shapland, J., Hibbert, J. I., Anson, J., Sorsby, A. and Wild, R. (1995) *Milton Keynes Criminal Justice Audit*, Sheffield: Institute for the Study of the Legal Profession, University of Sheffield.

Sharp, R. and Green, A. (1975) *Education and Social Control*, London: Routledge and Kegan Paul.

Sharpe, K., Broadfoot P., Osborn, M., Planel, C. and Ward, B. (1997) 'National identity in context: some notes on the significance of "national context" in the explanation of differential pupil identities and learning outcomes in English and French primary schooling', paper given at the British Educational Research Association Conference, York, September.

Shilling, C. (1997) 'The undersocialised conception of the embodied agent in modern sociology', *Sociology*, 31.4: 737–754.

Silver, Harold (1994) *Good Schools, Effective Schools: Judgements and their Histories*, London: Cassell.

Silver, Hilary (1994) 'Social exclusion and social solidarity: three paradigms', *International Labour Review*, 133: 531–578.

Slee, R. (1998) 'High reliability organisations and liability students – the politics of recognition', in Slee, R., Tomlinson, S. and Weiner, G. (eds) *Effective for Whom?*, London: Falmer.

Slee, R. and Weiner, G. (1998) 'Introduction: school effectiveness for whom?', in Slee, R., Tomlinson, S. and Weiner, G., *Effective for Whom?*, London: Falmer.

Smith, D. (1987) 'Whatever happened to Educational Priority Areas?', *Oxford Review of Education*, 13.1: 23–38.

Smith, D. J. (1994) *The Sleep of Reason*, London: Century.

Smith, D. J. (1995) 'Youth crime and conduct disorders: trends, patterns and causal explanations', in Rutter, M. and Smith, D. J. (eds) *Psychosocial Disorders in Young People: Time Trends and their Causes*, published for Academia Europaea, Chichester: Wiley.

Smith, D. J. and Rutter, M. (1995) 'Time trends in psycho-social disorders of youth', in Rutter, M. and Smith, D. J. (eds) *Psychosocial Disorders in Young People: Time Trends and their Causes*, published for Academia Europaea, Chichester: Wiley.

Smith, G. A. N. (1996) 'Urban education: current position and future possibilities', in Barber, M. and Dann, R. (eds) *Raising Educational Standards in the Inner City*, London: Cassell.

Smith, T. and Noble, M. (1995) *Education Divides – Poverty and Schooling in the 1990s*, London: Child Poverty Action Group.

Social Exclusion Unit (1998) *Truancy and School Exclusion*, London: The Stationery Office.

Stenhouse, L. (1971) *Culture and Education*, London: Nelson.

Stephenson, M. (1996) 'Cities in schools: a new approach for excluded children and young people', in Blyth, E. and Milner, J. (eds) *Exclusion from School: Inter-professional Issues for Policy and Practice*, London: Routledge.

Stronach, I. (1988) 'Education, vocationalism and economic recovery: the case against witchcraft', *British Journal of Education and Work*, 3.1: 5–31.

TACADE/Lions (1986) *Skills for Adolescence*, Manchester: TACADE.

TACADE/Lions (1990) *Skills for the Primary School Child*, Manchester: TACADE.

TACADE/Lions (1994) *Skills for Life*, Manchester: TACADE.

Tate, N. (1995) 'Friends, subjects, citizens . . .', *Guardian*, 5 September, Education Guardian: 8.

TES (1997) 'Poverty gap', *Times Educational Supplement*, 4217.

Thompson, J. B. (1990) *Ideology and Modern Culture*, Cambridge: Polity Press.

Titmuss, R. (1962) *Income Distribution and Social Change*, London: Allen and Unwin.

Tomlinson, S. (1996) 'Conflicts and dilemma for professionals in special education', in Christensen, C. and Rizvi, F. (eds) *Disability and the Dilemmas of Education and Justice*, Buckingham: Open University Press.

Tooley, J. (1993) *A Market-led Alternative for the Curriculum: Breaking the Code*, London: Institute of Education.

Townsend, P. (1979) *Poverty in the United Kingdom*, Harmondsworth: Penguin.

Townsend, P., Davidson, N. and Whitehead, M. (1992) *Inequalities in Health* (containing the Black Report and *The Health Divide*), Harmondsworth: Penguin.

Troyna, B. and Vincent, C. (1996) ' "The ideology of expertism": the framing of special education and racial equality policies in the local state', in Christensen, C. and Rizvi, F. (eds) *Disability and the Dilemmas of Education and Justice*, Buckingham: Open University Press.

Tsang, M. C. (1994) *Cost Analysis of Educational Inclusion of Marginalized Populations*, Paris: UNESCO, International Institute for Educational Planning.

Turner, B. S. (1993) *Citizenship and Social Theory*, London: Sage.

Urwin, S. (1995) 'Social reproduction and change in the transition from youth to adulthood', *Sociology*, 29: 293–315.

Utting, D., Bright, J. and Henricson, C. (1993) *Crime and the Family: Improving Childrearing and Preventing Delinquency*, London: Family Policy Studies Centre.

van Veen, D., Day, C. and Walraven, G. (1997) 'Youngsters at risk and urban education: problems and the role of research', in Day, C., van Veen, D. and Walraven, G., *Children and Youth at Risk in Urban Education: Research Policy and Practice*, Leuven, Belgium: EERA and Garant.

Wade, H. W. R. (1988) *Administrative Law*, Oxford: Clarendon Press.

Walker, A. and Walker, C. (1997) *The Growth of Social Exclusion in the 1980s and 1990s*, London: Child Poverty Action Group.

Walmsley, R., Howard, L. and White, S. (1992) *The National Prison Survey 1991: Main Findings*, Home Office Research Study no. 128, London: HMSO.

Weiner, M. (1981) *English Culture and the Decline of the Industrial Spirit 1850–1950*, Cambridge: Cambridge University Press.

Welton, J. (1985) 'Schools and a multi-professional approach to welfare', in Ribbins, P. (ed.) *Schooling and Welfare*, Lewes: Falmer.

Westergaard, J. (1992) 'About and beyond the "underclass": some notes on influences of social climate on British sociology today', *Sociology*, 24.4: 575–587.

Whitehead, A. (1962 [1932]) *The Aims of Education and Other Essays*, London: Ernest Benn.

Willis, P. (1977) *Learning to Labour: How Working Class Kids Get Working Class Jobs*, Farnborough. Saxon House.

Woodhead, C. (1995) *A Question of Standards: Finding the Balance*, London: Politeia.

Woodhead, C. (1996) 'What can the Ridings teach us?' *The Times*, 21 November: 22.

Wright, E. O. (1995) 'The class analysis of poverty', *International Journal of Health Services*, 25.1: 85–100.

Young, C. M. (1987) *Young People Leaving Home in Australia: The Trend towards Independence*, Monograph 9, Canberra: Australian Family Formation Project.

Young, M. F. D. (1971) *Knowledge and Control: New Directions for the Sociology of Education*, London: Collier Macmillan.

Index